American Revolution

by Steve Wiegand

Award-winning political journalist and history writer

for
dümmies®
A Wiley Brand

American Revolution For Dummies®

Published by: **John Wiley & Sons, Inc.**, 111 River Street, Hoboken, NJ 07030-5774, www.wiley.com

Copyright © 2020 by John Wiley & Sons, Inc., Hoboken, New Jersey

Published simultaneously in Canada

For general information on our other products and services, please contact our Customer Care Department within the U.S. at 877-762-2974, outside the U.S. at 317-572-3993, or fax 317-572-4002. For technical support, please visit https://hub.wiley.com/community/support/dummies.

Wiley publishes in a variety of print and electronic formats and by print-on-demand. Some material included with standard print versions of this book may not be included in e-books or in print-on-demand. If this book refers to media such as a CD or DVD that is not included in the version you purchased, you may download this material at http://booksupport.wiley.com. For more information about Wiley products, visit www.wiley.com.

Library of Congress Control Number: 2019911981

ISBN 978-1-119-59349-2 (pbk); ISBN 978-1-119-59350-8 (ePDF); ISBN 978-1-119-59351-5 (epub)

Manufactured in the United States of America

C10013316_082219

Contents at a Glance

Table of Contents

Introduction

J ohn Adams once wrote that "the history of our Revolution will be one continued Lye [*sic*] from one end to the other." Adams, second president of the United States, courageous statesman — and often a world-class grump — went on to sarcastically note that historians would doubtless report Benjamin Franklin "smote the Earth and out sprang George Washington." Then Franklin electrified Washington with a lightning rod "and thence forward these two conducted all the Policy, Negotiations, Legislatures and War."

Over the past two centuries, historians have poured out millions of words about the American Revolution, although no one to my knowledge has recounted it quite like Adams predicted. Tempting as it is to take an entirely fresh and novel approach, I'm not going to, either. But in the pages that follow, I am going to try to tell the story of one of the more remarkable events in human history: The creation of a nation unlike any other before it, born from a handful of scraggly colonies clinging to the east coast of a raw and sprawling continent.

Conceived in a war of words, and born from a war of blood against what was then the world's most powerful empire, America was then reborn with more words. They were written on documents that still resonate, for a country that Thomas Jefferson said represented "the world's best hope" and Abraham Lincoln redefined as the "last best hope of earth."

I don't think the history of the American Revolution is over yet. Now, before you jump to the not-totally-unreasonable conclusion that you are reading the work of a drooling imbecile, hear me out. It just may be that you are confusing the *American Revolution* with the *Revolutionary War*. A lot of people do. In fact, they've been doing it since, well, the Revolutionary War.

"There is nothing more common that to confound the terms of the American Revolution with those of the late war," wrote Dr. Benjamin Rush in 1786. That was just five years after the fighting between the American colonies and Great Britain had ceased, and three years after the two sides had signed a peace treaty in a second-floor room of a posh Paris hotel.

Rush had served with distinction as surgeon general of the colonials' army (even though he favored bloodletting for almost every ailment and for stomach troubles prescribed his own brand of "bilious pills" that were at least 50 percent mercury).

He was also one of 56 men who signed the Declaration of Independence. In pointing out the difference between the revolution and the war, he explained the latter was "nothing but the first act of the great drama . . . it remains yet to establish and perfect our new forms of government."

Rush was right (about the revolution, not the bloodletting). The American Revolution can be properly viewed as an ongoing event. It was, and is, an idea, an expedition, a continual work-in-progress. It's about devising the best way for human beings to get along with each other; to form social structures that allow us to govern ourselves with justice and fairness and compassion; and to respect the rights and freedoms of the individual while balancing them against the common good.

Establishing such a system — what George Washington called "the last Great Experiment for promoting human happiness" — is a tall order, and one that we continue to fine-tune with every presidential edict, congressional act, and Supreme Court decision. We're not done yet, and may never be done.

So, this book is about just the beginning of the journey, how it got started, who started it and how the route changed over those first years and decades. It's a bumpy and sometimes confusing trip, so buckle your seat belts and keep your eyes on the road.

About This Book

This book is not a textbook, nor is it an exhaustive encyclopedia covering everything that happened during those formative decades before and after America's beginning. Instead, I've tried to focus on the key events of the time, the whys and hows behind the events, and most of all, the people who made them happen. The aim is to give a basic foundation of information about the American Revolution and maybe entertain, amuse, and even irk you a bit along the way.

A word or two about the irking. This is not a completely objective, totally dispassionate, right-down-the-middle history book. There is no such thing. I've tried to stick to facts — or at least the most widely accepted historical interpretations of the facts — but the bottom line is that my own thoughts, biases, and interpretations will inevitably intrude. Sorry.

If there are factual mistakes, please let me know, and I'll fix them in the next edition. If you simply don't agree, congratulations. The freedom to disagree is one of the things the American Revolution was all about. If you take a look at Chapter 19, you can find a short list of other books on this topic. I've included at least a few that were written from either decidedly conservative or definitely liberal perspectives, so you can compare this book with some you might find more comforting, or more confrontational.

Lastly, I've included some anecdotes, quotes, and personality portraits that are meant to liven up the proceedings a bit. Learning about the past is certainly an important undertaking. But it doesn't have to be dull.

Conventions Used in This Book

To help you amble along the revolutionary trail, I use the following conventions:

>> *Italics* are used both to emphasize a word to make a sentence clearer and to highlight a new word that's being defined.

>> **Bold** highlights keywords in bulleted lists.

I've also tried whenever possible to use the exact language, spelling, and punctuation when quoting from letters, newspapers, or other historical documents. I think it adds to the authenticity and flavor of the topic. The few times I modernized things was when I thought the actual wording was too archaic to be easily understood.

What Not to Read

As you meander around the book, you'll encounter blocks of text in shaded boxes. They contain quotes; mini-profiles of both famous and semi-obscure people; the origins of things; factoids and numbers; and other historical debris.

You don't need to read them to get what's going on. They're just there as little extras that I've thrown in at no additional charge. Feel free to read them as you find them, come back to them later, or save them for recitation at your next poker game.

Foolish Assumptions

I'm assuming you picked up this book because you have some interest in the American Revolution (thus the cleverly selected title). If your interest is deeper than "some," great — feel free to plow through it from beginning to end. But if "some interest" is just about right for you, no problem. Feel free to skip around to the parts that catch your fancy most, be it Chapter 14, on the drafting of the U.S. Constitution, or even Chapter 19, which lists other good books on the subject. It won't hurt my feelings. Much.

Beyond the Book

In addition to what you're reading right now, this product also comes with a free access-anywhere Cheat Sheet that is a smorgasbord of information about how the American government was set up and functions, a couple of mini-bios of interesting folks, and a collection of factoids to amaze your friends and confound your foes. To get this Cheat Sheet, simply go to www.dummies.com and search for "American Revolution For Dummies Cheat Sheet" in the Search box.

Icons Used in This Book

Throughout the book, you'll find icons in the margins or alongside boxed sidebars that alert you to particular aspects or features of the text. Here's what they mean:

TECHNICAL STUFF

The names, numbers, and other stats behind the news are the focus of this icon.

REMEMBER

This icon alerts you to a fact or idea that you may want to stash in your memory bank.

Where to Go from Here

Hmmm, tough question. If you're reading this introduction, I'm betting you'll take a crack at what follows. I guess the best advice I can come up with is to consider that the American Revolution isn't over. And when you read about, watch, or listen to the news, keep in mind that the way America started is a pretty important part of where it's going — or should be.

1
The Roots of Revolution

IN THIS PART . . .

Centuries before anyone whistles "Yankee Doodle," religious and political ideas and events lay the foundation for the American Revolution.

The Old World meets the New, and it's not always pretty.

The American colonies participate in world wars and begin to feel strains of alienation from the Mother Country.

Chapter **1**

A Revolutionary Story

One of the dictionary definitions of *revolution* is "an overthrow or repudiation and the thorough replacement of an established government or political system by the people governed." Another is "a radical, transformative change." Yet a third is "a movement in a circular course, returning to its starting point."

The American Revolution, I think, fits parts of all three of those definitions. Americans certainly overthrew and repudiated the established government under which they had been living. The result was certainly a radical, transformative change for them — as well as much of the rest of the world for centuries to come. And as Americans have moved through the 240-plus years since the Declaration of Independence, we have often revisited our starting point, not only to give us a sense of direction, but to provide ourselves with reassurance we are still on the right track.

But I'd add a fourth definition when it comes to the American Revolution: "The ongoing process of perfecting the best way of governing ourselves." So, think of this chapter as providing a map for the rest of the book, which shows you where that process has taken us so far.

Setting the Stage

Before there was a United States of America, there were colonies, and before there were colonies, there were continents unvisited by Europeans, and before they could visit, the Europeans had to come through a whole lot of changes.

The changes ran the gamut from new ways of looking at religion to different kinds of governing. The two issues rarely stayed out of each other's way. **Chapter 2** takes a look at how economics, politics, and varying methods of worship combined to push Europeans, particularly those from England, Spain, and France, into a fierce competition to dominate the New World.

Progressing with Pilgrims — and for profit

As England came to dominate the portion of the North American continent now recognized as the United States, settlers took different approaches to settling. Some came to escape religious persecution in the Old World and establish their own little pieces of heaven on earth. Others came for money — or at least the profits that might be made in the new land.

Both kinds of newcomers encountered and endured a host of hardships. That's what **Chapter 3** covers, along with a look at how specific religious groups branched out to form their own distinctive colonies.

Fighting the natives and the home folks

Given the fact that Europeans in the 17th and 18th centuries were almost always fighting with each other, it was probably dismally inevitable they would end up at war with the people already in America when they arrived. **Chapter 4** follows the clash of cultures in different regions of the new land between the Native Americans and the newcomers.

It also examines early efforts by the various colonies to form alliances — and early rebellions against authorities representing the home country.

Growing up fast

Britain's American colonies exploded during the first half of the 18th century, in more ways than one. There were spurts in population, economic prosperity, and political clout, all of which were positive signs that things were going well for the colonists.

But negative growth occurred as well: The population of kidnapped and enslaved Africans soared. A series of world wars, some of them directly involving America, took place. When the final war ended, British America had rid itself of the threat posed by the French Empire and was ready to confront a new threat — posed by Britain. That's all in **Chapter 5**.

Divorcing the Mother Country

The American colonies generally came out of the French and Indian War in great shape. Millions of acres of virgin land had been won from the French and were ripe for settling. The mother country, Great Britain, was the most powerful nation on earth.

But lurking below the façade of Britain's greatness were enormous war debts that had to be paid. And since the colonies benefitted from Britain's protective cloak, British officials thought it natural that the colonists help pick up part of the bills. As **Chapter 6** shows, the colonists thought otherwise. A series of taxing efforts by Parliament resulted in a series of downright surly responses from Americans.

Warming up for war

For five-plus years, America and Britain had managed to confine their differences to rhetorical battles and bloodless economic boycotts. But the conflict takes a decided turn to the violent in **Chapter 7**. There's a massacre in Boston, along with a tea party.

Then a group of Americans from 12 of the 13 colonies get together in Philadelphia to compare notes and ask the king to knock it off. But tensions grow, until on a crisp clear morning in April 1775, a shot is fired — and heard 'round the world.

Declaring independence

Even after the shooting began at Lexington and Concord, many Americans and Britons held out hope that some kind of reconciliation could be reached before too much more blood was shed. But as **Chapter 8** reveals, the American leaders hedged their bets by setting up an army and picking the best general they could find to lead it — even if no one realized they were making such a good pick at the time.

More battles were fought, and the chances of accommodation dimmed. A scuffling writer newly arrived from England fanned the flames for a complete break from Britain. In July 1776, America declared its independence, in what is one of the most important political documents in human history.

Winning a war, the hard way

It certainly looked like a mismatch: the most powerful country on earth, with one of the most experienced and professional military organizations, versus a collection of 13 disorganized colonies that had to basically start from scratch to build an army and navy — and had very few raw materials to start with.

America did have at least one thing going for it, in the person of a military leader who had limited military skills but seemingly unlimited determination. As **Chapter 9** shows, George Washington would need every bit of that determination to win a war against Great Britain. This chapter follows the course of battles; the hardships endured by the American forces; the British leaders' uncanny knack for making blunders at critical times; and how things wound up after more than six years of fighting.

Making it a global affair

The American Revolutionary War didn't just occur in America. In fact, it was actually a world war, involving at least a half-dozen nations fighting on several continents. **Chapter 10** follows the action from India to the Caribbean, and explains how Britain having to fight on fronts all over the globe greatly hampered its efforts to hold on to its American colonies.

The chapter also takes a look at the American rebellion from the British perspective, as well as the leadership team King George III put together to fight the war and the flak he got from those in the British government who opposed it. That opposition, plus the timely and invaluable aid America received from France, led up to remarkably favorable peace treaty for the new United States.

Fighting among ourselves

While the Revolutionary War was a worldwide conflict, it was also a domestic civil war. Many Americans opposed independence from Britain, for a wide variety of reasons. **Chapter 11** examines how the difference of opinions had tragic consequences, pitting neighbor against neighbor and even splitting families.

The chapter also looks at how the war and the struggle for independence affected various groups of Americans, including women, African Americans, and Native Americans, and what roles these groups played in the fight. Finally, it covers how the war effort was exploited for financial gain by some Americans, how neglect and exploitation nurtured resentment among the men fighting the war — and why they continued to fight.

War's Over — Now Comes the Hard Part

Winning the war was only part of the American Revolution. Now a collection of 13 once-dependent colonies had to form some kind of independent nation. **Chapter 12** covers the awkward period between the Battle of Yorktown, which ended the major fighting, and the gathering in Philadelphia to create a government system Americans could live with.

Sorting out the Founding Fathers

Before getting to Philadelphia and the Constitutional Convention, **Chapter 13** examines the controversy among historians as to who deserves the title Founding Fathers or whether the term is meaningful. Then it gives you mini-profiles of ten, uh, "significant contributors" to the American Revolution.

Drafting new rules — and selling them

It was a long, hot summer of debating, arguing, writing, rewriting, and re-rewriting. The result, as **Chapter 14** explains, was the U.S. Constitution, a blueprint for a new system of government. But coming up with the document was only half the battle. In **Chapter 15**, the other half is waged: selling the idea to the American people and then drafting a Bill of Rights to sweeten the deal.

Getting Government Off the Ground

The men who drafted the Constitution were reasonably thorough about establishing the legislative branch of the new government. But they left some sizeable blanks to fill in when it came to the executive and judicial branches. **Chapter 16** fills in the blanks (or at least explains how they filled in the blanks), and covers getting the government financed. I also throw in the rise of party politics and say goodbye to George Washington.

Picking fights over presidents and parties

Choosing George Washington for president was easy; choosing his first two successors was pretty messy, mostly because of the convoluted process established by the Constitution. **Chapter 17** covers the mess, along with the rise of political parties in America and a feud with France.

Sorting out the Revolution's results

The American Revolution made an impact far beyond the new country's borders. A very brief **Chapter 18** summarizes some of the Revolution's effects elsewhere, as well as the reverberations it has had on U.S. history, and what should be kept in mind about it as the 21st century moves on.

For further reading. . . .

Think of **Chapter 19** as a mini-bibliography. I list some books on the American Revolution from various perspectives and on various parts of the topic. It's designed to whet your reading appetite — after you memorize this book, of course.

The Good Stuff at the Back of the Book

If you like lists — and who doesn't? — there are three of the *For Dummies* hallowed Parts of Tens chapters in the back of this tome. **Chapters 20, 21, and 22** provide things you didn't know about the Founding Fathers; some unsung heroes of the American Revolution; and pithy quotes from or about the struggle for independence.

As an added bonus, **Part 6** contains The Declaration of Independence, the Bill of Rights, and a timeline of 25 key events during the first half century of the American Revolution. Enjoy.

Chapter **2**

Here Comes Europe

L
ike a well-mixed salad, many great events are the result of seemingly disparate ingredients. The American Revolution was no exception. Combine greed,
God, and government with self-absorbed kings, virgin queens, rebellious
monks, and daring pirates. Add generous portions of sugar and tobacco. In a
century or two, you've got the makings of a revolution.

In this chapter, the preceding ingredients are blended, more or less, into a
recounting of institutional changes in post-Medieval Europe — particularly Spain,
France, and England — that helped shape events down the road in America. I also
touch on how European powers came to explore, exploit and tentatively settle in
the New World.

If you don't like salad, think of this chapter as sort of an inventory of ideas, issues,
and actions that helped shape the character of the American colonies, which in
turn laid the foundations of the American Revolution. And don't worry if it all
seems a bit disconnected. It will come together. Eventually.

Shaking Up the Old World

As Europe meandered from the Middle Ages, it began wrestling with some major
changes in the way people worked, worshipped, and governed themselves.

Trading economies

The economy of Western Europe during much of the Middle Ages was basically a collection of small and generally self-sufficient systems. They revolved around lowly peasants producing just enough food and manufactured items to subsist on, and using the rest to pay powerful nobles for letting them use the land and for providing military protection from outside threats.

But the various religious-sparked Crusades into the Middle East introduced Europeans to all kinds of nifty new products, including silks, dyes, exotic fruits — and an entire condiment-shelf's worth of spices that not only made food more palatable, but helped preserve it. To get this stuff, Europeans traded things like wool, timber, and metals.

TECHNICAL STUFF

This trading, in turn, led to the rise of *city-states*, particularly in Italy. Instead of vast-but-isolated agriculture-based tracts ruled by almost-omnipotent families, the city-states were urban areas whose economies often centered on producing particular goods or served as trading centers. Although powerful dynastic families often ruled them, the power might be shared by guilds of people who specialized in producing goods or trading them. Business ability and market skills made this *merchant class* less dependent on the whims of barons or dukes. Trade with other parts of the world intensified, and so did the quest for new markets and more products.

Another factor in this economic shift — and keep in mind it was gradual and uneven in its geography and timespan — was a morbidly drastic change in Europe's labor market. The various "Black Death" plagues — bubonic, pneumonic, septicemic — of the 14th century killed as many as 25 million people, about one-third of the continent's entire population. That meant fewer workers, which meant that labor was more valuable. Life got marginally better for some people who could parlay their skills into jobs instead of virtual slavery.

Rocking religion

At about the same time, religion and the role it played in people's lives was facing big-time convulsions. For centuries, the Rome-based Catholic Church had dominated most of Europe, and the church's popes felt free to interfere in the politics and policies of kingdoms, duchies, and just about anywhere else they felt like interfering.

But in the early 14th century, French kings, who were tired of papal intrusions into secular affairs, began to pick their own popes. Over the next century, it wasn't unheard of for Europe to have three or four "popes" at the same time. It took until the early 15th century for the various factions to sort it out and agree to return to a system of one pope at a time.

By then, however, the squabbling between the very tops of the secular and religious food chains had emboldened some scholars from within the Catholic Church itself. Several of these *Protestants* began to publicly protest financial corruption among the clergy, as well as other sleazy practices and procedures that were either ignored, or even approved, by the Church hierarchy.

The critics included John Wycliffe, an English scholar who argued, among other things, that instead of Latin, Catholic mass should be conducted in languages that church-goers actually understood. Another was Jan Huss, a Czech theologian who openly preached dissent and was burned at the stake for his troubles.

They were followed by Martin Luther, a German monk, and John Calvin, a French theologian. Luther particularly objected to the Church's practice of granting *indulgences,* which basically amounted to get-out-of-Hell-free passes for people who paid clergy to have their sins forgiven. In 1517, Luther posted a list of 95 theses on the door of a church in Wittenberg Germany. His central arguments were that the Bible, not the pope, was the key to figuring out what God wanted, and that faith was the key to salvation, not necessarily performing good works or adhering to Church-sanctioned rituals.

Calvin set up shop in the Swiss town of Geneva and sketched out an entire vision for Protestant Society, which viewed activities such as drinking and dancing as immoral. Calvin preached that man was essentially depraved and unworthy of salvation; that only a select few were "predestined" by God to be saved, and there wasn't really any need for a clergy.

REMEMBER

Both *Calvinism* and *Lutheranism* would become key elements in the role religion would play in the formation of governments in the New World. In the meantime, this religious *Reformation,* as it came to be called, helped trigger a fierce backlash by supporters of the Catholic Church that kept Europe well-drenched in the blood of wars waged in the name of God.

Consolidating secular power

All this religious protesting came in handy for various European monarchs, who were looking for ways to throw off the heavy hand of the popes when it came to running their countries. The kings were also looking to merge their countries' feudal fiefdoms into more centralized governments. They were tired of constant battles and feuds among, and with, nobles who enjoyed absolute power in their own regions and either paid little attention to royal wishes or schemed against the monarchies.

TECHNICAL STUFF

As kings began using force, diplomacy, bribery, and whatever else worked to weaken the nobility, they also fostered the concept of the *nation-state*. In essence, the idea was that people should feel they shared both political and cultural ties. For example, a farmer from York and a fishmonger from London should think of themselves first as Englishmen rather than Yorkshiremen or Londoners because they both lived on the same island, spoke more or less the same language, and might even have common ancestors.

The advantages of a nation-state, if you were a king, included making it easier to raise taxes, wage wars, and justify expansion into other territory, all in the name of being good for the entire nation. Of course, it helped maintain the system if the country was at war or faced with the threat of it because a common enemy united the home folks. So Europe hosted what seemed like continuous warfare between and among various nations. There was a Thirty Years War, an Eighty Years War, and even a Hundred Years War — which dragged on for 116 years.

REMEMBER

The rise of international commerce, the schism between Catholic and anti-Catholic forces, and the quest by monarchs to accumulate and monopolize political power all played important parts in how the New World would be perceived and dealt with by the major European nations that explored and conquered it, and how those who eventually settled in the New World would perceive and deal with life there.

MAGNA CARTA

It has been described as "the greatest constitutional document of all times," and a copy of it once sold at auction for more than $20 million. Yet in 1215, when a villainous English king affixed his seal to it to make it official, it wasn't worth the parchment it was written on.

In essence, the Magna Carta (Latin for Great Charter) was a peace treaty agreed to between John of England and a rebellious group of about 100 barons, whose chief beef with the king was having to pay for a lot of bad military decisions he had made. Drafted by the Archbishop of Canterbury, the 3,500-word document listed 63 rights, rules, and stipulations that ranged from a guarantee widows could not be forced to remarry, to exempting minors from having to pay interest on inherited debts, if the money was owed to a Jew.

King John reneged on the deal as soon as he could. He induced Pope Innocent III to annul the document because "it was illegal, unjust, harmful to royal rights and shameful to the English people." Then the king died of dysentery 16 months later, seemingly making the whole issue moot. In addition, all but three of the original measures were eventually amended or dropped.

But the document's overall importance far outweighed its specifics, or even the circumstances of its creation. Many legal scholars and historians see the Magna Carta as the first example in Western history of a monarch agreeing to abide by legal rules written by others. The eminent British jurist Alfred Thompson Denning called it "the greatest constitutional document of all times — the foundation of the freedom of the individual against the arbitrary authority of the despot." While variations of the document were reaffirmed 33 times by other English monarchs, its most important statement remained: "We will sell to no man, we will deny or delay to no man either justice or right."

The Magna Carta was often cited by America's Founding Fathers as a buttressing argument for their assertion of the rights to challenge an oppressive ruler, to spell out the conditions of governance, and the liberties of the governed that could not be restrained. In fact, when the First Continental Congress met in 1774 to draft a Declaration of Rights and Grievances against King George III, delegates decorated the title page with a column. At the top was a cap symbolizing Liberty. At the base were the words "Magna Carta."

Moreover, the venerable document has been cited numerous times in U.S. federal court cases. The issues ranged from a sexual harassment suit against President Bill Clinton to challenges of the detention and treatment of suspected terrorists by the administration of President George W, Bush. The judicial citations generally reinforced the idea that no person is above the law.

So venerated has the Magna Carta become in the American consciousness that in 1957 the American Bar Association paid for the construction of a memorial at the site of its signing in Runnymede England. Fifty years later, the financier and philanthropist David M. Rubenstein paid $21.3 million for a Magna Carta copy issued in 1297. He subsequently permanently "loaned" it to the National Archives in Washington, D.C. There it resides by two documents it helped shape: The Declaration of Independence and the United States Constitution.

P.S.: The reluctant regent who agreed to the Magna Carta is the same Prince John who is the bad guy in all the Robin Hood movies. He became king on the death of his brother, Richard I — the Lion-Hearted. John was succeeded by his 9-year-old son, Henry III, who reigned for an impressive 56 years. The story is that Henry had to make do with a bracelet to mark his coronation because his dad either lost or sold the crown.

Scoping Out the New World

One thing you could say with conviction about Christopher Columbus was that he was persistent — and also arrogant, egotistical, charming, stubborn, dictatorial, and physically striking, with reddish-blonde hair that turned white by the time he was 30, and standing 6 feet tall in an age where the average European male barely reached 5 foot 6 inches.

Born a weaver's son in Genoa Italy in 1461, Columbus ran a map-making business with his brother Bartholomew and developed himself into a first-class sailor. In the 1470s, he began shopping the idea of finding a western route to the riches of South and Southeast Asia, which was popularly known in Europe as the Indies. The idea was to replace the eastern overland routes that had been closed or greatly restricted when the Ottoman Turkish Empire conquered the trading center of Constantinople in 1453.

With his brother, Columbus began making the rounds of European capitals, searching for royal sponsorship of his idea. In return for 10 percent of all the loot he found, the title of Admiral of the Oceans, and a guarantee that his heirs would become governors of all the countries he discovered, Columbus promised to make some lucky nation very rich and powerful.

Monarchs in France and England weren't interested. The king of Portugal was much keener on the news that his own guy, Bartolomeu Dias, had made it down the west coast of Africa and around the southern tip into the Indian Ocean. Going that way seemed a lot better than going west to get east. But in Spain, Columbus piqued the interest of Queen Isabella, who agreed in 1486 to ponder the idea. Six years later, she finished pondering, and Columbus embarked with three small ships called *caravels* and a crew of 90 men.

Contrary to popular belief, scholars and competent seamen already knew the earth was round, and there was no concern about sailing off the edge of the world. What they didn't know was just how big the world was. Columbus figured it would be roughly 2,500 miles to the Indies, sailing west. He was off by about 7,500 miles. But after 10 weeks, and just as the mutinous mutterings of his crew were getting pretty loud, an island in what is now the Bahamas was sighted around 2 a.m. on Oct. 12, 1492.

Moving on to what is now Cuba and then an island Columbus called Hispaniola (now the Dominican Republic and Haiti), the Europeans encountered friendly natives they called Indians. "They must be good servants and very intelligent," Columbus noted in his journal, "because I see that they repeat very quickly what I tell them, and it is my conviction they would easily become Christians, for they seem to not have any sect . . . with fifty men all can be kept in subjection, and made to do whatever you desire."

His calculations in this regard were as off as much as his calculations of the earth's circumference. After leaving 39 men behind at a nascent trading post called La Navidad, Columbus sailed back to Spain. He returned the following year with a fleet of 17 ships and 1,200 men, only to find the trading post had been wiped out by the natives. There was also very little gold or precious spices to be found in the region.

Two more voyages ended similarly, and Columbus died disappointed, but not unbowed, in 1506. "By the Divine will," he wrote shortly before his death, "I have placed under the sovereignty of the king and queen an other world, whereby Spain, which was considered poor is to become the richest of countries."

Following Columbus

Despite the shattering implications of Columbus's discoveries, the truth was that most folks weren't lining up to be on the next ship to the Americas. The trip meant sailing across unknown seas in cramped, leaky vessels no longer than a tennis court, subsisting on provisions that would gag a cockroach, and coping with comrades who just might turn murderous at the first sign of trouble. Those who did follow in Columbus's path were often avaricious and cruel. But they were also undeniably brave and determined.

Among Spain, France, and England — the Big Three European nations as far as the future of North America was concerned — Spain was in the best position to follow up on the Columbus trips, and not just because it had sponsored him in the first place. In 1469, 17-year-old Ferdinand II of Aragon married his 18-year-old second cousin, Isabella I of Castile. The marriage greatly hastened the unification of Spain's major city-states.

REMEMBER

By 1492, the couple had finished driving the Moors out of Spain after centuries of trying. The fighting made the Spanish military well-seasoned for overseas scraps. In addition, Spain was undivided when it came to religion (especially after Spanish Jews were compelled to convert to Catholicism or get out, and Ferdinand and Isabella were formally dubbed "Catholic King and Queen" by the pope). That meant a more unified home front than some of Spain's rival nations. Finally, the country's rulers after Ferdinand and Isabella were part of the Habsburg Empire, the powerful dynasty that controlled much of the rest of Europe. All that added up to putting Spain in a very nice position to invest in further exploring the New World.

Dividing things up

Of course, other countries, particularly Portugal, also wanted in on the action. With the possible exception of the Polynesians, the Portuguese were the world's best navigators in the 15th and 16th centuries. They had been the first Europeans to sail around the tip of Africa and into the Indian Ocean. In an effort to keep things peaceful between the two countries, Pope Alexander IV drafted the *Treaty of Tordesillas* in 1493. The pact divided the New World between Portugal and Spain.

But the treaty reserved the around-the-tip-of-Africa route for the Portuguese. So Spain, which by this time was aware that Columbus had discovered a whole new land and not bumped into India, began looking for a western route that would get to the east. In 1513, Spanish explorer Vasco de Balboa reached the Pacific Ocean after crossing the Isthmus of Panama.

And in 1521, Ferdinand Magellan, a Portuguese mariner working for Spain, finally realized Columbus's dream of reaching the East Indies by sailing west. Magellan landed in the Philippines after rounding the southern tip of South America and sailing across the Pacific. Magellan was killed in a battle in the Philippines. But one of his five ships — and 18 of his original crew of 237 — made it back to Spain in 1522, completing the first circumnavigation of the globe.

As impressive as the Magellan voyage was, the Spanish really hit the jackpot in Central and South America. In 1519, Hernando Cortez began a two-year quest to conquer the Aztec Empire in Mexico, with the aid of weapons that ranged from horses to smallpox. In 1532, Francisco Pizarro began his conquest of Peru's Inca Empire.

REMEMBER

Both domains yielded fabulous amounts of precious metals. Between 1500 and 1600, it was estimated the Spanish *conquistadores* shipped back 200 tons of gold and 16,000 tons of silver, so much that it permanently cemented the transition of Europe's economic system from trade-and-barter to cash-and-currency. It also made Spain the richest country in Europe.

A decade later, Hernando de Soto and Francisco Coronado found less treasure but a lot of interesting scenery while staking Spain's claim to what would become the southeastern and southwestern portions of the United States. Juan Cabrillo, meanwhile, was claiming much of what would become the American West Coast.

REMEMBER

The explorations and conquests not only made Spain rich, and by extension powerful, but set it on a course to control one of the greatest empires the world has ever seen. By the 18th century, the Spanish Empire covered 7.7 million square miles — about 13 percent of the Earth's entire land mass — and was inhabited by about 68 million people, or 12 percent of the world's population. Other countries clearly had some catching up to do.

Freezing and furring with the French

Francis I was understandably upset when he heard the news that the pope had divided the New World between Spain and Portugal. "The sun shines for me as all the others," the French king sniffed. "I should like to see the clause in Adam's will which excludes me from a share of the world."

Unfortunately for Francis, and France, for much of the 16th century, the country was not in any great position to compete with Spain, or even Portugal for that matter. While the feudal system was still relatively strong in Spain, France was torn internally by a rising merchant class striving for political power and an entrenched nobility striving to keep it to themselves. The country was also plagued by fights with neighbors, including Spain and various portions of Germany and Italy.

Worse, France was ravaged by a series of internal religious wars between Catholics and Protestants, most of whom were followers of the theologian John Calvin and were called *Huguenots*. Between 1562 and 1598, the wars claimed an estimated 3 million lives from violence, famine, and disease associated with the fighting. So convoluted was the turmoil that one French ruler, Henry IV, switched from Protestant to Catholic to Protestant and back to Catholic, both to keep power and stay alive. (He was eventually assassinated anyway.)

Still, the French did manage to get in some exploring. In 1524, Giovanni de Verrazano, an Italian working for France, traversed nearly the entire length of the North American east coast. Verrazano made two more voyages, theorizing that the continent was probably just a narrow strip of land separating the Atlantic and Pacific oceans. On his third trip, however, he was killed and eaten by angry, and presumably hungry, natives in the Caribbean, and was thus thwarted before he could prove his theory.

In 1534, explorer Jacques Cartier sailed to Newfoundland, and a year later up the St. Lawrence River, which he hoped would lead to China. It didn't. Cartier nonetheless kept seeking a *Northwest Passage*. The route was widely believed to exist and promised to provide a water route to the east. Cartier also brought back to France what he thought were gold and diamonds but turned out to be iron pyrite and quartz.

REMEMBER

There was, however, a valuable resource in the cold Northern regions the French was probing: the fur of various animals. It would prove to be an important commodity, not only for its intrinsic value but for its role in how France would colonize its part of the New World. It was also something of a consolation prize in light of the fact that French efforts to establish colonies in what is now Florida and the Carolinas were wiped out by the Spanish. That relegated France to the climactically less hospitable northern part of the continent.

In 1603, Samuel de Champlain landed near Newfoundland on the first of what would be more than 20 trans-Atlantic voyages by the man who would be dubbed "The Father of New France." Descended from a sea-going family, Champlain founded in 1608 what became the city of Quebec. He was the first European to describe the Great Lakes and for several decades worked tirelessly to establish a French presence in North America.

Staying home with the English

Like France, England was late out of the gate when it came to the New World. In 1497, the Italian explorer John Cabot was hired by Henry VII of England to explore the Americas. Cabot reached Newfoundland, following much the same route taken by the Vikings 500 years before. He made a second trip the following year. All but one of his five ships, however, disappeared, along with Cabot. And that was about it for early English exploration. By 1510, the monarchy had begun directing its resources to building up the English navy rather than financing future New World voyages.

Also like France, England was wracked with religious differences that became inextricably linked to royal politics. In 1534, Henry VIII in effect divorced the Roman Catholic Church and set himself up as head of the Church of England. The split came after the pope refused to annul the first of Henry's six marriages, which the king kept initiating in a quest to sire a male heir.

In addition to establishing his own church — and looting and destroying most of the Catholic churches and monasteries in England — Henry pushed hard to expand the powers of the English monarchy. He bribed some nobles and church leaders and executed others. He also invaded France twice, fought with Scotland, and bankrupted the country. But his 38-year reign saw next to nothing done in the way of English forays into the Americas.

REMEMBER

Henry's immediate successors were likewise none too keen on exploring. His daughter, Elizabeth I — who never married and thus earned the sobriquet "Virgin Queen" — became mildly interested in the 1570s, when English *privateers* (a sort of cross between patriot and pirate) like Francis Drake and John Hawkins began coming home with ships full of loot they had taken from Spanish ships and colonial ports. She was particularly impressed by Drake, who from 1578 to 1580 sailed around the world and came home with an estimated $9 million in appropriated Spanish treasure. Drake and Hawkins were both knighted for these and other efforts.

About the same time, Humphrey Gilbert, a solider, member of Parliament, and an unusually bad sailor, convinced Elizabeth he had received word, via a dream, from the biblical figures Solomon and Job, that a Northwest Passage through

North America to China really existed. Duly impressed, the queen gave Gilbert a letter permitting him to discover and occupy any lands not already claimed "by any Christian prince" and settle them "agreeable to the form of the law and powers of England." Gilbert promptly sailed with a fleet of seven ships and almost as promptly was driven back to port by a storm. After getting lost in the fog on another trip, he tried again in 1584. This time he was lost at sea, last seen on the deck of his ship, reading a book.

SWEET AND STINKY

Gold and silver weren't the only New World commodities that proved profitable to Europeans. In fact, both Spain and England cashed in on two very different crops that nonetheless shared a vital component in their success.

Spain's was sugar. Cane crops had been grown successfully for years on Spanish-controlled islands in the Eastern Atlantic. In 1493, Christopher Columbus brought some sugar cane cuttings with him on his second voyage to the Americas. The plant thrived, and in 1516, the first sugar produced in the New World was presented to King Carlos I of Spain. Within 15 years, sugar was as commercially important to the Spanish colonial economy as gold.

It also produced a bonus byproduct. Planters discovered that juice left over after the cane had been crushed could be mixed with water and left out in the sun to create a tasty — and potent — drink they called *rum.* It was particularly handy on long sea voyages because it didn't spoil easily. The result was a sugar boom, with plantations popping up all over the Caribbean.

The English miracle product was tobacco. On his journeys around the Americas, Sir John Hawkins had noticed the local inhabitants lighting leaves packed in a small cup at the end of a hollow cane, which "they do suck through the cane the smoke thereof, which smoke satisfieth their hunger and therewith live for four or five days without meat or drink."

Hawkins brought some tobacco back to England in 1565, but it took years to become popular. It finally became quite the Elizabethan court rage by the end of the 16th century. Even Queen Elizabeth was said to have tried it, although her successor, James I, thought it "loathsome to the eye, hateful to the nose, harmful to the brain (and) dangerous to the lungs." It nonetheless caught on — big-time. By 1639, more than a million pounds of Virginia-grown tobacco was being shipped annually to the Mother Country.

And the common denominator? Their viability as cash crops depended almost entirely on slavery.

Despite Gilbert's misadventures, several of Elizabeth's closest advisers badgered her to launch more America-bound expeditions. "I conceive great hope that the time approacheth, and now is that we of England may share . . . both with the Spanish and Portuguese in part of America and other regions as yet unconquered," wrote Richard Hakluyt, one of the queen's councilors.

The time did approacheth for English colonies in the New World, but the early results would prove to be pretty dismal.

Settling In

With the exploring and conquering phases either done or well under way, the European Big Three adopted varying approaches to making their presence in the New World permanent. The differences would eventually play a key role in which nation would succeed in dominating North America.

Enslave and extract

Spain's approach was the most direct: Enslave the indigenous people; convert them, by force if necessary, to Christianity; extract whatever valuable and/or useful resources there were to be had; and ship them back to Spain.

The system was in essence a one-way trade route, with the exception of African slaves shipped to the Americas to replace the native peoples who had died off from overwork or disease. That meant Spanish colonists had little incentive to develop industry or come up with other economic innovations. In addition, the almost total dependence on slaves or other forced labor — a system called the *encomienda* — meant workers had no reason, other than fear, to show initiative.

TECHNICAL STUFF

The government system of Spanish colonies was equally one-way. A *Council of the Indies,* established in 1524, acted as an advisory panel to the king, regulated the military, and served as a supreme court for civil and criminal matters — all while thousands of miles away. In the Americas, *viceroys* were the direct representatives of the crown and served as sort of dictators-in-residence. While cities and regions might have councils of local residents, the final authority rested with a relative handful of royal appointees.

Despite the generally infamous, brutal treatment of the locals who fell under Spanish control, the Catholic Church took a seemingly Jekyll-and-Hyde approach to the issue. In 1514, for example, Pope Leo X declared that "not only the Christian religion but Nature cries out against the slavery and the slave trade." Yet only the year before, a papal proclamation required the natives to convert to Christianity or be either executed or enslaved. One chief who was being burned at the stake for refusing to convert reportedly said he was afraid to do so because "he might go to Heaven and meet only Christians."

The Spanish system of colonization worked best where there were enough exploitable resources to hold the attention of the government in Spain and enough local slave labor to reap the resources. That wasn't the case in most of the area held by the Spanish in North America.

Finding few Frenchmen in New France

France was also interested in extracting as much of a valuable resource as it could from its New World holdings. But finding fur meant going into, and moving around in, country controlled by powerful and well-organized native nations. French hunters, trappers, and fur traders (known as *coureurs de bois,* or "runners of the woods") soon learned it was easier to barter fairly with the tribes than to fight.

REMEMBER

Instead of beads and baubles, the French traded things the tribes could actually use, such as blankets, axes, knives, cups, and even guns. They also sensibly limited settlements, not only to lessen the chances of angering the natives, but also to keep from running off the furry quarry.

But as a result, French colonization was slow and sparse. In 1628, the Company of New France was chartered and charged with developing both trade and settlements. It proved much better at the former. For one thing, the main colony of Quebec was restricted to Catholics only. For another, fur trapping and trading were solitary occupations, unlike farming, where having a big family was an asset.

So despite efforts that included censuring bachelors and fining the fathers of daughters who still weren't married at the age of 16, the population of New France stayed small. By 1700, English colonists in North America outnumbered their French counterparts by 6 to 1. That eventually spelled trouble for the French when wars in Europe spread to the Americas.

Getting rich — and rid of the riff-raff

There were at least two things Elizabeth I didn't care much about during her 41-year reign as queen of England. One was religion: "I have no window to look into men's souls," she said in explaining her antipathy toward persecuting Catholics. The second was colonizing the Americas. "I marvel not a little that since the first discovery of America," lamented her close adviser Richard Hakluyt, "we of England could never have the grace to set fast footing in such fertile and temperate places as are yet unpossessed."

The queen's reluctance to seek colonies (the word "colonies" didn't even enter the English language until the 1550s) was based mostly on the costly and time-consuming effort to subdue rebels in Ireland, and on Elizabeth's fear it would stretch the country's resources too much at a time when invasion from Spain always seemed imminent.

REMEMBER

That fear was realized in 1588 when Phillip II, tired of raids by English privateers and doubtless still smarting from Elizabeth's earlier rejections of his marriage proposals, amassed an enormous armada of ships carrying an army of 30,000 soldiers and sent it toward England. Fortunately for the English, a combination of bad Spanish planning, brilliant English seamanship, and a nasty storm combined to wreck the armada. It took a while — 16 years — but the two nations finally signed a peace treaty in 1604. By that time, Elizabeth was dead, and her successor, James I, was more amenable to the idea of colonization. Calls for the creation of an English empire by men like Richard Hakluyt began to gain a wider audience.

TECHNICAL STUFF

One audience sector was a growing middle class of merchants, entrepreneurs, and speculators looking for ways to make lots of money. One way was to pool their money into organizations called *joint-stock companies*. The companies would finance colonies that would produce goods Europe wanted and harvest New World resources England needed, such as timber.

In addition, colonizing seemed an ideal way to get rid of some of England's burgeoning population, particularly from the less desirable segments of society, or what one observer indelicately referred to as "human offal." Petty criminals could earn a second chance by trading prison terms for passage to America. The hopelessly poor could indenture themselves as colonial servants or apprentices for terms from four to seven years, in return for the promise of cheap or even free land and elevated societal status.

In 1606, James I granted a charter to two joint-stock companies to settle on "that parte of America commonly called Virginia," which was named in honor of Elizabeth I's alleged virginity and stretched from what is now the Carolinas to what is now Canada. The settlers — and their descendants — would enjoy "all liberties, franchises and immunities . . . as if they had (been) abiding and born within our realm of England."

REMEMBER

The idea of English liberties for those on American soil had thus been firmly established. Establishing a firm colony on American soil would prove a much more dicey proposition.

ROANOKE

Walter Raleigh was brash, avaricious, idealistic, and not overly concerned with honesty. He was also tall, handsome, glib, and a dapper dresser. He rather smoothly worked his way into Queen Elizabeth's favor, so it wasn't a complete surprise when the queen put aside her indifference to colonization and granted Raleigh his request to set up a settlement in America. In 1584, Raleigh picked an island off the coast of North Carolina he called Roanoke and sailed back to England.

After being knighted for his efforts, Raleigh returned the following year with 7 ships and 600 men. About 100 were left on the island, including a scientist, an apothecary, a surgeon, and some "skilled" craftsmen. Apparently they weren't skilled enough, as they had to be rescued from starvation by Sir Francis Drake, who happened to be sailing by with a cargo of 300 African slaves he had stolen from a Spanish ship. (It's said Drake made room for the colonists by dropping the slaves in the sea.)

In 1587, Raleigh tried again. This time the settlers included 17 women and 11 children, (soon to be 12 when Virginia Dare became the first English baby to be born on American soil). But the return of a promised supply ship was delayed by the battles with Spain's Armada. By the time the ship arrived in 1590, the settlers had disappeared. Searchers found five chests, containing rotting books, maps, and pictures, and the letters CRO carved on a tree. There was also the word Croatoan, which may have referred to another island. Despite several searches, no trace was ever found of the inhabitants of England's first colony in America.

As for Raleigh, he was eventually imprisoned in the Tower of London for 13 years as a traitor, during which time he wrote a history of the world. When he was released, he got into trouble again while searching for the fabled city of El Dorado in what is now Venezuela. He was beheaded in England, at the request of Spanish authorities. His last words to the executioner were said to have been "this is a sharp medicine, but it is a physician for all diseases and miseries . . . strike, man, strike!"

Chapter **3**

"In God We Trust"

I t's indisputable that religion was a major driving force behind the settlement of the English colonies in America. But just which particular religion God favored was — as is has always been in human history — a sharp bone of contention. Equally contentious was determining the dividing line between the authority of the State and the authority of the Church. Or Churches.

In this chapter, followers of various religions and religion subsets set up camp in the colonies and wrestle with the issues of religious tolerance and the role of God in government. But the first successful English colony in America was driven not by prophets, but by profits.

Colonizing for God and Profit — But Not in That Order

Despite being a Scot by birth, James I became the English king in 1603 because Elizabeth I died childless, and as her first cousin once removed, he was basically her closest relative (never mind that Elizabeth had ordered James's mom, Mary, Queen of Scots, beheaded for treason). James was already king of Scotland and Ireland, and he liked being king.

In fact, like Elizabeth, James loved the idea of governmental power being concentrated in the hands of the monarch. He also hated any suggestion absolute monarchies weren't a good idea — so much so that he had the word "tyrant" banned from the famous English-language version of the Bible he commissioned, and which is still referred to as the King James Bible. (It was that kind of stuff that earned him the nickname Wisest Fool in Christendom.)

Unlike Elizabeth, James was at least mildly enthusiastic about the idea of English colonies, particularly if the government didn't have to pay for them. So when two companies — the Virginia Company of London and the Virginia Company of Plymouth — applied for royal charters to establish settlements on the American east coast, James said sure.

The charters did include a religious element, in that they instructed the settlers to educate Native Americans about the Christian God and divert them "from the highway of death to the path of life, from superstitious idolatry to sincere Christianity."

But mostly the charters stressed capitalism, which took capital, which took investors. For £11 2 shillings (roughly $3,200 in 2018 U.S. dollars), a share buyer got 100 acres of land and an additional 100 acres if he actually went to the colony, plus a portion of the company's profits. Thus the colonies were to be as self-sufficient and unreliant on government support as possible. In the long run, that became a key factor in their success — and also nurtured the idea of independence from the mother country.

REMEMBER

As important in terms of America's future was a provision that established a 13-man council in London (the members of which were eventually appointed by the company) to oversee English colonies in general, but also a 13-member council in Jamestown "to Govern and Order all Matters and Causes." That meant royal-sanctioned local control of local matters, a system of which colonists would become very fond.

Promotion of colonization was both relentless and shameless. As one poetic ad suggested:

"To such as to Virginia Do Propose to Repair,

And when that they shall thither come, Each Man Shall have his Share.

Day wages for the Laborer, And for His more Content,

A House and Garden Plot shall He have And much is Further Meant."

Another inducement claimed that in the New World, "Wild boar is as common as our tamest bacon is here." In reality, there were no native wild boars in America. Nonetheless, about 600 inspired individuals and 50 commercial firms invested.

The Plymouth, Virginia company quickly ran aground. It set up a settlement on the Kennebec River in what is now Maine in 1607. Called the Popham Colony, it lasted about a year before being abandoned due mostly to personality clashes and political differences among the settlers. They did manage to construct the first English-built ship in North America, which they used to sail back to England, and that was the end of colonization in the north for more than a decade.

But the London company's colony, which started in what is now Virginia a few months before the effort in Maine had begun, proved more permanent, even if way more problem-plagued.

Stumbling into Jamestown

The 105 colonists who reached Virginia in May 1607 (39 had died on the way over, a foreshadowing of things to come) were clearly mindful of how much their king thought of himself. They named the wide, deep, and easily navigated river they sailed on for 40 miles inland from the coast the James River and obsequiously, if unimaginatively, called their settlement Jamestown.

REMEMBER

While their diplomatic skills were polished, however, the newcomers' settling skills were dismal. Some were indentured servants, others upper-crust adventurers whose chief aim was to find gold and get back to England as soon as possible. Almost all were clueless when it came to frontier skills, such as hunting, fishing, farming, or anything else that might be useful. One of the few who actually had some ability dismissed the bulk of his companions as "ten times more fit to spoyle a commonwealth than either begin one or help to maintain one."

Unfortunately, the site chosen for the colony matched the skills of the colonists in terms of being lousy. It was swampy and heavily forested, which made clearing it for farming an onerous task. The water swarmed with bacteria and the air with mosquitoes. That translated to malaria, dysentery, and Yellow Fever. The first Native American attack came two weeks after the settlers arrived. It was little wonder that half of those who had survived the ocean crossing were dead in six months. That any survived at all was due almost entirely to the efforts of a 27-year-old English soldier-of-fortune who had fought for the French and Austrians, been knighted by a Transylvanian prince, and been a slave of the Turks.

The name's Smith. John Smith.

He was charismatic and diplomatic, an accomplished self-promoter, and a terrific liar. But most important to the Jamestown settlers, John Smith was tough. After a career as a mercenary for various nations, Smith signed on with the Jamestown colony as a soldier. He arrived in Virginia in chains, as a result of brawling on the voyage over and being accused of mutiny. At a trial by a jury of his peers — the first in America — Smith was acquitted. He even won a sizeable libel verdict against one of his accusers. From that auspicious start, Smith quickly became the glue that held the colony together.

He spent the first summer pushing the construction of a triangular protective barricade, hunting, and mapping the region around the settlement. He returned from one such trip to find the other colonists loading themselves in a boat to leave. Smith persuaded them to stay by leveling a cannon at the boat and suggesting they disembark. On another occasion, he hanged a mutineer. A fellow council member was accused of spying for the Spanish and executed.

Smith also became the colony's chief negotiator with the locals, who were led by a chief named Powhatan. At one point — according to Smith — negotiations were going badly, and the chief decided to conclude them by bashing in Smith's head. But Powhatan's daughter, a lovely and precocious teenager named Pocahontas, "got (Smith's) head in her arms, and laid her own upon his to save him from death."

By the fall of 1608, Smith had been formally elected head of the colony — the first such election on American soil by the English — and issued an edict that "he who doeth not worke shall not eat." But the following year, Smith was badly injured when some gunpowder in a canoe exploded near him, and in the fall of 1609, he departed for England. Then things in Jamestown got really rough.

The Starving Time

As Smith was getting things organized, the company was replacing him. Sir Thomas Gates, the new Jamestown governor, left England in May 1609 with a fleet of nine ships carrying supplies — and from 500 to 600 colonists, including women and children. Most of the colonists were emigrating under a new company policy that promised to grant them and their offspring land after seven years of basically working for the company. Seven of the ships — the ones carrying most of the colonists — made it to Jamestown by fall. But the other two, carrying the new governor and most of the supplies, were shipwrecked in Bermuda by a hurricane.

After rebuilding the ships, Gov. Gates arrived at Jamestown in May 1610 to be greeted by a scene lifted straight from a post-apocalyptic horror movie. Most of the new settlers were as inept at pioneering as the original settlers. Rats had destroyed most of the colony's food stores; raids on nearby Native American camps to steal food had proved futile. What followed came to be called *The Starving Time.*

Of the 500 or so colonists who had landed at Jamestown in 1609, only about 60 were still alive. The rest had succumbed to starvation, disease, madness, murder — and worse: One survivor later wrote that they had been reduced "to doe those things which seem incredible, as to dig up corpses outte of graves and to eat them." So stunned was Gates that he decided to abandon the colony altogether. As they were leaving, however, a three-ship relief fleet miraculously intercepted them. Jamestown had once more been saved.

Gates and his top aide, Sir Thomas Dale, quickly reinstituted the military-type discipline John Smith had established. The 13-member governing council, which had all but disappeared anyway, was abolished.

TECHNICAL STUFF

In 1611, a formal — and inordinately harsh — legal code was adopted, establishing Lawes, Divine, Moral and Martiall. It included rules against ignoring the Sabbath, dressing immodestly, and loafing. Killing poultry without a license, running away to live with the local tribes, and 18 other offenses were punishable by death. The stated purpose of the draconian code was to restore order to the colony. But having laws wasn't enough. To survive, the colony needed some way to make a living.

Smoking up an economy

One of the people who arrived in Jamestown with Gov. Gates was a 25-year-old businessman named John Rolfe. Arriving with Rolfe were some tobacco seeds he had somehow obtained before leaving England. They had been smuggled out of the Spanish colony of Trinidad at the risk of a death sentence for the smuggler.

At the time, Spain had a near-monopoly on good tobacco, grown on its holdings in the Caribbean. And lots of people in England wanted good tobacco. Along with other Europeans, the English ascribed all sorts of medicinal properties to the plant, perhaps as a way of justifying their addiction to it. Tobacco, it was said, could help heal sword wounds, clear congested lungs, and ward off plague, among other marvelous attributes. But even avid smokers didn't like the stuff that was grown on the American mainland. It was acrid, lacking the sweetness of good Spanish tobacco.

Enter Rolfe (who, by the way, later married Pocahontas, the Native American princess who had purportedly saved John Smith's life). In 1611, Rolfe began growing his smuggled seeds in Virginia soil. It did well, and in 1614 he shipped four barrels of leaves to England. By 1619, the Jamestown colony was shipping 20,000 pounds a year, and by 1639, an astounding 1.5 million pounds. The plant was grown everywhere it could be grown in the colony, which was pretty much everywhere. It even became a medium of exchange, used for paying fines, salaries, and dowries. Jamestown had finally hit it big.

But there were two major drawbacks to tobacco growing, the solutions to which would have major roles in America's future troubles with England, and with itself. The first was that, while easily grown, tobacco quickly wore out the soil. That forced growers to move farther west, much to the displeasure of the Native Americans already there. The second was that it was very labor-intensive, and Virginia was short on labor. The "solution" to that problem arrived in the hold of a Dutch ship.

Setting up slavery

Among his journal entries for Aug. 20, 1619, John Rolfe wrote "there came in a Dutch Man-of-War that sold us 20 Negars" (see Figure 3-1). The "negars" were African slaves from the kingdom of Ndongo, now part of Angola. They had been kidnapped by a rival kingdom and sold to Portuguese slavers on their way to Brazil. The slavers' human cargo had then been seized by an English privateer sailing from a Dutch port. (That should give you some taste of the international scope of slavery at the time.) Of the 20 slaves, 15 were bought by the colony's governor for work on his 1,000-acre tobacco plantation and the rest by other colonists.

LANDING NEGROES AT JAMESTOWN
FROM DUTCH MAN-OF-WAR. 1619

FIGURE 3-1:
The arrival of
African slaves in
Jamestown.

Library of Congress

In the early years of slavery in Virginia, the line between a slave and an indentured servant was somewhat murky. Theoretically, both could seek freedom after time of servitude was up — in slave cases, five years. But any debts they incurred, real or imagined, extended their indenture. Either way, relatively few slaves gained their freedom, especially as compared to the number of indentured servants who did become free.

Colonists preferred indentured servants to slaves for practical reasons. Servants were easier to communicate with and accustomed to English customs. They could also be worked harder and treated worse because they were generally temporary help and not property in which capital had been invested. By 1650, only an estimated 300 Africans were in the Virginia colony, compared to 4,000 indentured servants.

But those numbers gradually began to shift as slaves became more affordable. In 1662, the Virginia assembly passed a law that automatically made slaves of the children of slaves. By 1670, Virginia's slave population had reached 2,000; by 1700, 12,000. Slavery had not only taken root, it had sprouted.

Welcoming brides-to-be

Sir George Sandys, a member of Parliament and a founder of the Virginia Company of London, came up with the idea of sending 90 "well-chaperoned" women, classified as *young maidens,* to the colony. Sandys figured it was easier in the long run to produce future colonists on-site, in the form of children, than to induce adults to make the trip across the Atlantic.

The prospective brides, who arrived in August 1619 — about the same time as the African slaves — were volunteers. As additional inducements, in addition to free passage to the colony, they got a dowry of clothing, linens, and other furnishings. But if the brides were there of their own free will, they weren't free: Jamestown bachelors had to fork over 125 pounds of tobacco (worth about $5,000 in 2019 currency), payable to the company, to wed one of the women. That assured the women their future husbands were probably among the wealthiest men in the colony.

One thing the deal didn't guarantee the women, however, was equality. The month before the brides arrived, the colony's new General Assembly considered a proposal to give wives a legal share in land ownership "because in a plantation, it is not known whether Man or Woman be the most necessary." Voted on by an all-male body, the measure failed.

Assembling in an Assembly

For connoisseurs of historical paradox, it should be noted that just three weeks before the first African slaves appeared at Jamestown, so did the first representative legislature in America. This consisted of 22 colonists, 2 from each of 11 regions of the colony. It was called the General Assembly (later the House of Burgesses when it was split into two legislative bodies) and was the brainchild of the colony's new governor, Sir George Yeardley, and Sir George Sandys, the same fellow who came up with the idea to ship brides to Jamestown.

The Assembly, the members of which were voted on by male colonists age 17 and over, functioned as the Virginia colony's House of Commons. It had the authority to meet at least once a year, make laws, and serve as the highest court of justice. The governor, who was himself an appointee of the Virginia Company, was assisted by a panel of six councilors. He retained veto power over Assembly decisions, but the setup assured colonists at least some voice in their own governance.

Under Yeardley's guidance, the assembly threw out the harsh 1611 legal code and replaced it with a milder version. It included laws requiring, among other things, that colonists bring their guns with them to church services (in case of Indian attack), refrain from gambling, and work at something. Then after "sweating, stewing and battling flies and mosquitoes" for five days, during which one elderly delegate apparently keeled over and died, they decided it was too hot to continue and went home.

As would be expected from a king who lusted for absolute control, the creation of the General Assembly outraged James I. In 1624, he annulled the company's charter, and Virginia became a crown colony under direct royal control. James apparently had every intention to abolish the General Assembly. Fortunately for fans of representative democracy, he died before he could follow through.

It might not have mattered anyway. There were no royal troops in the colony to enforce royal edicts. As a result, James's successor, his son Charles I was inclined to accept the consent of the governed as a condition of keeping commercial operations running smoothly. Otherwise, the flow of tobacco might have gone up in smoke.

Purifying and Separating

Protestant English rulers had divorced themselves from the Catholic Church in large part because they could not abide sharing power with popes. But Protestantism opened its own can of worms. The theology behind it had itself sprung from rebellion, and it encouraged people to read and learn from the Scriptures without the direct guidance of clergy. That inevitably led to differing interpretations of them, which in turn led to different ways of worship.

Not surprisingly, conflicts developed. And religious conflicts in 17th century England weren't just a Sunday thing. The church parish was the center of virtually every community's daily life. It handled not only ecclesiastical matters, but also many roles many would consider governmental functions, from fixing roads to running relief and other social programs. "Men are governed more in peacetime by the pulpit than by the sword," a contemporary politician observed.

REMEMBER

The biggest conflict centered on Protestants who thought the Church of England (a.k.a. the Anglican Church) that had been created by Henry VIII was still too close in its liturgy and structure to the Catholic Church from which Henry had split. These critics wanted to "purify" the Church of England, thus being dubbed *Puritans.* The Puritans' ranks were heavily sprinkled with educated members of the middle class, including lawyers, leading merchants, and even members of Parliament.

A much smaller group of dissidents, drawn more from farmers, shopkeepers, and craftspeople than from the middle class, had no interest in trying to fix the nation's official religious institution: They wanted to break away altogether. They became known as *Separatists,* although they called themselves *The Saints* and became known to history as *Pilgrims.*

Whatever they were called, James I didn't like any of them. The king viewed those who defied his authority as head of the Anglican Church as being just a tiny step away from defying his authority as the nation's political leader. It was true that James had initially worked with Puritans on the creation of the magnificently written version of the Bible that bears his name and on strengthening Protestantism both in England and in the rest of Europe.

But as Puritans grew more numerous and the movement became more political, the king began to crack down. When some Puritan-controlled parishes banned the playing of sports on Sundays, James overruled them. When James ordered certain specific practices in church services, such as kneeling at communion, the Puritans objected. Puritans who held government offices were harried or booted out. By the mid-1620s, many of them decided it was time to leave the mother country. A small group of Separatists had already beat them to it.

Plowing into Plymouth

In 1608, about a year after the founding of Jamestown, an 18-year-old farmer's son named William Bradford sneaked out of England with a small group of Separatists and settled in the small Dutch city of Leiden. As the years passed, Bradford became a silk and cotton weaver, married, and had a son. In his free time, he devoured books, teaching himself to read in six languages. Moreover, the Dutch authorities didn't care what religious beliefs he held.

REMEMBER

Still, something didn't feel right. A decade into their stay, the Separatists were troubled that their children were losing, or had already lost, any sense of their English heritage. It was time to move on, they decided, and the place to move was America.

The move took three years of planning and negotiations with the English powers-that-be. Sir George Sandys, the Virginia Company cofounder who had done much to stabilize Jamestown, was not particularly sympathetic to their plight, but his company needed colonists. Sandys helped them secure a charter entitling them to 80,000 acres near what is now New York City.

TECHNICAL STUFF

It took one false start and the abandonment of a leaking sister vessel, but on Sept. 16, 1620, a group of 102 men, women, and children who had briefly returned to England from Holland left the English port of Southampton. They were aboard "a staunch, chunky slow-sailing vessel" called the *Mayflower*. It was about 90 feet long and 25 feet wide amidships. And while it leaked and carried at least 30 more people than it should have, its passengers noted that it didn't stink, at least not at first. For most of its life, the *Mayflower* had carried wine between France and England, rather than animals, cheese, or something equally odoriferous.

Now it carried Bradford, his wife (they had left their son behind with relatives, deeming the passage too dangerous), and 35 other Separatists, to whom Bradford would refer to as Pilgrims years later when he wrote his memoirs. There were also 65 non-Separatist settlers, some of whom had been chosen because they had skills that would be useful in the colony, such as carpentry or blacksmithing.

Along with its passengers, the ship's cargo included musical instruments, enough furniture for 19 cottages, a book on the history of Turkey, and provisions from spices and turnips to oatmeal and dried ox tongues. A shoemaker named William Mullins brought 139 pairs of boots and shoes.

Despite a rough crossing that took 65 days, only one passenger and one crew member died on the voyage, and one baby was born. Tragically, however, Bradford's wife fell overboard and drowned shortly after the ship dropped anchor in a broad shallow bay they called Plymouth, near the site of abandoned Indian cornfield.

"A Civil Body Politick"

Two important things happened on the way over to America. One was that as a result of fierce storms, the Mayflower was blown at least a hundred miles north of its intended landing site. That meant they were essentially squatters and lacked any legal right to establish a colony where they were.

The second was a brief document signed on Nov. 21, 1620, by 41 male passengers, in which they agreed to "covenant and combine ourselves together into a civil Body Politick, for our better Ordering and Preservation" (see Figure 3-2). It also pledged them to draft "equal Laws, Ordinances, Acts, Constitutions and Officials . . . as shall be thought most meet and convenient for the General Good of the Colony."

FIGURE 3-2: Pilgrims signing the Mayflower Compact, Nov. 11, 1620.

Library of Congress

REMEMBER

The *Mayflower Compact*, as it came to be known, was occasioned by the mutterings of some of the non-Pilgrims (whom Pilgrims called Strangers) who claimed that since they weren't settling on the land described in the charter, they weren't bound by the charter's rules. To prevent chaos, the Pilgrims drew up the compact. The document also gave them some political cover because it made clear they weren't rebels and still considered themselves loyal subjects of King James.

The compact lacked any details about the colony's governmental structure or specific laws. Even so, it was a remarkable document, in that it was not a pact between a ruler and the ruled, but among peers all voluntarily promising to respect the rights and equal standing of each other.

Leaving their mark

Despite their planning, the Plymouth colony had a very rough start, in part because they arrived at the beginning of a New England winter. Like the Jamestown colonists, half of the Plymouth settlers died in the first six months — including the shoemaker Mullins, his wife, and his son. But unlike most of Jamestown's citizens, the Pilgrims were hard workers.

They were also flexible. The original idea had been to function as something of a commune, with crops and other stores to be collectively gathered and distributed. But when the system produced less-than-desirable results the first year, colony leaders divided the land into individual parcels and let families fend for themselves. The colony did much better the second year.

The Plymothians benefited from having an intelligent and able leader. William Bradford, the weaver-turned-immigrant, was elected governor after the original governor died in 1621. He served in the office for most of the rest of his life, which ended in 1657. They also had a reliable, though diminutive, military leader in Myles Standish (his nickname was Captain Shrimpe).

Finally, they were extremely lucky because the local Native Americans, the Wampanoag, proved not only to be hospitable neighbors, but had one among them who spoke English. His name was Squanto. He had been kidnapped twice by Europeans and enslaved, escaped, and returned to America only to find his entire tribe had been wiped out by a disease probably introduced by Europeans. But Squanto was apparently not one to hold a grudge. Until his death about a year after the Pilgrims arrived, Squanto served as an invaluable interpreter and adviser.

With Squanto as a go-between, the Wampanoag showed the newcomers some planting techniques. They traded the Pilgrims furs for some of the newcomers' surplus corn, thus giving the colonists something to send back to their financial backers in England. By the summer of 1621, the Plymouth settlers had enough to be thankful for that they could afford to host a few days of feasting with the locals. (Just 242 years later, President Abraham Lincoln made Thanksgiving a national holiday.)

The Plymouth colony never hit a Jamestown-like tobacco jackpot and by 1692 had been absorbed into the larger Massachusetts Bay Colony. But the impact of its approach to government far outstripped its size or longevity as a colony. Plymouth became a symbol of self-governance, and the Pilgrims, in the words of eminent historian Samuel Eliot Morrison, became "the spiritual ancestors of all Americans."

"Like a City Upon a Hill": The Puritans

On June 14, 1620, a handsome 350-ton, 28-gun ship named the *Arbella* arrived off the coast of Salem, Massachusetts. It was the flagship of an 11-ship fleet carrying an estimated 1,000 settlers, 40 cows, 60 horses — and John Winthrop, a wealthy 41-year-old lawyer who had given up a comfortable lifestyle in England for the uncertainties of colonial life in America.

REMEMBER

Upon arrival, Winthrop, the group's leader, gave a short speech that was essentially a pep talk. He urged the settlers to think of themselves as exceptional, as examples to others of what could be accomplished through determination, hard work, and a willingness to sacrifice for principles and beliefs.

"We shall be like a city upon a hill," he said. "The eyes of all people are upon us . . . the Lord will make our name a praise and glory, so that men shall say of succeeding plantations: 'The Lord make it like them of New England.'"

Winthrop's assemblage, which became known as the Massachusetts Bay Colony, was as unique in its establishment as had been those of the gold seekers of Jamestown or the pious Pilgrims of Plymouth. In England, harassment of Puritans by the crown and Anglican Church had intensified. Winthrop, for example, had been pushed out of a cushy judicial post because of his religious views. As a result of the persecution, increasing numbers of Puritans were looking to exit the country.

In 1629, a group of Puritans essentially took over a joint-stock company that had already set up a small colony in Salem. By voting to move the company's headquarters to America, the Puritans eased out the non-Puritan stockholders, who were uninterested in emigrating. Control of the company ensured the colony almost total independence.

Setting up shop around Boston Harbor

On arriving in Massachusetts, Winthrop's group dispersed to a half-dozen sites around what became known as Boston Harbor, with the settlement of Boston becoming the capital. Then they set to work. Despite his lofty status as governor, Winthrop worked side by side with servants and laborers, according to an obviously impressed colonist, "and thereby so encouraged the rest that there was not an idle person to be found."

Clearly a hard worker, Winthrop was also one paradoxical Puritan. He was deeply religious, but a pragmatic businessman. He supported such egalitarian practices as trials by jury, tax-supported schools, and requirements that the heads of households educated their children and servants. But he regarded democracy as "the meanest and worst" of all forms of government and rather quickly tried to install himself as political boss of the colony.

As the colony grew, its financial system moved from one of subsistence to a diversified market economy. The colonists established fur, fishing, and shipbuilding industries. They developed crafts, such as silversmithing and printed their own books. Seeking wealth was not regarded as sinful because accomplishing it meant God liked you. "In America," noted the Puritan writer Edward Winslow, "Religion and Profit jump together."

But even if being rich was not a sin, the Puritans could be pretty puritanical in other areas. Pulling hair, falling asleep in church, and abusing one's mother-in-law were offenses that could get one fined or set down in the stocks. Adultery was punishable by death until 1632, when the penalty was reduced to a public whipping, followed by the forced wearing of the letters AD sewed onto the clothing.

Adultery aside, the Puritan colonists did enjoy other recreations: fishing for sport, picnicking, music, readings, and even dancing, as long as there was no touching. Even Gov. Winthrop, who apparently had no discernable sense of humor, enjoyed smoking a pipe and recreational shooting. He also had 14 children, so. . . .

Growing pains

The success of the Massachusetts Bay Colony was not lost on the folks back in England. While the Anglican Church's Archbishop of Canterbury, William Laud, sneeringly described the colony's residents as "the Swine Which root in God's Vineyard," a lot of English Puritans began shopping for ship tickets. Through the rest of the 1630s, an estimated 200 ships carried around 20,000 settlers to New England. The newcomers were part of what was called *The Great Migration*, which saw an additional 50,000 people move to the warmer climes of English colonies in the Caribbean.

TECHNICAL
STUFF

All these new arrivals, however, spelled political trouble for the establishment in the Bay Colony. The charter had envisioned the creation of a *General Court*, whose members would be the free male adults of the colony. The Court would meet up to four times a year, make laws, adjudicate them, and elect a governor, deputy governor, and 18 other deputies called *assistants.* But only 8 freemen showed up at the first meeting. They promptly voted themselves in as assistants and changed some of the rules laid down by the charter.

One of them was to restrict voting privileges only to members of what became known as the Congregational Church. That disenfranchised about 80 percent of the male adult population. Meanwhile, everyone had to pay taxes to support the Church. It was clearly a form of taxation without representation, an issue that would become a key target of American colonists' anger with Great Britain in the next century.

In 1634, newcomers to the colony demanded to see the original charter and were outraged when they found it called for the General Court, not the assistants, to make the laws and for all freemen to be members of the Court — conditions Gov. Winthrop and his allies had ignored. As a compromise, Winthrop agreed to having two deputies elected from each town in the colony to form the Court.

It was a compromise that cost him his job. The new Court voted Winthrop out as governor and voted itself the power to tax, distribute land, and grant the vote to freemen as they arrived in the colony. Winthrop accepted his defeat with grace and dignity and would be reelected governor three more times before his death in 1649. Not only had a form of representative democracy secured a foothold on American soil, but the nonviolent resolution of the power struggle augured well for a political system still trying to find its footing.

Slipping away from the church

As the various communities around the Bay Colony developed, their local churches set up their own organizational structures, and even variations of the liturgy they followed. That helped establish a taste for local control among the colonists and encouraged more active participation by congregants. But it also weakened the central structure of the colony's religious institution.

TECHNICAL STUFF

To be a church member, an individual had to have a *conversion experience*, which was a deeply personal encounter with God that had to be accepted as genuine by the congregation. But as the second generation of colonists grew up, fewer people were professing to be "born again." That meant their children could not be baptized, which meant church membership was shrinking. In the 1660s, a Half-Way Covenant was proposed that allowed the children to be baptized as long as their parents accepted the church's doctrine, even though they weren't full-fledged congregants.

As confusing as all this was, it did have some unintended consequences. The proposal caused bitter — and public — disputes among the colony's leading clergy, which diminished their public image; it led to splits within and between congregations; and it gradually diluted the churches' influence.

REMEMBER

By the end of the 17th century, the Massachusetts colony's governmental structure had evolved from a members-only theocracy to at least the semblance of representative democracy. The former had no separation of church and state because the church was the state. In the latter, the argument about church and state separation would not center on if the two should be separated, but by how much.

In the decades in between, other American colonies were founded on faith and wrestled with their foundations.

Dissidents, Catholics, and Quakers

Despite their own persecution, or maybe because of it, the Puritan colonies were remarkably intolerant of other religions, or even of those members of their own faith who got a little too loud in criticizing Puritan theology.

Dissidents and members of other faiths who wandered into Boston, Salem, or other Massachusetts locales risked being banished, beaten, and on at least one occasion, hanged. "If they beat the Gospel black and blue," a Puritan minister explained, "it is but just to beat them black and blue." Rather than get beat or join up, those unwelcome in the land of the Puritans sometimes moved on.

Running to Rhode Island

Roger Williams was clever, energetic, sociable, and an expert in the languages of Native American tribes in New England. As far as Puritan leaders were concerned, he was also a man with dangerous ideas and a big mouth.

Williams, who came to Massachusetts at the age of 29 from England, became an informal assistant to the pastor in Plymouth and "his teachings were well-approved," according to Plymouth leader William Bradford. The approval lasted about a year, or until Williams began agitating on behalf of the local Native Americans. The tribes, he said, had been ripped off by the English settlers, who not only didn't even try to teach them about Christianity, but also stole or swindled them out of their land.

As time passed, Williams became pastor in Salem — and began stirring up trouble on another front. This time it was what he considered a too cozy relationship between the church and state. The connection was "ulcered and gangrenous." Moreover, forcing people to worship in a particular way "stinks in God's nostrils."

Naturally the authorities took umbrage to this opinion, and in 1635, Williams was ordered to leave the colony for spreading "newe and dangerous opinions." His exile was delayed while he recovered from an illness, but being sick didn't keep him quiet. This time, the colony's leaders ordered him completely off the continent and were ready to do it forcibly.

Privately tipped off by none other than John Winthrop, the Bay Colony leader who liked Williams in spite of his opinions, Williams fled in 1636 to what is now Providence Rhode Island. There he bought land from two local tribes, built a church, and eventually won a colony charter from Parliament. While Puritan leaders referred to the colony as "the Sewer of New England," dissidents, rebels, and people just tired of being pushed around found it an oasis of tolerance.

Rhode Island offered complete freedom of religion (even for Quakers, whom Williams personally disliked); no compulsory church attendance; and no public tax support for any sect or faith. "No person . . . shall be in any wise molested, punished, disquieted or called in question for any difference in opinion in matters of religion" the colony's charter said.

ANNE HUTCHINSON

Anne Hutchinson left behind no personal written documents and held no public office, but she was almost certainly the first important European woman in America. Born Anne Marbury in England in 1591, Hutchinson was the daughter of an Anglican cleric who was also a school teacher. She thus received a better education than most girls of her era. At the age of 21, she married a fabric merchant who became both wealthy and the father of her 15 children.

The couple moved to Boston in 1634, and when not busy having children herself, Hutchinson became an accomplished and much-sought-after midwife in the town. Gov. John Winthrop, who came to despise her, nonetheless referred to her as "a woman of ready wit and bold spirit."

Hutchinson frequently hosted get-togethers of women, and a few men, at which the main topic of discussion was often religion. She had strong opinions on the subject. Chief among them was that salvation came from an "inner grace" and not in doing good works, although it was a good idea to do good works for their own sake. Moreover, the church had no business determining whether someone was worthy enough in God's eyes to belong to the congregation.

Of course, this viewpoint put her at odds with the Puritan powers, who tried everything to shut her up and/or smear her — including disinterring a malformed stillborn baby at whose birth Hutchinson had assisted, in an effort to imply she was a witch. In 1637, Hutchinson was put on trial for heresy. But her accusers couldn't make a case because her opinions had been stated mostly in private gatherings. Instead, she was convicted of slandering various ministers and exiled in 1638.

After initially seeking refuge in Rhode Island, Hutchinson moved after her husband died to what was then the Dutch colony of New Netherland, with seven of her children. In 1643, the family was massacred by local Indians angry about the intrusion of white settlers. Ever the sore winners, Puritan church leaders celebrated news of her death by ringing Boston church bells for 24 hours.

REMEMBER

While Rhode Island remained relatively small, it was the first colony to offer both complete religious freedom and the complete separation of church and state — concepts that would be remembered when drafting a new nation's constitution. In addition, it introduced the idea of religions — and other sets of ideas — being allowed to compete with each other. That trait would spill onto other aspects of the American character.

Leasing Maryland

If you can't be the king, it's sometimes good to be his secretary. George Calvert was in that very role to James I, and when he left the job, James made him the first Lord Baltimore. An Anglican-turned-Catholic, Calvert had a yen to start an American colony, both to make money and to serve as a haven for his fellow Catholics.

He tried first in Newfoundland in 1620, but the colony, called Avalon, flopped in the face of disease, an inhospitable climate, and attacks by the French. Undaunted, Calvert tried again, this time farther south. In 1634, King Charles I agreed to lease Calvert land around Chesapeake Bay, just north of the Virginia colony — much to the displeasure of the Virginians, who both coveted the territory and feared potential competition in the tobacco industry.

The rent for the colony, named Maryland after the king's wife, was one-fifth of all the gold and silver found there, plus two authentic Native American arrows, to be delivered each Easter to the royal castle at Windsor. Unfortunately for the king, he got a lot more arrows out of the deal than precious metals. Unfortunately for Calvert, he died just four weeks before the charter received final approval. But his son Cecil stepped in and took over.

The first batch of about 300 settlers was a mix of Catholics and Protestants, Calvert figuring that mixing in Protestants would make the colony more palatable to its Protestant-dominated neighbors. It did, so much so that when Maryland prospered because of the success of its tobacco growing, a whole lot of Protestants moved in.

In an effort to prevent Catholics from eventual persecution, the colony's General Assembly passed a Toleration Act in 1649 that mandated religious tolerance for most, but not all, beliefs. It not only excluded Jews as well as atheists, it imposed a death sentence on anyone who denied the divinity of Jesus Christ.

Even with the built-in exclusions, however, the act didn't last. In 1692, Puritans overthrew Calvert's hold on the colony, banned the public practice of Catholicism, and prohibited Catholics from voting. It would take an American Revolution to restore religious freedom.

Quaking in Pennsylvania

If it didn't hurt to be the king's secretary when starting a colony, it was downright helpful to be the son of a well-respected English admiral. That was especially true when you belonged to a religion that almost everyone hated.

Sir William Penn had enjoyed an illustrious career as a naval officer and member of the House of Commons. His son, also named William, had endured a career that saw him serve briefly as a soldier and also serve briefly in jail. This latter service was a result of William the younger's embrace of the Religious Society of Friends.

The Friends were known as *Quakers* because they supposedly sometimes quaked with religious fervor. Quakers refused to doff their hats in the presence of civil and social "superiors"; would not take oaths of any kind; refused military service; declined to support the Anglican Church; and talked funny, using "thees" and "thous" instead of "you."

Penn became a Quaker after his military service and was eventually jailed for, among other things, writing inflammatory pamphlets and refusing to remove his hat in court. His father got him out and also extracted a promise from Charles II to look after his son when the admiral died.

Penn the son eventually struck a deal with the king in 1681 that essentially boiled down to Charles giving Penn 45,000 square miles of land in America in return for Penn taking a lot of the troublesome Quakers out of England and writing off a large debt Charles had owed to Penn's father. (In current currency, the deal amounted to about 10 cents an acre.)

The king named the new colony Pennsylvania (Penn's Woodland) after the admiral. Penn tirelessly advertised his new colony, calling it *The Holy Experiment.* He established good relations with the region's Native Americans and generously handed out land at low prices. While originally aimed at creating a safe place for Quakers, the colony had no official religion and promised religious tolerance for everyone (although under pressure from the king, Jews and Catholics were not allowed to vote or hold elective office).

A well-planned capital city called Philadelphia (Greek for "brotherly love") was established, with broad streets laid out in orderly transecting rows. By 1700, Pennsylvania was the third-largest English colony, behind only Virginia and Massachusetts, and by 1750, Philadelphia was not only the largest American city, but its cultural center. The lessons learned in the various colonies' struggles to find a balance between freedom of religion and freedom from religion, and to establish a government separate from any individual religion's precepts but respectful of the beliefs of all its citizens were not lost on the Founding Fathers. The trick was finding a way to avoid constantly relearning them.

DUTCH TREAT

After the Netherlands finally won independence from Spain after 80 years of fighting for it, the country aimed most of its colonial aspirations at Asia and the Far East. But in 1609, it did commission the English explorer Henry Hudson to look around North America for it. Hudson didn't find the fabled Northwest Passage, but he did find a richly wooded and well-watered region that in 1624 became the colony of New Netherland.

The colony, whose capital was started in 1626 and dubbed New Amsterdam, was established by the Dutch West Indies Company to function as a center for its fur-trading operations. Spurred by neither religious zeal nor politics, the company's directors were relatively indifferent to everything but business, and the cultural atmosphere was a good deal more relaxed than in the surrounding Puritan colonies. The capital became a bustling seaport, so cosmopolitan that a 1640s visitor counted 18 different languages being spoken on its streets. To defend against Native American attacks, a big wall was constructed along one side of Manhattan Island, in a region that would eventually become known as Wall Street.

The English, however, regarded the Dutch as trespassers in their backyard. In 1664, a squadron of English ships captured New Amsterdam without firing a shot. King Charles II promptly renamed the city and colony after his brother, the Duke of York. (That may or may not have been a better choice than naming it after one of his eight illegitimate children, the Duke of Cleveland.)

The conquest of New York gave England an unbroken string of territory from Maine to the Carolinas. The short-lived former Dutch colony gave the America waffles, sauerkraut, Easter eggs, bowling, and Sinterklaas — better known today as Santa Claus.

Chapter 4

Together and Apart

Well before the Revolutionary War began, English colonists had plenty of practice fighting, with both Native Americans and the colonial powers-that-be. Sometimes the colonists banded together, but mostly not. There were immense obstacles in traveling to, and communicating with, each other — and no colony was too excited over the idea of ceding any of its independence to someone else.

This chapter recounts the often-tragic relations between the continent's newcomers and its original residents — and the colonists' rehearsals for rebellion.

A Clash of Cultures

Even before they landed in America, many Englishmen had convinced themselves they were already the moral superiors to Spanish colonizers when it came to dealing with the New World's indigenous population. "With all cruel inhumanity," wrote Richard Hakluyt, the chief cheerleader for English colonization, "they (the Spanish) subdued a naked and yielding people . . . did most cruelly tyrannize them and against the course of all human nature did scorch and roast them to death."

Indeed, in approving the first English colonies in America, King James I had instructed colonists to treat Native Americans as humanely as possible, while bringing "the infidels and savages living in those parts to human civility" and make efforts to Christianize them. Unfortunately for both sides — but mostly for the locals — it didn't work out that way.

REMEMBER

Native Americans generally regarded the English settlers with a mixture of friendly, or at least neutral, curiosity, at least at first. The newcomers were interesting creatures. They were also a source of valuable products, such as metal implements and guns. The natives quickly realized, however, that these new immigrants not only had plans to stay indefinitely — and were likely to multiply — but had alien customs and beliefs and clearly no plans to assimilate into the Native American way of doing things.

"Your coming is not for trade," sagely noted Powhatan, the father of Pocahontas and leader of a confederacy of 31 tribes in Virginia, "but to invade my people and possess my country."

The English tended to myopically view the Native Americans as a homogenous group, with no substantial differences among the various tribes and confederacies. They also didn't — or wouldn't — grasp that the Native Americans had different concepts of land ownership.

REMEMBER

For the native peoples, land was typically owned by the community and not the individual. At the same time, a tribe might claim huge tracts of acreage that it wasn't using for anything. Both ideas were alien to settlers who crossed an ocean in search of their most cherished dream — being master and mistress of their own spaces.

In addition, many English settlers simply didn't regard the Native Americans as worthy of respect as human beings. "Though these Indians dwell among the English, and see in what plenty a little industry enables them to live," the Puritan minister Samuel Stoddard wrote in 1722, "yet they choose to continue in their stupid idleness and to suffer all the inconveniences of dirt, cold and want, rather than to disturb their heads with care, or defile their hands with labour."

The Virginia Wars

In the Virginia colony, relations between the Native Americans and England's first American settlers ranged from uneasy to murderous. After an initial attack on the Jamestown settlement, the tribal confederacy led by Powhatan negotiated with John Smith to broker peace. The deal was occasionally marred by things like kidnapping Powhatan's daughter and holding her as a hostage to prevent further attacks, or raiding the locals' cornfields when food supplies got short in Jamestown.

Even so, large-scale bloodshed was avoided. While it was a capital offense to teach a native how to use a gun and trade with the tribes was restricted, it was also unlawful to injure Native Americans in any way that would threaten peace between the two sides.

Fighting Opechancanough

When Powhatan died, his brother Opechancanough (say that three times fast) replaced him. The new chief had an implacable hatred for the European newcomers. In 1622, he led a wave of surprise attacks on the settlements around Jamestown. (Jamestown itself was saved only because of a warning from a friendly Native American.) More than 350 settlers were killed — about a quarter of all the English in the colony. "Before the end of two Moones, there should not be an English in all the countries," Opechancanough reportedly told his followers.

REMEMBER

He miscalculated. The colonists retaliated by burning Indian villages and cornfields. In 1623, they invited tribal leaders to a peace parley, then poisoned more than 200 natives, shot 50 more, and scalped many of them. When appalled Virginia Company leaders in London criticized the tactic, colonial leaders retorted "we hold nothing injust [*sic*] that may tend to their ruin . . . with these foes, neither fair war nor quarter is ever to be held."

Intermittent war continued until 1642, when a peace agreement was reached. It lasted for all of two years, or until Opechancanough — now in his early 90s — led another wave of surprise attacks. This time 500 colonists were killed. But Opechancanough was captured and shot in the back by one of the colonists after being paraded past jeering settlers.

The colony's leaders imposed even harsher restrictions on trading with the tribes, creating government-sanctioned monopolies that enriched a favored few settlers and angered the rest. They also foisted new rules on the tribes, forbidding them from trading with anyone outside the colony, and warning that if a Native American killed a white man, the rest of the tribe "would be answerable for it with their lives and liberties."

Stealing hogs leads to battling Bacon

In 1675, a group of Native Americans who had been cheated in a deal with a plantation owner retaliated by stealing some of his hogs. He retaliated by killing some of the Native Americans. They retaliated by razing his plantation and killing one of his employees. That was followed by the murders of 24 Indians during another bogus "peace parley," and another war was on.

The Virginia colony's governor, Sir. William Berkeley, decided to fight a defensive war. He ordered construction of ten forts, conscripted colonists to man them, and heavily taxed the plantation owners to pay for it all.

Bad idea. Colonists chafed at the draft, at the harsh discipline meted out at the forts — and at the taxes. There were also mutterings that Berkeley was being soft on the Indians because he had lucrative side deals with the agents his office licensed to trade with the tribes. Led by Nathaniel Bacon, a prominent planter who was Berkeley's cousin-in-law and who had a history of fractious relations with local tribes, some colonists formed their own militia and marched off to fight the Native Americans independent of the colonial government.

Bacon's troops succeeded mostly in spreading the war by attacking several tribes that had not been previously involved. But eventually the colonists' firepower, and general ruthlessness, prevailed, and peace was reached in 1677.

REMEMBER

In the meantime, however, a Berkeley-Bacon showdown would shake the American colonies, reverberate across the Atlantic, and foreshadow revolutionary events to come. You can find out more about it in the section "Revolting with Bacon" at the end of this chapter.

Dividing and Conquering

New England's Puritan settlers initially avoided bloody wars with Native Americans in part because of the good early relations established by the Plymouth Pilgrims, and in part because there weren't a whole lot of locals with which to deal. "The Natives, they are all dead of small Poxe," Massachusetts Bay Colony Gov. John Winthrop noted on his arrival in 1630. "The Lord hath cleared our title to that (land) which we possess."

REMEMBER

Winthrop was a bit premature in declaring game over. As more settlers arrived and spread out to regions away from the core area of Boston Harbor, tensions grew. Worse, when it came to dealing with Native Americans, the New Englanders readily adopted the policies established by their Virginia brethren: All Indians were basically alike; all were culpable for any transgressions against settlers, and retaliation should be brutal and overwhelming.

Unfortunately for the Native Americans when it came to dealing with the inter-lopers, the first of these assumptions — that there was a cultural homogeneity among various tribes — was patently false. Generations-old grudges and disputes between and among tribes often led them to sometimes side with the newcomers against other Indians. The English colonists soon learned to exploit that weakness when needed, while continuing to treat the Native Americans as all the same in other matters.

Failing to unify in the face of colonists' aggression would help lead to defeat after defeat for Native Americans. It also may have served as a lesson for those they were fighting when it came time for the "New Americans" to face off with the old home country.

Wiping out the Pequots

The failure of the tribes to unify was tragically exemplified in 1636, when a prominent New England trader was killed by members of a tribe in Rhode Island. A Bay Colony militia attacked the offending tribe, but didn't accomplish much in terms of revenge. It then attacked and burned a Connecticut tribal village suspected of harboring the killers.

The Connecticut tribe, called the Pequots, had been accused by the colonists of other crimes and misdemeanors in the past. While protesting their innocence, the Pequots also sought help from the neighboring and powerful Narragansett tribe. As the Pilgrim memoirist William Bradford noted, the Pequots presciently warned the Narragansett that if they didn't help their fellow Native Americans now, "they did but make way for their own overthrow" later. But the Narragansett not only turned down the request for help, they ended up opposing the Pequots.

Moreover, according to Bradford, the Pequot plan for fighting the English settlers was also visionary: "They (the Pequot) would not come to open battle with them (the colonists), but fire their houses, kill their cattle, and lie in ambush for them . . . they well saw the English could not long subsist but they would either be starved with hunger or be forced to forsake the country."

What they didn't see, however, was the English appetite for total warfare. After Pequot hit-and-run raids on several settlements, a large colonial militia force — reinforced by warriors from tribes hostile to the Pequot, including the Narragansett — launched a surprise attack on a Pequot village, near Connecticut's Mystic River in May 1737. The village was mainly populated by women, children, and old men, since most of the tribe's warriors were at a more heavily fortified village nearby.

From 400 to 700 Pequots were killed in the attack, which consisted of burning the village and then shooting or clubbing the inhabitants as they fled the fire. "Sometimes the Scripture declareth women and children must perish with their parents," one of the settlers' leaders subsequently argued. ". . .We had sufficient light from the Word of God for our proceedings."

CASINO COMPENSATION

A condition of the Pequots' surrender was that the tribe's name would no longer be mentioned in New England (although a derivation of it popped up in the novel *Moby Dick*, when author Herman Melville named Captain Ahab's ill-fated whaling ship the *Pequod.*)

But not all of the world's Pequots were gone. In 1983, the federal government formally recognized some far-flung lineal descendants as the Mashantucket Pequot Tribal Nation. In 1992, with the help of loans from a Malaysian businessman, the Pequot opened a casino on tribal lands in Connecticut. In time, the Foxwoods casino became one of the largest in the world, providing enough revenues to branch into, among other things, a golf course, posh hotel, pharmaceutical network, spa, and a second casino in Mississippi.

By 2018, the tribe was one of Connecticut's five largest employers and one of the state's biggest taxpayers. Pequot was no longer a dirty word.

REMEMBER

Almost all of the rest of the tribe was eventually hunted down and killed or sold as slaves to neighboring tribes or to English colonies in the West Indies. Gov. Winthrop kept three of the captives as slaves for his own household, noting in his journal that the rest were traded for "some cotton and tobacco, and negroes." While some historians have quibbled over use of the term, the Pequot War is often cited as one of the earliest examples of genocide on American soil. However correct the term, the Pequots had all but disappeared.

Defriending the Wampanoag

The smashing of the Pequot tribe marked the end of open warfare in New England for nearly 40 years. Native Americans continued to be bullied and bewildered, however, by the English colonists. The Puritans insisted the natives obey Puritan laws. Those included proper observation of the Sabbath, even if they weren't Christian, and not blaspheming — a vague offense even to some Puritans and completely baffling to Indians — that nonetheless in some cases carried a death penalty.

One of the tribes most baffled by this behavior was the Wampanoag. This was the very same people who had befriended the Pilgrims at Plymouth when they first arrived, almost certainly saved them from starvation, and shared with them what is commemorated at countless warm-and-fuzzy fourth-grade pageants as the First Thanksgiving. (See Chapter 3 for more on the Pilgrims.)

In 1662, the tribe acquired a new chief, named Metacom, whom the colonists called King Philip because he and his brother had asked for English names, and because of his reputed fondness for clothes from Boston shops. As the number of settlers and their cattle increased, and as it dawned on the Wampanoag that maybe they and the newcomers had different ideas about what land ownership meant, tensions rose.

Starting in 1671, Plymouth officials began periodically summoning Metacom/Philip to answer vague charges of plotting against the colonists. The chief complied with demands to surrender his tribe's guns and sign treaties, pledging obedience to Puritan laws and allegiance to the English king.

But in the summer of 1675, the pot boiled over. A Christianized, or "praying Indian," whom the Wampanoag believed to be an English informant, was found murdered. Three members of the tribe were hanged for the killing, despite the lack of substantive evidence. Fed up, the Wampanoag attacked the town of Swansea, burning a few homes. The war was on.

Fighting Philip's War

Following a guerilla-fighting strategy, the Wampanoag raided towns, settlements, and farms, took what they needed to sustain their warriors, and destroyed the rest. Encouraged by the Wampanoag successes, other tribes in Massachusetts and Rhode Island joined in — including the Narragansett tribe that had refused to help the Pequots 40 years before.

Town after town was attacked: Deerfield, Northfield, Dartmouth, Taunton, Brookfield. Native American forces came within 20 miles of the colony's capital of Boston. Before the fighting was over, 20 New England towns had been completely destroyed and dozens more severely damaged.

Colonial leaders, stunned by the breadth and ferocity of the attacks, drafted every man between the age of 16 and 60, decreeing the death penalty for shirkers, banning travel from towns without permission, and ending trade with any Indians.

Both sides sunk to barbarism. Burning buildings with besieged families still inside was a common practice. Captives were occasionally tortured and routinely executed or enslaved.

Eventually, the colonists' superior firepower and the lack of a consistently reliable source of food and supplies for the tribes began to tip the scales toward the settlers. The final blow came when tribes not involved in the fighting refused pleas to join Philip's forces, and either stayed out of it or even joined the English side to curry favor, gain plunder, or exact revenge for old feuds. In August 1676, Philip was killed in a surprise attack. His head was cut off and displayed on a stake at Plymouth for the next 25 years, and his wife and son were sold to the West Indies as slaves.

REMEMBER

It's been argued by some historians that King Philip's War was the bloodiest in American history in terms of the number of casualties as a proportion of the total population. An estimated 6 percent to 10 percent of the military-age colonists were killed; the Indian dead numbered in the thousands. "God hath consumed them by the Sword and by Famine and by Sickness," wrote the Puritan clergyman Increase Mather.

The monetary costs to the New England colonies was also huge, creating debts that took years to pay off and badly damaging both the economy and the normal processes of government.

The war did teach the colonists that most European-style military tactics were useless in the American wilderness, and that the hit-and-run tactics employed by the Native Americans might just be the way to fight. They also learned that colonies working together might just be the way to win.

Getting Together

One of the lessons colonists learned in fighting Native Americans was that it was a lot more effective to coordinate their efforts than to fight as individual colonies. But deciding unification was a good idea and actually unifying turned out to be two very different things.

Confederating in New England

Almost as soon as they were done all but wiping out the Pequots, several New England colonies began talking about banding together in some sort of common-purpose group. The idea sprang at least partially from their fear that the region's Native American tribes would beat the colonists to it and at some point decide to unite.

REMEMBER

It took nearly six years of kicking it around, but in May 1643, the colonies of Massachusetts, Plymouth, Connecticut, and New Haven formed the *Confederation of the United Colonies of New England*.

The group's charter declared its purpose was to be "a firm and perpetual league of friendship for offense & defense . . . both for preserving and propagating the truths of the Gospel and for mutual safety and welfare."

Each of the colonies' legislatures — *general courts* — was to elect two representatives to the confederation's commission, which was to meet at least once a year and also on "special occasions," such as the start of a war. The representatives had to be members of the Puritan church. The commission's president would be selected from among the representatives on an annual basis, but had no powers other than to moderate at meetings.

The commissioners could declare war, make peace, and divvy up military expenses among the member colonies in proportion to their population. But approval of the taxes levied to pay for military operations had to be approved by all of the colonies' general courts. The commission could also make recommendations to individual colonies, settle border disputes (of which there were many), and provide for the capture and return of fugitives, particularly runaway indentured servants.

No colony was bound by anything unless its general court approved, and the Confederation guaranteed the independence of each colony to make its own rules within its own boundaries.

Bickering into oblivion

The pulling-together plan looked good on paper, but quarreling among the colonies began almost immediately. Massachusetts, which as the largest and most prosperous colony was something of a regional bully, vetoed a request by some communities in what is now Maine to join, mainly because Massachusetts leaders had designs on annexing the area. No one wanted to let Rhode Island in. It was full of what most Puritans regarded as weirdos and troublemakers, and it wouldn't agree to repatriate runaway servants.

Connecticut and New Haven (the latter of which was absorbed by the former in 1664) didn't support helping Massachusetts grab some land from the French, and Massachusetts declined to help Connecticut and New Haven get a chunk of real estate controlled by the Netherlands. Massachusetts and Connecticut argued about the land formerly owned by the Pequots. And Plymouth was so small, no paid much attention to anything it wanted. As a result, the Confederation accomplished almost nothing in its first three decades of existence.

The alliance did come in handy, however, when King Philip's war broke out. The member colonies each agreed to supply specific quotas of draftees for the war and finance the military effort.

But once the fighting stopped, Massachusetts made clear it was sorely vexed by the fact that while the costs of mutual defense had been apportioned according to the populations of the colonies, it only got the same number of seats on the commission as everyone else. That meant its citizens paid more than the other colonies' citizens, but didn't get more of a say in Confederation decisions. That issue would pop up again for future Americans trying to form a representative democracy.

REMEMBER

The issues all became moot in 1684, when the Confederation was dissolved by English officials who had begun to reassert their dominance of the region by revoking colonial charters. But the inspiration provided by the New England Confederation would far outstrip its influence at the time.

It was the first stepping stone toward forming a union of individual colonies. As can be seen in Chapter 5, it helped spur efforts in 1754 of seven colonies to form a union — and in 1776, when 13 colonies began exploring the same idea.

Getting news and getting around

In addition to the political obstacles colonies faced in getting together, there were the problems of trying to move around and communicate with each other.

Roads were few, and often not worth finding: In Massachusetts, snow actually improved travel by filling in the chasmlike potholes. It wasn't until 1766 that regular coach service opened between Philadelphia and New York — and that took three days to travel 94 miles. New York to Boston was five to six days, and that was in good weather.

Travel by water along the coast, particularly for longer distances, was generally quicker, but unpredictable, dependent on tides, storms, dodging pirate attacks, and the vessel's seaworthiness. Even then, going from New York to England was often easier than going from New York to Charleston. Benjamin Franklin, for example, made eight trips back and forth across the Atlantic to Europe during his lifetime, which is almost certainly more times than he visited South Carolina.

Getting mail was akin to winning the lottery: a pleasant surprise that seldom happened. Carried by post-riders, it traveled only when enough of it piled up at one location to be deemed worth the trouble to deliver to another. It's estimated that fewer letters were mailed in all of the American colonies for the entire year of 1753 than within New York City in one day in 1904.

TECHNICAL STUFF

Even getting local news was dicey. While the first printing press in America arrived in 1636 at Cambridge, Massachusetts as an enterprise of a new college called Harvard, the first newspaper didn't appear until 1690. Called *Publick Occurrences*, it promised to come out once a month "or if any glut of occurrences happen oftener." (It only came out once and then stopped publication.) By 1740, there were only 16 newspapers throughout the 13 colonies, none of them daily. By 1776, there only 37, with a total circulation of 5,000 in a country of 2.5 million.

Most colonists therefore stayed close to home, with little knowledge of what was going on in other colonies. Human nature being what it is, that, of course, led to a region's inhabitants developing suspicions and stereotypes about other regions. Based on one bad experience with a Boston merchant, a Virginian might regard all New Englanders as self-righteous, inhospitable, and less than honorable in business. The Bostoner, in turn, might regard all Virginians as morally lax, overly familiar, and dumber than a bag of hammers.

The English colonies had been settled at different times (see Figure 4-1) by different peoples and for different reasons. They had also generally been left alone by the English government. That was about to change.

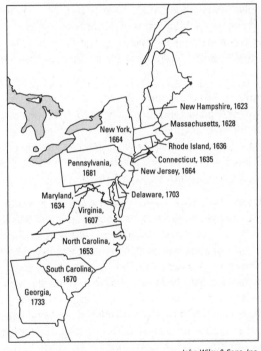

FIGURE 4-1:
The 13 American colonies and their dates of establishment.

John Wiley & Sons, Inc.

Meanwhile, in the Mother Country . . .

For much, if not most, of the 17th century, England had followed what became known as a policy of *salutary neglect* when it came to its colonies in America. It basically meant, in the words of a British prime minister, "If no restrictions were placed on the colonies, they would flourish." Part of the reason for this approach was frankly that the American colonies weren't nearly as important to England's economy at the time as its Caribbean islands were. But a bigger part was that for much of the century, England was so preoccupied dealing with domestic issues, it had little time to spare on colonial matters.

Here's what was going on in England, and how that affected the English colonies in America. If it seems really complicated, that's because I left out a lot of the details. Otherwise it would seem ridiculously complicated:

>> **Charles becomes king, 1625.** The 24-year-old son of James I was even less friendly to Puritans than his dad, and his policies and those of Archbishop of Canterbury William Laud, a close adviser, motivated thousands of English Puritans to emigrate to the New World.

>> **Charles dissolves Parliament, 1629.** Angered by England's deliberative body formally criticizing his financial and religious policies, the king shut Parliament down for 11 years and essentially ruled England alone. With fewer politicians looking over their shoulder from home, the colonists in America were pretty much on their own.

>> **Charles summons a new parliament, 1640.** The king needed money to fight a war against Scotland and couldn't get it without parliamentary support. But he found the new Parliament — with an increasing number of Puritans and other Protestants who didn't like what they deemed his Catholic-leaning ways — as objectionable as the first one that he had dissolved. So he dissolved this one, too. It didn't affect America much.

>> **A civil war breaks out, 1642.** Thwarted in trying to bend Parliament to his will, Charles summoned his Royalist, or *Cavalier,* supporters and war began with the Parliamentarians, or *Roundheads* (so-called because a lot of them sported short bowl-shaped haircuts). In America, Virginia and English colonies in the Caribbean generally sided with the Royalists, while New England sided with Parliament. The divide was enough to cause the New England Confederation to break off trading with the Royalist-supporting colonies. But the only real bloodshed occurred at a skirmish in Maryland near the Severn River, between a Puritan group and a Catholic group. The fight occurred in 1655 — four years after the fighting stopped in England.

>> **Charles I is executed, 1649.** After fleeing to Scotland as the tide of battle turned against him, the king was eventually ransomed by the Scots to the Roundheads. When the king's supporters began a new wave of fighting, the Parliamentarians, led by a stern Puritan-soldier named Oliver Cromwell, decided the best thing to do was cut off the king's head. So they did. The news variously stunned and thrilled colonists in America.

>> **Cromwell names himself Lord Protector, 1653.** No one could find a mutually agreeable political system to replace the monarchy with, so Cromwell appointed himself virtual dictator. That was fine with the New England Puritans, not so fine with the Royalist sympathizers in the Southern colonies, where many English Cavaliers began fleeing.

>> **Charles II becomes king, 1660.** Cromwell died in 1658 and was replaced briefly by his son Richard. But Richard turned out to be a nincompoop, and the English still couldn't come up with a system of government that enough of them liked. So the eldest son of the beheaded Charles I was restored to the throne. While much of England celebrated, as well as the American South, the *Restoration*, as it came to be called, made New England Puritans very uneasy — with good reason, as it turned out.

Restoring and Rebelling in New England

Charles II was a witty fellow. When a court minister joked that the king never spoke foolishly and never acted wisely, Charles is reported to have retorted the paradox was easily explained, "for his discourse was his own; his actions were the ministry's." He also didn't order the minister's tongue cut out. (Charles's good sportsmanship did have limits: After being crowned, he had Cromwell's body dug up and beheaded, in revenge for his dad's execution.)

Both the king's humor and tolerance were marked departures from the reign of Cromwell, who was puritanical enough to have ordered all the theaters in London closed. Charles not only reopened them, but allowed female parts in plays to actually be played by females.

However, the king also ordered strict conformity to the restored Anglican Church and also turned his attention to the American colonies.

Cracking down on Massachusetts

In 1664, Charles sent a royal commission to the Massachusetts Bay Colony with general instructions to remind the colony who was boss. One sore point with the king was the lax enforcement of England's *Navigation Acts.* These were a series of laws that restricted colonial trade by banning foreign ships from carrying American cargoes; limited the export of many products only to English ports; required American imports to come mostly from England; and imposed import and export duties. Most colonists routinely ignored them, and there was virtually no English government presence to enforce them.

The king's three-member commission was also charged with ending the Puritans' practice of viciously persecuting Quakers; insisting that members of the Anglican Church be allowed to openly practice their faith; demanding that the colony's leaders take an oath of allegiance to the crown; reminding the colony that it must follow English law; and redistributing chunks of Massachusetts that it had snatched from surrounding colonies.

"The king did not grant away his sovereignty over you when he made you a (charter) corporation," commissioners warned. "'Tis possible that the charter you so much idolize may be forfeited."

Massachusetts leaders responded by ignoring much of what the commissioners demanded and rejecting the rest. They also got lucky, because things got unlucky for Charles II, at least temporarily. In 1665, London was swept by both a devastating plague outbreak and a massive fire, both of which consumed much of the king's attention.

In addition, England found itself embroiled in a series of naval wars with the Dutch, who were understandably upset that England had seized its colony of New Amsterdam and renamed it New York. In 1667, a Dutch flotilla sailed up the Thames River, destroyed most of an English fleet moored there, and to rub salt in the wound, stole two of the best English ships. The humiliating defeat forced Charles to sign a peace treaty.

The reign of Randolph

After another war with the Netherlands ended in 1676, the king renewed his interest in New England. This time he sent an arrogant bureaucrat named Edward Randolph. After a protracted legal and political battle with the Massachusetts hierarchy, Randolph became Collector of Customs for New England — the first salaried English government official in New England.

Randolph, whom one chronicler called "the Evil Genius of New England," began zealously enforcing the Navigation Acts, seizing 36 ships in his first three years. He also began a continual power struggle with Massachusetts officials. Colony leaders forced him back to England, where he presented a scathing report to Charles II about their lack of respect for English law, the monarchy — and, of course, himself.

The crown reacted by revoking the Massachusetts Bay Colony's 50-plus-year-old charter in June 1684. It became a crown colony, with a royal governor authorized to run military operations, collect a tax on landowners that was payable to the king, and veto anything passed by the colonial assembly. Then, as far as the colonists were concerned, things got worse.

The taxing Governor Andros

In February 1685, Charles II died and was succeeded by his brother, James II, who happened to be a Roman Catholic and had even less love for Puritan New England than his brother had. Eight months after his coronation, James declared the creation of the *Dominion of New England.* The act combined Massachusetts, New Hampshire, and Rhode Island into a single crown colony, overseen by a grand council appointed by the king and a royal governor. It was later extended to include New York and what is now part of New Jersey.

The new governor, Sir Edmund Andros, brought two companies of English soldiers with him. He was a ruthlessly efficient and experienced colonial administrator, with a knack for making people really dislike him. He not only strictly enforced the Navigation Acts and suspended the colony's hugely popular and relatively democratic town meetings, but squeezed every shilling he could out of the colony. Taxes on liquor were doubled. All land titles were ordered reconfirmed, for a fee. A service charge was even imposed on paying taxes.

To make things more galling for the colonists, Andros was drawing an exorbitant annual salary of £1,200 — about $358,000 in 2018 U.S. dollars. When colonists complained about the crown's policies and tactics, Andros' secretary — Edward Randolph — archly replied, "It is not to his Majesty's interests that you should thrive."

But both the governorship of Andros and the reign of James II were short-lived. Fearful of a Roman Catholic dynasty developing after James had a son, the English deposed him in a bloodless coup in November 1688 and replaced him with a Protestant Dutch prince, William of Orange. (For those of you keeping score on English royalty, William was the grandson, on his mother's side, of Charles I, the English king who was beheaded. He was also the husband of his first cousin, Mary, who was the daughter of James II. That made James both William's father-in-law and uncle. I think.)

The *Glorious Revolution,* as the coup was called, meant the return of Protestant rulers to the English throne. When the news reached Boston a few months after it took place, it also meant the end of the Andros Administration. In April 1689, a band of 200 armed rebels demanded Andros surrender his authority. The English troops assigned to keep order prudently declined to fire on the rebels, and Andros and his secretary Randolph were jailed for months before being shipped back to England. Similar rebellions occurred in other areas of New England.

But to the disappointment of the Massachusetts colony's old guard, the former charter was not reinstated. Instead, new charters that established royal governors and councils for the New England colonies were put in place. The colonies were allowed to keep their elected legislatures, but the right to vote was extended to non-Puritans.

REMEMBER

The new system ensured an ongoing tension between the colonies' local government and the English crown's administrators and bureaucrats. But there was a temporary silver lining for the colonists: While the Navigation Acts stayed on the books, their enforcement was sporadic. For the most part, a few well-placed bribes ensured the kind of unfettered business to which the colonists had become accustomed.

Revolting with Bacon

In the Southern colonies, a family feud took on class overtones and sparked a spate of rebellions. As mentioned earlier, in "The Virginia Wars" section of this chapter, Virginia Gov. William Berkeley and his cousin-by-marriage, plantation owner Nathaniel Bacon, Jr., had a sharp disagreement in 1676 over how to fight Native Americans.

Berkeley was a tyrannical 70-year-old aristocrat and longtime Virginia resident who was contemptuous of those he governed, considering them "a people who six parts of seaven . . . are Poore. Endebted, Discontented and Armed." Bacon was a 28-year-old relative newcomer to the colony. He was clever and charismatic, but also a bully with a greatly inflated ego and a hot temper.

Berkeley wanted to play defense when it came to Indian-fighting, building forts, drafting colonists to man them, and taxing the populace to pay for it. Bacon preferred going on the offensive and attacking every tribe he could find, even those who were not at war with the colonists. To that end, Bacon drummed up a militia of fellow plantation owners and other settlers in the western end of the colony who were most at risk from attack. The militia also attracted poor farmers and recently freed indentured servants and slaves.

Then things got weird. To save his, excuse the pun, bacon, Bacon apologized for challenging Berkeley's authority; Berkeley forgave him. The governor called for new elections to the House of Burgesses to come up with a new war plan. The new house — to which Bacon was elected — instead enacted a sheaf of what became known as Bacon's Laws, even though he didn't attend the session and had nothing to do with them. The laws included such reforms as term limits on officeholders and extending voting rights to all free white adult males, whether they owned land or not.

Bacon, meanwhile, repudiated his previous apology and marched on the colonial capital of Jamestown with a militia of from 500 to 700 men and demanded at gunpoint to be made a general. He was given his commission, after which Berkeley immediately branded him a rebel and began raising a force to fight Bacon's militia and not the Native Americans. As inducements, Berkeley offered tax exemptions and a share of the plunder from the possessions of Bacon's followers.

Bacon responded by burning down much of Jamestown and greatly expanding his vision of the rebellion beyond Virginia.

When after one of Bacon's fiery harangues, a follower remarked, "Sir, you speak as though you (desired) a total defection from his Majesty and our country," Bacon replied, "Why, have not many princes lost their dominion so?" Heady with his initial success, Bacon also issued a Declaration of the People, which demanded Berkeley and his top aides surrender — and also demanded that everyone swear allegiance to Bacon, under pain of arrest.

And then Bacon suddenly died in October 1676, apparently of dysentery. The rebellion fizzled. After mopping up the last rebels, Berkeley hanged 23 of them. An English naval squadron carrying about 1,000 soldiers — and royal pardons for the rebels — arrived too late to participate. After a crown investigation, Berkeley was recalled to England, where Charles II was said to have remarked of the governor that "the old fool has hanged more men in that naked country than I did for the murder of my father!"

REMEMBER

Before it ran out of gas, however, Virginia's rebellious atmosphere spread to neighboring colonies. In Maryland, a group of about 60 dissidents assembled at the capital to denounce heavy taxes and the revocation of voting rights. The group's two leaders were promptly hanged for treason and another man exiled for advocating freedom of speech.

In North Carolina, a new tax on tobacco exports triggered a rebellion in which the governor was arrested and thrown out of office. Both he and his rebellious replacement wound up in London pleading their cases. The rebel, John Culpeper, was tried for treason. He was acquitted, but removed from office.

Sizing up the Impacts

One thing all of the English colonies' early rebellions had in common was that they were aimed at individuals or specific circumstances. That naturally limited their appeal for other colonies to join in. Even if the causes had wider appeal, lousy transportation and communication systems would have made wider alliances difficult.

But they did exemplify a spirit of independence and a willingness to challenge authority. Those grew stronger as inhabitants of the English colonies began to multiply, spread out — and increasingly begin to think of themselves as Virginians or Rhode Islanders rather than as citizens of European countries. That was a key step toward thinking of themselves as Americans.

And if nothing else, they added weight to the argument that, as Thomas Jefferson put it, "Insurrections proceed oftener from the misconduct of those in power than from the factions and turbulent temper of the people."

PSYCHEDELIC SALAD

While English colonists were frequently on the lookout for novel New World products that might catch on in Europe (remember tobacco?), not everything they found was deemed marketable.

Take *datura stramonium*, a weed that Virginia colonists encountered, ingested — and learned to treat with respect. Of course, they didn't always tip off newcomers to the colony about the plant's effects. Thus, when a group of English soldiers sent to help quell Bacon's Rebellion added some (actually, more than some) to a meal, everyone got a big laugh out it, except the soldiers.

"They turn'd natural Fools," wrote the contemporary historian Robert Beverly. "One would blow up a Feather in the Air; another wou'd dart Straws at it with much Fury; and another, stark naked sitting upon a Corner, like a Monkey, grinning and making Mows upon Them . . . a Thousand such simple Tricks they play'd, and at Eleven Days, return'd to themselves again, not remembering anything that had pass'd."

Beverly identified the plant as *the James-Towne Weed,* which later evolved to *Jimson Weed.* And the soldiers were lucky to get off with just looking silly. Although sometimes used as a folk remedy to treat asthma or as an analgesic, the weed is part of the nightshade family and lethal in even relatively small doses. Good thing it never caught on. Like tobacco.

Chapter **5**

The Fight for a Continent

As the 18th century unfolded, Britain's colonies in mainland America underwent an amazing growth spurt in population, diversity, and economic and political clout. This chapter chronicles the causes and effects of these dizzying expansions — particularly how they changed the colonies' relations with the mother country.

Many colonists also experienced a shift in how they worshiped. A few even took a swing at forming a political union. And to top it off, the colonies were sometime-hosts to a series of international conflicts, where the ultimate Grand Prize was control of a major chunk of North America.

Growing toward Revolution

In 1751, Benjamin Franklin did some figuring. The 45-year-old Franklin estimated that the population of the American colonies had doubled during his lifetime and predicted it would double again in 24 years. He was off by a considerable margin. About 1.1 million colonists, servants, and slaves were living in America in 1751. By 1776, there were 2.6 million, half again as much as Franklin had predicted.

Most of the boom was homegrown. American colonists were apparently an amorous bunch (or didn't have much else to do at night): It's estimated that up to one-third of New England brides at the time of the Revolutionary War were pregnant before they were married. They were early starters, too: Females who reached the age of 21 and were still unwed were sometimes referred to as *antique virgins.*

There was also a practical side to procreation for the overwhelming majority of colonists, who lived on farms: Large families meant more people to work the land. Whatever the motivation, the size of many American families was astounding.

Franklin — printer, inventor, scientist, author, and almost certainly the most famous American in the world at the time — wrote of a Philadelphia woman who had 14 children, 82 grandchildren, and 110 great-grandchildren by the time she died at the age of 100. That was particularly impressive record of fertility when you consider the high infant mortality rate. One woman was reported to have lost 20 children at birth or soon thereafter.

And they apparently didn't waste much time: The anecdote-laden Mr. Franklin (whose own father sired 15 children) also told of a particularly practical — and not overly sentimental — woman who used refreshments left over from her first husband's wake to serve to guests at her next wedding.

Pouring in from all over

Of course, not everyone was the offspring of that one woman in Philadelphia. Starting around 1720, tens of thousands of Scots, Irish, Germans, Swiss, and natives of various Scandinavian countries flocked to the American colonies, often in organized groups. By 1790, about 20 percent of America's population was from somewhere other than England or Wales.

Many were fleeing religious or political persecution, but almost all were also lured by the promise of land, which was cheap, good — and plentiful, particularly west of the already-settled regions along the Atlantic coast.

They were joined in the colonies' western reaches by a wave of *second sons,* young men whose older brothers stood to inherit the family land and were therefore compelled to stake their own claim elsewhere, as well as people driven by restlessness, ambition, or a desire to just start over. They included the fathers of men like Thomas Jefferson, Abraham Lincoln, and Andrew Jackson.

And as with every immigrant wave, there was a criminal element. In 1717, Britain began a formal policy of shipping some of its societal dregs to the colonies. By mid-century, it was estimated that 10 percent of the city of Baltimore's population were former British thieves, pickpockets, and worse. Some of them became good citizens; some didn't. But the policy nonetheless prompted the prominent Virginia planter William Byrd II to write a friend in England, "I wish you would be so kind as to hang all your felons at home."

While around 90 percent of the populace lived in small towns or farms, American cities were also growing. In 1700, New York City and Philadelphia had populations of about 5,000 each and Charleston (then "Charles Town"), South Carolina about 2,000. Boston, the largest city, held about 6,700. By 1775, Philadelphia had surpassed Boston as the most populous, with 40,000, followed by New York (25,000), Boston (16,000), and Charleston (12,000). In fact, Philadelphia by 1775 was quite possibly second only to London in the British Empire in terms of size, and maybe first in attractiveness: A German visitor in 1770 remarked Philadelphia was "allowed by foreigners to be the best of its bigness in the known world."

But as the American colonies' population grew through high birth rates and hefty immigration levels, it also grew from the arrival of thousands of people who weren't here voluntarily.

Coming in chains

In 1725, an estimated 75,000 slaves were in the American colonies, the overwhelming majority of them Africans. By 1790, there were more than 700,000. At least some slaves were in all but three states (Massachusetts, Maine, and Vermont). By 1750, nearly half of the human beings in Virginia were owned by the other half. In South Carolina, slaves actually outnumbered nonslaves by about 1.5 to 1.

REMEMBER

The explosive growth was due to the tragically simple triumph of economics over morality. The British, who had once condemned other nations for slave trading, had found African slaves well-suited — and eventually financially indispensable — for harvesting sugar on British colonies in the West Indies. American colonists in the South needed them for harvesting labor-intensive crops, such as tobacco, rice, and later, cotton.

American colonists at first preferred indentured servants because they were easier to communicate with, were familiar with English culture, and cost less (see Chapter 3). But as demand grew and as enslaved Africans seemed to adapt better to plantation work than indentured Europeans, the preference changed. So did the economics.

For example, an indentured servant might cost a plantation owner £2 to £4 (roughly $500 to $1,000 in 2019 U.S. dollars) a year to maintain over the length of their servitude. An African slave might cost ten times that much to buy, but was the owner's property for the life of the slave and could be bred. As one owner put it, breeding slaves — or even raping them — was "a pleasant method to secure (more) slaves at a cheap price."

The view of slaves as economic necessities was by no means limited to the South. "I do not see how we can thrive until we get a stock of slaves sufficient to all our business," wrote Emanuel Downing, a Massachusetts lawyer, "for our children's children will hardly see this great continent filled with people, so that our (indentured) servants will still desire freedom, to plant for themselves."

Not all colonists were enamored with the rapid increase in the colonies' slave population, although the reasons for their disapproval were not always based on solely moral grounds. Some feared widespread rebellions as the numbers of slaves increased.

In fact, slave rebellions did occur, from New York to South Carolina. But all involved relatively few slaves, and all were put down, almost always with horrific punitive measures that ranged from mass hangings to burning slaves alive. In addition to setting off alarm bells about the growing number of slaves, the revolts did result in some dubious reforms. In South Carolina, for example, laws were passed that required slave owners to provide better food and clothing — and limit the slaves' workday to no more than 15 hours.

REMEMBER

Other colonists wanted to limit the importation of slaves to drive up the values of those already in America. But British officials refused to consider limits, fearing they might slow things down economically. The slave trade had become one of the main components in the British and American economies by the mid-18th century, a key component of what was known as the *Triangular Trade*. This consisted of New England–produced rum being sent to Africa to exchange for slaves who were then shipped to the British West Indies and traded for sugar that was then taken to New England to be made into rum.

Lots of people made money at every stop, including the British government, which collected duties and other fees. Thus, slavery became, in the words of one slave trader, "the Hinge on which all the Trade of this Globe moves on and the best traffick the kingdom hath." It was a key cog in the economic machine that joined Britain and the colonies — and the machine was humming along quite nicely.

Doing Business with Mom

Like virtually all European powers of the 16th through 18th centuries, Britain's economic theory was based on *mercantilism*. The idea was that there was a finite amount of wealth in the world; the chief economic goal of a country was to get as much of it as it could, and the chief duty of a country's citizens — in particular its colonies — was to help the country get it.

The American colonies, therefore, had three goals to pursue as far as the British were concerned:

>> **Produce** goods Britain needed or wanted and sell them only to Britain.

>> **Buy** stuff only from Britain.

>> **Avoid** competing with Britain by not producing similar goods.

The first goal was fairly easy to attain, since America had a lot of things Britain both wanted and needed: Tobacco, indigo, and rice in the Southern colonies; timber, furs, fish, and naval supplies in the Northern colonies.

Timber, for example, was so abundant in America and so scarce in Britain that a British merchant might sail to Boston, sell his cargo, use the proceeds to commission the construction of another ship, and sail both back to Britain loaded down with raw lumber.

Selling only to Britain was an irritant. But on the positive side, American producers were guaranteed access to the sizeable British market — and the British government paid bounties to encourage production of especially desirable American products.

The second rule — buying stuff only from Britain — was more problematical and therefore generally ignored. American colonists bought wine and salt from Spain's Madeira Islands and molasses and slaves and gold from France's Caribbean islands, even while the mother country was at war with the other European nations.

The third rule — not competing — was also a tough one to comply with. As colonists ventured into various manufacturing endeavors, colonial governors were ordered to "discourage all Manufactures and to give accurate accounts (of production levels) with a view to their suppression." Laws were passed to prevent American hat makers from selling hats to other colonies and limit the overall number of hat-makers. Shipping wool or woolen yarn or cloth was forbidden. To slow down the American manufacture of sail cloth, ships built in the colonies could be equipped only with sails of British-made cloth.

Enforcing trade laws — or not

Enforcement of all the various trade laws was the province of the London-based eight-member *Board of Trade,* which in turn answered to the king's *Privy Council.* No one on the board or council was likely to collapse from overwork, however. Regulations were often vaguely worded and seldom enforced with any enthusiasm. Bribery of customs agents was routine, and strict enforcement would have been tough in any case since there were too few agents and too much empire to cover.

While the council had the authority to veto any laws passed by the colonial assemblies that ran afoul of British trade laws, it did so in less than 6 percent of the cases that came before it. And despite the arbitrary and sometimes silly nature of the trade laws, they actually affected only about 15 percent of colonial goods anyway.

It was true that Britain kept a tight lid on the bank. In fact, no banks were in the American colonies. In keeping with the mercantile theory that all wealth should accrue to the mother country, *hard currency* — gold and silver — as well as British pounds were funneled back to Britain and in short supply in America.

Instead, British companies extended lines of credit that colonists could use to buy British goods, or receipts for goods that colonists then used as a sort of cash. They also bartered: One Harvard student paid his tuition, according to a receipt, with "a Watertown goat, which died." The colonists also printed their own currency, which was illegal and generally worth little.

REMEMBER

But despite the difficulties of running an economic system with 3,000 miles of ocean in the way, both sides did well. American colonies, which had absorbed about 10 percent of all British exports in 1701, were consuming 40 percent by 1774. At the same time, the economic output of the colonies, which in 1700 was about 4 percent of Britain's, was 40 percent by the 1760s.

The British statesman Edmund Burke marveled in 1775 that what it had taken England 1,700 years to accomplish economically would be achieved "by America in the course of a single life! . . . For some time now, the Old World has been fed by the New."

Doing okay in America

Of the European and North American nations during the 18th century, only the Netherlands, Great Britain, and the American colonies managed to maintain their standards of living while increasing their populations — and America grew much faster than either of the other two.

Americans also ate better, or at least more. It was estimated that by mid-century, the average American male colonist consumed 200 pounds of meat annually, which may have helped account for the fact that he was on average two inches taller than his European counterpart. "Hoggs in America feed better than Hyde Park duchesses in England," joked a British visitor.

REMEMBER

America developed a distinct and rather sizeable middle class. A typical worker in Philadelphia in mid-century might make £60 a year (about $16,300 in 2019 U.S. currency) and pay £2-3 ($550–$800) in taxes — as much as twice the salary and half the taxes of his English cousin. In 1755, the average farm in Connecticut was reckoned to have 10 head of cattle, 16 sheep, 6 pigs, 2 horses, a team of oxen, and enough grain and produce to sell 40 percent of it as cash crops. By the 1770s, Americans could afford to spend part of their incomes on imported goods considered luxuries, such as ceramics, cutlery, spices, and lace curtains.

"You may depend upon it," said William Allen, one of the richest men in Pennsylvania, "that this is one of the best poor man's countries in the world."

Colonists were feeling financially feisty — and the feistiness carried over to their politics as well.

Flexing Political Muscles

In 1751, the eminent Philadelphia botanist John Bartram noted with some satisfaction that newcomers flocking to the American colonies for land were also "excited by the desire of living under governments and laws formed on the most excellent model on earth."

Bartram was referring to the British structure of an executive — the monarchy — and a two-body Parliament with the non-elected House of Lords and the elected House of Commons. In theory, that's the way American colonial governments were set up. Each colony had a governor appointed by or approved of by the king. Each governor had a council usually composed of wealthy and influential colonists, many of whom had powerful political connections in Britain. An assembly of representatives was elected by the colonists.

One of the reasons Britain had set up its mainland American colonies with charters and so much self-governance in the first place was to save money. Administrators and bureaucracies 3,000 miles away were expensive. But the price of being thrifty was that American colonists became used to running things on their own. In addition, the English civil wars and Glorious Revolution, as well as the numerous mini-rebellions in the colonies themselves, had whetted the appetites of Americans for self-rule even more.

And the American colonies were not a desired posting for members of the British foreign service. They were too American. One newly appointed governor of the New York colony was depressed enough about his assignment that he hanged himself the week after he arrived.

So good officials asked for, and generally got, sent to the West Indies, or India, or even Nova Scotia, which had a more British feel to them. As a result, the British officials who did arrive in America were rarely among the empire's best and brightest. They were often despised and ridiculed by the colonists and slighted or ignored by their superiors in Britain.

REMEMBER

But the main difference between the colonies' governmental structure and that of the mother country was that in Britain, the king and his ministries had considerable control of government spending. In America, elected assemblies did. Colonial governors were free to veto any assembly-passed laws they didn't like. But they did so at great personal financial peril, since the assemblies' powers included setting the governor's salary.

The assemblies also set tax and fee levels, appointed local commissioners and tax collectors, and ran elections. Governors often countered by buttering up the colonies' rich and powerful, who controlled big portions of the economy and could exert some influence over things, particularly in the longer-settled regions of the colonies along the coast. But in general, the balance of power tipped in favor of the assemblies.

Most free white males over the age of 16 who owned at least some land could vote. This greatly displeased many of the colonies' Old Guard, whose families had controlled much of the colonies' wealth. "It is as bad as a state of Warre for men who are all in want to have the making of Laws over Men that have Estates," grumbled a rich South Carolina plantation owner.

REMEMBER

One result of the Little Guy having so much say in government was that government was kept small and therefore inexpensive to operate. Most costs were covered by fines, land sales, duties on sales, and so on. Direct taxes were extremely low and sometimes nonexistent: New Jersey and Pennsylvania had no taxes at all for several decades. In fact, American colonists were among the least-taxed people on earth.

And with things going along pretty well on the economic front, they began to loosen up a little when it came to tolerating each other, religiously speaking.

GOVERNORS AND MONKEYS

New York Gov. William Cosby was, by most accounts, a corrupt and generally incompetent bozo. Appointed by King George II to run the colony in 1732, Cosby helped himself to tax revenues, gave away land he didn't own, packed the colony's courts with cronies, and generally ignored his duties. His behavior did not go unnoticed, and a political war erupted.

Enter John Peter Zenger. A German-born printer, Zenger was induced by Cosby's foes to start a newspaper, the *Weekly Journal*. Among the paper's primary purposes was to get under Cosby's skin. This was accomplished by printing anonymous articles that likened Cosby and his supporters to runaway monkeys and dogs. Understandably upset, Cosby responded by having Zenger charged with *seditious libel* — public statements designed to encourage insurrection against authority. Zenger was jailed and languished there for nine months because his bail had been set at an amount equivalent to about $168,000 in 2018 currency.

Enter Andrew Hamilton. A Philadelphia lawyer, Hamilton became Zenger's attorney after the printer's first lawyer was disbarred by Cosby. Hamilton employed a novel defense: Zenger had indeed published the offending articles, but the articles were basically true, and truth should trump libel. The jury, Hamilton argued, was not deciding Zenger's fate, but pondering "the cause of Liberty." The judge, a pal of the governor, promptly instructed the jury to ignore the argument. But the jury promptly ignored the judge, and after ten minutes of deliberation, acquitted Zenger.

The case did not immediately establish a legal precedent. In fact, it wasn't until 1805 that the New York Assembly passed a law allowing truth to be a defense against libel. But it did help lay a legal foundation to prevent government officials from stifling publication of material they don't like. It also helped reaffirm an old — and continuing — American custom of juries sometimes ignoring the law in favor of justice.

Relaxing Religiously

The New England colonies had been there less than a century, but by the early 1700s some of their Puritan leaders were already despairing that the shining City Upon a Hill was turning into a Sodom-by-the-Sea. A society founded on and operated by strict religious orthodoxy was, in the words of Massachusetts Judge Samuel Sewall, giving way to "sensuality, effeminateness, unrighteousness and confusion."

Women were leaving their husbands; prostitutes could be found entertaining sailors at Boston's bustling harbor. Rum exporting was a major industry, and not all of it was being exported, as attested to by the fact there were now more taverns in the city than churches.

Even funerals were becoming so ostentatious that the colony's General Court tried — and failed — three times to set spending limits on final send-offs. "Religion brought forth Prosperity," the theologian Cotton Mather sourly noted, "and the daughter destroyed the mother."

There was no question that America's improving economic conditions had led to shifting cultural and societal norms, and it wasn't only in New England. "Pennsylvania," the German writer Gottlieb Mittelberger observed, "is heaven for farmers, paradise for artisans, and hell for officials and preachers."

But the shift didn't necessarily mean American colonists were becoming less devout. In fact, by the 1730s a movement that became known as the *Great Awakening* marked a massive religious revival that reflected both a growing sense of religious tolerance (except toward Roman Catholics) and an increasing desire on the part of many Americans to declare independence from institutional controls.

REMEMBER

In general, the Great Awakening was a combination of simplifying worship by deemphasizing — or ignoring — the ceremonies and authority of traditional church-based religions and urging the individual to find his or her own way to God by personal study and introspection. Its preachers leavened the terrors of eternal damnation in Hell with the joys of finding a path to Heaven.

Dangling Bugs and Road-Show Religion

The catalyst of the Great Awakening was a tall, delicately built genius named Jonathan Edwards. A brilliant theologian who had entered Yale at the age of 13, Edwards was the school's head tutor by the age of 21. He was also a scientist, writing dazzling papers on subjects from atomic theory to spiders. And he was a spellbinding public speaker.

"The God that holds you over the pit of hell, much as one holds a spider or some loathsome insect over the fire, abhors you and is dreadfully provoked," he thundered in a sermon called "Sinners in the Hands of an Angry God."

But Edwards also preached that when not angry, God radiated his goodness into everyone, not just a chosen few. By grasping that goodness, anyone could attain the beauty of salvation.

Edwards was joined, and eventually surpassed in popularity, by a small, cross-eyed and melodramatic preacher from England named George Whitefield. Nicknamed the Great Itinerant, Whitefield held mass revival meetings from Georgia to Massachusetts over a 30-year career. On one tour alone, he traveled 800 miles in 75 days and gave 175 sermons.

Equipped with a booming voice and theatrical instincts, Whitefield drew crowds in the thousands to his meetings. "People wallowed in the snow night and day for the benefit of (his) beastly brayings," a Boston Puritan acidly noted. Benjamin Franklin, however, was impressed. After attending a Whitefield revival, Franklin wrote that "from being thoughtless or indifferent about religion, it seem'd as if all the world were growing religious."

REMEMBER

The impact of the Great Awakening reached beyond the realm of religion. Its emphasis on the importance of the individual fostered the birth of new religious denominations, which in turn saw the founding of new colleges — Dartmouth, Brown, Columbia, and Princeton, for example — to ensure an adequate supply of ministers.

More important, it helped to break down barriers between colonies by creating a commonly shared experience. And as the first spontaneous mass movement in America, the Great Awakening heightened the individual's sense of power when combined with that of others.

Connecting the Snake

On May 9, 1754, a woodcut print appeared on Page 2 of the *Pennsylvania Gazette*, the colonies' most widely read newspaper. The picture, shown in Figure 5-1, depicted a snake chopped into eight pieces, with each piece bearing the initials of a colony or group of colonies. Beneath the snake was the legend "JOIN, or DIE."

FIGURE 5-1:
Benjamin Franklin's "JOIN, or DIE" woodcut.

Library of Congress

Designed by — who else? — Benjamin Franklin, the woodcut's purpose was to urge the colonies to band together in a common defense against the omni-present threat of attack from Native Americans and quite possibly France.

As part of an effort to prepare for such attacks, Franklin was one of about 20 representatives, selected by the royal governors of various colonies, to convene in Albany, New York in July 1754. The convention was the brainchild of George Montagu Dunk, Earl of Halifax and First Lord of the Board of Trade in London. His Lordship's goal was to persuade a powerful group of six tribes — the Mohawk, Oneida, Onondaga, Cayuga, Seneca, and Tuscarora — to side with the British in any upcoming fight, or at least stay neutral.

The tribes, also known as the Six Nations or *Iroquois Confederacy,* hated the French because France had sided with ancient enemies of the confederacy in past fights. But they were also distrustful of the British. By the end of the conference, however, the tribes agreed to stay on the sidelines, took their wagonloads of "presents," including 400 guns, and went home.

Franklin, meanwhile, had been doing some thinking about his chopped snake. Over the course of a few days, he and other delegates came up with an idea to permanently join the American colonies. A *Grand Council* would be established to deal with mutual defense, frontier expansion, and Native American relations.

The council would be supported by taxes paid in proportion to the colonies' sizes, and delegates apportioned in proportion to the amount of taxes paid. Under the plan, small colonies like New Hampshire and Rhode Island would get two representatives each, while large colonies like Massachusetts and Virginia would get seven each. The council could legislate, make war and peace, and select a governor-general to preside over meetings and function as sort of a council manager.

REMEMBER

On July 10, the assembled delegates approved the idea. But neither British officials nor colonial assemblies were wild about it, the British for obvious reasons and the assemblies because they feared a loss of autonomy. Not a single assembly endorsed the plan.

"I am still of the opinion that it would have been happy for both sides of the water if it had been adopted," Franklin noted years later in his memoirs. "The colonies, so united, would have been sufficiently strong to have defended themselves (against the French); there would have been no need of troops from England; of course, the subsequent pretense for taxing America, and the bloody contest it occasioned would have been avoided."

But the Albany Union didn't happen, and the chain of events that Franklin outlined had already begun even before the delegates had drawn up the idea.

Waging World Wars

Except for a few skirmishes here and there, the three European superpowers — Britain, France, and Spain — had managed to stay out of each other's way in the New World for most of the 17th century. One reason was there was still a lot of wilderness between their territories. Spain's claim was mainly in South and Central America and what is now the American Southwest. France's domain was to the north and west of the British colonies, which clung to the Atlantic coast or nested on islands in the Caribbean.

Each power had taken a different approach to colonizing. Spain viewed its colonies as resources to exploit and the native populations as slaves. France had only half-heartedly encouraged immigration, in favor of maintaining good relations with the natives to foster the fur trade. And Britain had encouraged its colonies to develop as semi-independent profit-driven entities, dealt with the Native Americans by negotiating treaties or killing them, and imported African slaves to fill the demand for cheap labor.

But in 1688, the first of what would be four world wars broke out. Over the next 75 years, the Big Three and some other European nations would intermittently clash in both hemispheres and on several continents and seas. The first three wars began in Europe and spread to America. The fourth began in the woods of Virginia — and nurtured the growing seeds of revolution.

King William's War

The first of the three warmup fights was known in Europe as the *War of the League of Augsburg* (Americans liked to shorthand the names of these wars by assigning them to British monarchs). Its chief cause was that the Catholic king of France, Louis XIV, didn't like that the English had thrown out their Catholic king, James II, in favor of the Protestant William III. After England sided with other countries against France in a territorial dispute, war erupted.

The fighting covered parts of Europe, India, the Caribbean, and South America, as well as North America. French-led Indians wiped out the village of Schenectady, New York; American colonists briefly captured the strategic stronghold of Port Royal in Nova Scotia. But after nine years of bloody and economically crippling fighting, both sides agreed to call it a draw. A subsequent peace treaty returned virtually all the territories the various combatants had controlled before the whole thing started.

Queen Anne's War

Known in Europe as the War of the Spanish Succession, it pitted Spain and France against England and her European allies, including the Dutch and Austrians. Beginning a scant four years after the end of the last war, this one was sparked after Louis XIV of France installed his 17-year-old grandson on the throne of Spain. England and other European countries objected to the idea, and the fighting began again.

This time colonists in South Carolina found themselves fighting Spaniards in Florida and successfully defending the town of Charleston, while New Englanders were again facing French-led Indians. The American colonists again captured Port Royal in Nova Scotia. But this time, Britain got to keep it. In 1713, a peace treaty awarded the British with all of Nova Scotia, Newfoundland and an area around the entrance to the St. Lawrence River.

King George's War

Historians with a sense of whimsy — and there probably are some — like to start this war with a Welsh mariner named Robert Jenkins. In 1731, Jenkins's ship was seized in the West Indies by Spanish privateers, who accused Jenkins of smuggling, summarily sliced off one of his ears, and then handed it to him. They told him to give it to the British king and relay the message they would likewise cut off His Majesty's ear if he tried to smuggle in their territory.

Jenkins eventually delivered the message to British officials, who generally ignored it. But eight years later, as tensions between Spain and Britain mounted over trade rights in the West Indies, particularly in the slave trade, the incident was used to whip up support for another war.

The War of Jenkins' Ear was a relatively small-scale fight in the Caribbean. But it soon merged with a much larger conflict known in Europe as the War of Austrian Succession, which had to do with a dispute between Austria and Prussia. In America, colonists captured a key French outpost on Cape Breton Island called Louisburg, which commanded the Gulf of St. Lawrence. But Britain managed to lose its colony of Madras in India to the French.

When the war ended in 1748, the two nations traded the areas back to each other. That outraged the American colonists, who had lost 900 men — about one-third of their force — in taking and holding Louisburg, only to see it given back to the enemy without them having a thing to say about it. The bad taste it left in colonial mouths, especially in New England, substantially lessened their appetites for future fights as allies of Britain.

Unfortunately, they wouldn't have much choice. Just six years later, in the words of the British writer Horace Walpole, "The volley fired by a young Virginian in the backwoods of America set the world on fire."

"I Heard the Bullets Whistle . . ."

Early in the morning of May 28, 1754, a tall and athletically built 22-year-old Virginian stood at the top of an isolated ravine, as the group of colonial militia and Seneca Indians he was leading poured musket fire down on a group of French soldiers camped below.

After 15 minutes of fighting, the French surrendered. But as the young Virginian watched in horror, one of his Seneca allies suddenly bashed in the head of the now-unarmed French officer, who, it turned out, was leading a diplomatic mission and not a raiding party.

Things got worse. The colonists built a haphazard and poorly located fort to defend themselves against an attack from a much larger French force. (The Seneca told the militia leader it was a bad idea and left.) When the French attack came, about a quarter of the young Virginian's troops were killed or wounded. The colonists surrendered on July 4, a date that would take on much happier significance in 22 years. But their leader was forced, or tricked into, signing a statement admitting the murder of the French officer. The French then gallantly but inexplicably let the Virginian and his men go home.

All in all, it was a humbling beginning to any military career. Still, it helped convince the young man he wanted to be a soldier. "I heard the bullets whistle," George Washington wrote to his brother, "and believe me, there is something charming in the sound."

Setting up a showdown

Washington's defeat at the inelegantly named Fort Necessity triggered yet another worldwide conflict. This one was called the French and Indian War in America and the Seven Years' War in Europe. And this time, it wasn't about religion, monarchial successions, or a ship captain's ears — it was about land.

REMEMBER

As the American colonies began filling up, settlers hungrily eyed the vast expanses of what to them was empty open space to the west. It wasn't empty at all as far as the Native Americas living there were concerned, and it wasn't open as far as the French were concerned. But to American colonists and British officials it seemed unfair, as one of them put it, that "the French have stripped us of more than nine parts of ten of North America and left us only a skirt of coast along the Atlantic shore."

To rectify this "unfairness," British and American speculators secured the rights to about 500,000 acres in the Ohio River Valley from members of the Iroquois Confederacy, whose own claims to the land were highly dubious. The French countered by building a string of forts to defend what they considered their territory. Fighting ensued.

On paper, the French and British seemed evenly matched. Britain had the better navy, France the better army. Britain's colonies in North America had a vastly larger population than France's, but France's autocratic colonial system meant there was less infighting among officials. Plus the French had good relations with powerful Indian tribes, such as the Ottawa and Algonquin, who were eager to destroy British settlements, while Britain's Indian allies were either not all that strong, or in the case of the Iroquois Confederacy, not all that enthusiastic about fighting.

Getting off to a bad start

Initially, the war did not go well for Britain, even as it spread around the globe and encompassed disputes over fishing rights in Newfoundland, navigation rights on the Mississippi River, trade rights in the East Indies, and sugar plantation ownership in the West Indies.

In 1755, British General Edward Braddock arrived with two regiments and orders to destroy the French forts in the Ohio Valley. Braddock was undeniably brave (he had five horses shot out from under him in one battle), but also arrogant to the point of stupidity.

When he was warned that marching his troops single-file through heavily wooded terrain was an invitation for a Native American attack that would slice his force to pieces, Braddock haughtily replied that "these savages may indeed be a formidable enemy to your raw American militia, but upon the King's regular and disciplined troops, sir, it is impossible they should make any impression."

The remark echoed the opinions of most British military leaders, who were contemptuous of the American militia's lack of discipline, shoddy equipment, and fighting ability. One British general called them "the dirtiest, most contemptible cowardly dogs that you can conceive."

Most Americans had no love for France, which was still ruled by a monarch with absolute power. France was Catholic, imposed heavy taxes on its people, had a military draft, and operated a legal system that left things in the hands of judges rather than juries.

But many Americans also disliked the British military in their midst, particularly since His Majesty's generals had a penchant for taking over private residences to bivouac soldiers and allowing their troops to help themselves to food and other supplies without paying for them.

Thus, many colonists were not convinced the war was any of their business, particularly those whose homes weren't immediately threatened by marauding Native Americans. Several colonial assemblies refused to muster any militia at all until the British government guaranteed it would pick up the bills.

The indifference of his fellow colonists infuriated Washington, especially when they stymied efforts to enlist troops and gather supplies. "In all things I meet with the greatest opposition," he complained. "No orders are obeyed (without) a party of my soldiers or my own drawn sword's enforcement. Without this, a single horse for the most urgent occasion cannot be had."

Fumbling start, good finish

Accompanied by Washington, Braddock led a force of 1,400 against the French forts in the Ohio River Valley. As predicted, his troops were surprised by a French and Indian army. Braddock was killed, along with about two-thirds of his men. Washington, whose horse was killed and coat pierced with musket balls, led the retreat. The defeat was followed by a string of British losses in both North America and elsewhere over the next two years.

Things began looking up, however, in 1758, when a British politician with a hawk-eyed gaze, out-sized ego, and oodles of charisma took over the war effort. "I know that I can save this country," said William Pitt, "and that no one else can." A brilliant orator, Pitt was so well-liked by the average Britisher that his nickname was the Great Commoner. People would kiss his horse as they rode down the street. (Presumably the front part.)

Pitt, who is also considered by many historians to have been at least a little nuts, took a spend-first, worry-about-it-later approach to financing the war. He employed a strategy of forcing the French to divert much of their army to battlefields away from North America and then concentrating British efforts toward breaking France's back in the New World by taking Canada. And he cajoled American colonists into taking an active part in the fighting, promising the war would be conducted "at His Majesty's expense."

Pitt also ignored the tradition of putting senior generals in charge of things and picked the best and brightest military leaders he could find from among Britain's officers corps. These included 41-year-old Jeffery Amherst, who became the army's top commander, and 32-year-old James Wolfe.

In September 1759, Wolfe led a risky attack against the French stronghold of Quebec by landing an amphibious force at the base of a set of 600-foot cliff and scaling it while dragging up two cannons. Surprised at the audacity of Wolfe's move, French defenders foolishly left the city's fortifications to attack across open country and were routed in a 15-minute battle. Both the French commander, the Marquis de Montcalm, and Wolfe were killed.

Coupled with the conquest of Montreal by Amherst the following year, the British victories all but ended the North American portion of the war, which formally ceased in 1763 with the signing of a peace treaty in Paris.

Assessing the aftermath

The British Empire ended up with all of Canada, all of America east of the Mississippi River, Florida, and some Caribbean islands. Moreover, the victory cemented Britain's place as the most powerful nation in the world (see Figure 5-2).

FIGURE 5-2: Map of North America showing the regions controlled by European powers after the French and Indian War ended.

John Wiley & Sons, Inc.

The American colonists got rid of the French threat at their backdoor and gained a lot more territory in which to stretch out — or at least they thought they did. Future political and military leaders matured. And more than in any previous wars, men from the various colonies fought alongside each other, helping to ease regional differences.

The differences between the colonies and the mother country, however, which had multiplied and sharpened during the war, were about to get a whole lot more numerous and sharper.

2

The Fight for Independence

IN THIS PART . . .

British actions and American reactions pave a road to revolution.

Independence is declared — but not yet won.

A war is waged at home and around the world, and America loses right up until it wins.

Chapter **6**

Causes and Effects

I f you sauntered through the last chapter, you may be wondering right about now just what it was the American colonists really had to squawk about at the end of the French and Indian War. Things generally seemed to be going along pretty well, especially when compared to life in most of the rest of the world.

But one of the things that made the American Revolution unique was that it sprang as much from conditions that Americans feared might occur in the future as much as from past or current conditions. Parliament was seeking ways to assert its authority over the colonies at precisely the same time the colonies were increasingly regarding themselves as partners in the British Empire, not second-class subjects of it. The more British officials pushed, the more American colonists pushed back.

In this chapter, a series of British actions — and American reactions — over a host of issues accelerate tensions to the brink of violence.

Warring over the West

Many American colonists were giddy over the prospect of millions of virgin acres of land newly won from the French after long war. Some were newcomers looking for a place to start, while some — including the ambitious soldier-turned-planter George Washington — were hoping to get rich by cornering huge tracts that could be resold for handsome profits. But if the French and Indian War was over, the fights with Native Americans weren't. The biggest of these post-war fights was called *Pontiac's War* — and it was ugly.

Waging biological warfare

Both the British and French had curried favor with various tribes by lavishing gifts on them, from rum to guns and ammunition. With the war over, however, the gifts stopped. The French were all but gone from the Great Lakes and Ohio Valley regions, and the British military leaders were under orders to reduce spending as much as possible.

The orders delighted Gen. Jeffery Amherst, who had commanded British forces in North America during the French and Indian War. Amherst was left in charge of the British troops that remained as an occupying army on the continent after the war.

A capable career soldier, Amherst had a pathological hatred of Native Americans. When tribes protested at the halt in distributing "gifts," Amherst replied that if they caused trouble, "They must not only expect the severest retaliation but an entire destruction of all their nations."

In addition to cutting off supplies, the British built forts, gave away Indian lands, and generally treated the tribal leaders with contempt. By May 1763, a loose confederation of tribes under an Ottawa war leader named Pontiac had had enough. Pontiac, who was said to have had a vision of "a heaven where there are no white men," urged his colleagues to "exterminate from our lands this nation which seeks only to destroy us . . . nothing prevents us; they are few in numbers and we can accomplish it."

They gave it a good try. Within a month, every fort in the region except the ones at Detroit and Pittsburgh had been overrun and destroyed, in part because Amherst had stationed most of his troops in other parts of America and Canada. The warring tribes killed or captured an estimated 2,000 settlers and forced another 4,000 to flee east. About 400 British soldiers were killed and another 50 or so captured and tortured to death.

REMEMBER

Amherst responded by ordering the "total destruction" of what he called "the vilest race of beings that ever infested the earth." He enthusiastically endorsed a subordinate's plan to spread smallpox among the tribes by sending them blankets infected with the disease and to use dogs to hunt Indians down, "as well as to try Every other Method that can serve to extirpate this Execrable Race."

Eventually, the Indian coalition ran low on supplies and was crippled by a smallpox outbreak that apparently began before the infected blankets were delivered.

Tribes to the north and south refused to join in the fighting; the British managed to hold the key forts at Detroit and Pittsburgh, and French troops still in the Louisiana territory declined to get involved. By late 1765, the war was over. Luckily for the Native Americans, Amherst had been recalled to England. His replacement, Gen. Thomas Gage, chose rationality over revenge, and the war ended without harsh reprisals by the British.

Colonial militias had played only a minor role in the war, with many assemblies refusing to muster their militias or offer much cooperation. The British government noticed their absence.

Proclaiming the West off-limits

Even before news of Pontiac's war reached London, British officials were drafting a plan to keep peace on the Western frontier — by keeping American settlers out of the area. But news of the war made them put a rush on it.

On Oct. 7 1763, George III issued a proclamation that basically put all the newly conquered land east of the Alleghany Mountains, from Canada to the Gulf of Mexico, off limits to American settlement "until our further pleasure be known." The ban's enforcement would be carried out by the British army.

The stated purpose was to head off continual warfare with the region's Native American tribes, but British officials had at least two ulterior motives as well. One, in the words of a member of the Board of Trade, was to keep the area "as open and wild as possible" for the lucrative fur trapping trade.

REMEMBER

The other was to keep colonists in areas closer to the Atlantic coast, such as Nova Scotia, Georgia, and Florida, "where they would be useful to their Mother Country, instead of planting themselves in the heart of America, out of reach of the government, and from where (because of) the great difficulty of procuring European commodities, they would be compelled to commence manufactures, to the infinite prejudice of Britain." In other words, they would be too far away to buy things from Britain and get into the bad habit — as far as British merchants were concerned — of making things for themselves.

The proclamation did spur a mini-boom in some eastern areas (Benjamin Franklin bought 100,000 acres in Nova Scotia), but for the most part, it either angered Americans or elicited yawns. The fact was that hundreds, if not thousands, of settlers already lived east of the dividing line, and more were pouring in. To them, that had been one of the main purposes of the war with the French. Surely the British government wasn't serious about keeping all that land empty. George Washington, for one, didn't think so.

Washington, who was heavily invested with other Virginia plantation owners in a speculative land scheme in the West, wrote off the proclamation as a "temporary expedient to quiet the minds of the Indians" and urged potential investors in Western lands to "find and claim them without delay." "What Inducements have Men to explore uninhabited Wilds," he rhetorically asked, "but the prospect of getting good Lands?"

Warm-Up Quarrels

Putting lots of land off limits wasn't the only way British officials came up with to irritate American colonists. Other issues ranged from property rights to pine trees and from involuntary service in His Majesty's navy to paying clergymen in tobacco.

Wrangling over writs

In an effort to crack down on rampant smuggling, customs agents in Massachusetts were issued documents in 1760 called *writs of assistance*. These were basically open-season search warrants that allowed agents to break into and search anywhere at any time — stores, warehouses, and even private residences. An outraged group of 63 Boston merchants (some of whom were almost certainly smugglers) went to court to try to stop the writs from being renewed. And one of their lawyers was James Otis, Jr.

REMEMBER

In an impassioned argument that enthralled a packed courtroom, Otis contended that the practice was a violation of the basic rights of English subjects. "A man's house is his castle," he said, "and while he is quiet, he is as well guarded as a prince in his castle." Moreover, Otis argued, "when an act of Parliament is against common right and reason," the court had the right — and the duty — to overrule it.

It took almost three years for the courts to reach a final decision — and the merchants lost. After a temporary lull, the issuance of writs was renewed in the colonies. But Otis's oratory helped feed colonists' growing impatience with what they regarded as arbitrary and intrusive British rule. One courtroom spectator, 26-year-old John Adams, described Otis's speech as "a flame of fire . . . every man of an immense crowded audience appeared to me to go away, as I did, ready to take arms against writs of assistance."

Protesting parsons' pay

In Virginia, another young lawyer was making similar arguments — and winning similar acclaim — on a wildly different issue. This case involved a convoluted dispute over the salaries of clergymen. Because currency was scarce in the colonies, it was customary for Virginia clergy to be paid in tobacco. But because tobacco's value fluctuated wildly from season to season, the House of Burgesses decided to fix its value at twopence a pound when it came to paying salaries of parsons and some government officials. The clergy objected and took their case to London. The crown's representatives agreed with the parsons and overruled the colony's elected officials.

But when one of the ministers sued for back pay, he ran into an as-yet unheralded 27-year-old lawyer named Patrick Henry. Arguing for the colonial assembly, Henry daringly attacked the king himself in a passionate defense of Virginia's right to set its own laws. "A king, by disallowing acts (of) so salutary a nature, from being the father of his people degenerates into tyranny, and forfeits all rights to his subjects' obedience," Henry thundered.

The jury did find for the plaintiff and awarded him damages — of one penny. Henry was carried from the courtroom on the cheering spectators' shoulders. As with the writs, final resolution took several years, and by then the case had been overtaken by more pressing issues. But the case nurtured the idea that not only did colonists have the right to be represented in matters of taxation, but also when it came to making the laws they lived under.

Pouring more fuel on the flames

Other colonial grievances against British policies and laws were not widespread but widely varied in their subject matter.

In Boston, New York City, and other seaports, violence periodically erupted against the British navy's practice of *impressment*. Impressment was essentially a form of legal kidnapping, wherein "eligible men of seafaring habits between the ages of 18 years old and 55 years old" could be grabbed off the street or off merchant ships on the high seas by British "press gangs" and forced to join the navy. John Adams contended that anger over the practice heavily contributed to the colonies' eventual rebellion.

In Connecticut, New Hampshire, and Vermont, fights occurred over the White Pines Acts, which prohibited colonists from cutting down any eastern white pine tree with a diameter of more than 12 inches, even if the tree was on their property. The idea was that the crown had dibs on the bigger trees because they made great ship masts. The law was so hated that when a government surveyor who was thrown into a millpond after trying to enforce the rule filed a criminal complaint, a New Hampshire jury found the surveyor himself guilty of trespassing.

In New Jersey, New York, and Pennsylvania, there were tussles over whether colonists or the crown should decide how long a judge's term of office should be. And nearly everywhere, there was opposition to a push by Anglican Church officials to station a church bishop in the colonies so new ministers didn't have to go all the way to England to be ordained. The proposal, colonists argued, was a thinly disguised first step to establishing the Church of England as the Church of America.

"The Minds and Hearts of the People"

Most of the issues outlined in the last section were specific in nature and limited to either a single colony or just a few. Before I move on to events that were broader in scope, it's worth a few paragraphs to discuss something that's harder to define, but I think nonetheless contributed to the American Revolution. I'll call it the *American Character.*

The British colonies in America were settled by people who were by nature restless or rebellious, or both. Many — by some historians' estimates as many as half — were indentured servants or apprentices whose sole escape from the numbing poverty of the Old World was to sign away years of their life for a chance at a new beginning in the New World.

Others wanted the opportunity to live their religion in the open. Some saw it as the only way they would become masters of their own land. And some were just tired of being expected to doff their hats to their "betters" while walking down streets that belonged to them as much as anyone else.

They adapted new ways of doing things or invented them. If they didn't, they often died. They learned to take what the new land offered, dress for the climate, and fight like the natives. They came to regard their government systems as replicas of, and equals to, the British Parliament.

It took decades to evolve from English to English colonists to Americans. No single event, or even series of events, caused the shift, and no event or events triggered a hasty and irreversible rush to revolt. As the French writer Alexis de Tocqueville put it, "The revolution of the United States was the result of a mature and dignified taste for freedom, and not of a vague or ill-defined craving for independence."

Or as John Adams wrote, "The Revolution was effected before the war commenced. The Revolution was in the hearts and minds of the people."

Cents and Sensitivity

"We in America have certainly abundant reason to rejoice," the brilliant-but-erratic Massachusetts lawyer James Otis, Jr. wrote in 1763. "The British Dominion and Power may now be said, literally, to extend from sea to sea . . . the true interests of Great Britain and her (colonies) are mutual, and what God in his Providence has united, let no man dare attempt to pull asunder."

Within five years, however, Otis would describe the British House of Commons as "button-makers, horse jockey gamesters, pensioners, pimps, and whore-masters" and repeatedly proclaim in speeches and pamphlets that British efforts to tax American colonists without affording them representation in the British government was "tyranny."

What happened in between these two statements? (Other than the fact that Otis became mentally unstable, a condition exacerbated by having his head gashed in a tavern fight with a tax collector.)

Well, a lot happened. In 1763, both Britain and America were still basking in the afterglow of their shared victory in the French and Indian War. Britain had vanquished its European rivals and now had the dominant role in political and economic affairs. America had the French out of its backyard. But there was price to pay for all that, and deciding who was going to pay it had a lot to do with the marked change in the rhetoric of Otis and other Americans.

Paying for victory

TECHNICAL STUFF

The French and Indian war had been expensive. Britain's costs had amounted to an estimated £133 million, (roughly $30 billion in 2019 U.S. currency), about half of that spent on operations in North America. The national debt had doubled from the start of the war to the end. Moreover, to protect its newly won territory, regulate the fur trade, and keep a sharper eye on American colonists, it was reckoned Britain would need to keep 10,000 troops stationed in North America, as well as more customs agents and tax collectors. That could cost another £200,000 a year (about $45.5 million in 2019 U.S. dollars).

The notion of debt did not sit well with George Grenville, who had become the British prime minister in 1763. Grenville was self-righteous, cautious, and a tedious public speaker. He was also a born bean-counter. But after cutting post-war military spending, the nation's budget was still in the red. That left raising revenues, which meant raising taxes: Whose taxes was the hard part.

REMEMBER

From the British perspective, it seemed only fair that Americans kick in a portion — say, about one-third — of the needed revenue. After all, the war had been waged in part to protect them from the French and Indians. "He that accepts protection stipulates obedience," sniffed the British poet, playwright, and polemicist Dr. Samuel Johnson. "We have always protected the Americans, we may therefore subject them to government."

In addition, the colonists already enjoyed a much lighter tax burden than their English cousins — about 1 shilling per head per year in America compared to 26 shillings per head in England. And it was galling that Americans continued to dodge customs duties on goods they imported from the mother country, to the tune of about £500,000 a year (about $600 million in 2019 U.S. dollars.) If they just paid what the law already required them to, British leaders argued, it would more than cover the cost of stationing troops and other government officials in the colonies.

But British officials also had a less public motive: keeping the colonists in line. With enough revenues from America, Britain could afford to pay its governors directly, rather than depending on colonial assemblies to do so. That would restore the de facto power of the crown's direct representatives. "It may be time to exact a due obedience to the just and equitable regulations of a British Parliament," an aide wrote to William Petty, head of the Board of Trade, which oversaw colonial matters for the king.

On the other hand . . .

Many Americans took a much different view. They saw the issue as being forced to pay for a lot of insolent and rowdy soldiers in their midst, whom they didn't need or want: The French were gone, and the American militias could handle the Indians. As Philadelphia lawyer John Dickinson put it, a standing British army in America amounted to "a formidable force established in the midst of peace to bleed us into obedience."

Worse, Americans would be paying the upkeep on customs agents and tax collectors whose attitudes toward the colonists were viewed to be just as bad as the soldiers' attitudes. "Their offices make them proud and insolent," Benjamin Franklin noted, "their insolence and rapacity make them odious; and being conscious they are hated, they become malicious."

Moreover, their sole purpose was to enforce a lot of rules and regulations the colonists had no say in creating. That was the "taxation without representation" to which James Otis and others had repeatedly objected. Realistically, taxation with representation would probably have been no more palatable, since a few American representatives sitting in the House of Commons would have been routinely outvoted on any matters pertaining to the colonies.

Besides, the colonists already had champions in Parliament. Example: An exchange between Charles Townshend, who had succeeded William Petty as head of the Board of Trade, and Col. Isaac Barré, a House of Commons member who had served with distinction in the French and Indian War:

Townshend: *"Will these Americans, children planted by our care, nourished up by our indulgence until they are grown to a degree of strength and opulence, and protected by our arms, will they grudge to contribute their mite to relieve us from the heavy weight of the burden which we lie under?"*

SLAVERY'S SLIPPERY SLOPE

In 1769, Charles Stewart, a British customs officer stationed in Boston, returned to England. Stewart brought with him an African slave named James Somerset. In 1771, Somerset escaped, but was recaptured, whereupon his master put him on a ship bound for Jamaica, where Somerset was to be sold to a plantation.

But while in England, Somerset had been baptized a Christian, and his godparents interceded on his behalf, seeking a *writ of habeus corpus* — a legal term that asks a court to decide whether someone is being held illegally. An English court granted a hearing. Somerset's five attorneys — mostly paid for by Granville Sharp, a champion of the abolition of slavery — argued that no English law recognized the existence of slavery on English soil. Stewart, Somerset's owner, argued that his property rights were paramount. The judge sided with the slave.

"A foreigner cannot be imprisoned here on the authority of any law existing in his own country," wrote Lord Chief Justice William Murray, Earl of Mansfield. Somerset was freed.

While narrowly limited in terms of legal precedence, the case became widely known in the American colonies. In 1773, five slaves in Massachusetts cited the ruling in petitioning for their freedom, to no avail. But the case highlighted a politically troublesome issue for the colonies: how to press for rights and freedoms from Britain while denying them to hundreds of thousands of inhabitants of the colonies.

The paradox was not lost on the Massachusetts slaves: "We expect great things from men who have made such a noble stand against the designs of their fellow man to enslave them," they wrote. But the fear of alienating Southern colonies so heavily dependent on slave labor helped kill a proposal in the Massachusetts assembly to abolish slavery. "If passed," an assembly member wrote to John Adams, "it should have a bad effect on the union of the colonies."

The hypocrisy of what amounted to political expediency was music to the ears of America's enemies in Britain. "How is it that we hear the loudest YELPS for LIBERTY from among the drivers of Negroes?" noted the writer Samuel Johnson.

It was a question that would vex America for generations to come.

Barré: *"Planted by your care? No! Your oppression planted 'em in America. They fled from your tyranny to a then-uncultivated and inhospitable country . . . Those Sons of Liberty . . . they (Americans) I believe are as truly loyal as any subjects the king has, but are a people jealous of their liberties and will vindicate them if ever they be violated . . .".*

Barré's stirring speech was widely circulated and cheered in the colonies — so much so that towns would be named after him in five different American states. But rhetoric, no matter how impassioned, didn't pay anyone's bills — and a string of Parliamentary acts to collect from the colonies would become a lit fuse.

Sugar, Stamps, and Tea Make Trouble

To a 21st century observer, it might appear that in the years leading up to the Revolutionary War, the British handled nearly everything ineptly, while the Americans responded to nearly everything overdramatically.

There's a fair amount of validity to that observation. To Britain, America was getting too big for its britches. "The Americans must be subordinate," said the British statesman William Pitt, who was generally sympathetic to the colonists' concerns. "This is the Mother Country. They are children. They must obey, and we prescribe." But to America, Britain was an overbearing authority figure that was becoming a bully. As Benjamin Franklin put it — in verse: *"We have an old mother that peevish has grown;/ She snubs us like children that scarce walk alone;/ She forgets we're grown up and have sense of our own."*

But in addition to butting heads on regional issues from pine trees to parsons' pay, British authorities and American colonials began in 1764 to tangle over much wider and more serious issues.

The Sugar Act

In 1733, Parliament imposed a sixpence-per-gallon tax on all foreign-produced molasses (made from sugar) that the American colonies imported to make rum. The idea was to coerce the colonists into buying molasses from British colonies in the West Indies. But since the British colonies charged higher prices, Americans generally smuggled in foreign molasses, or bribed customs agents into letting them pay a tax as little as one penny per gallon.

No one cared much about it until after the French and Indian War, when Britain faced both a huge war debt and the ongoing expense of keeping a sizeable army in North America. So British Prime Minister George Grenville came up with a plan under which Americans would pay about one-third of the £200,000 per year (about $45.5 million in 2019 U.S. dollars) it would cost to support the America-based troops.

REMEMBER

Under Grenville's plan, approved by Parliament as the *American Revenue Act,* the duty on molasses was cut in half, to only threepence per gallon. But under the act, smugglers and tax dodgers would be pursued more enthusiastically and dealt with more harshly. Those so accused would face trial by a military judge rather than a colonial jury, and have to go all the way to Nova Scotia for the trial. There were other provisions as well, which ranged from higher duties on some imported goods to prohibitions against colonists selling products such as lumber to markets other than those in Great Britain.

Grenville thought the plan was quite reasonable. But his reasoning was harshly challenged by colonists, who condemned the act as unjust, unwarranted, and unconstitutional. It spurred the creation of communication networks called *committees of correspondence,* which were designed to spread information — and anti-British propaganda — throughout the colonies. A British critic called the system "the foulest and most venomous serpent ever issued from the egg of sedition." Be that as it may, it was effective, and helped set the foundation for the colonial congresses that would follow.

Besides misjudging colonial reaction, Grenville's timing was terrible. Following the end of the French and Indian War, both sides of the Atlantic were enduring an economic recession. During the war, colonial merchants had prospered by selling supplies to the troops (sometimes on both sides).

But with the fighting over, military markets dried up. Industries such as ship-building slumped. The colonies were also hit with several years of low crop production, particularly tobacco. Credit was scarce; demands for payment of existing debt intensified. As Americans slowed their purchases of British goods, the recession hit the mother country, too. An estimated 40,000 people were in debtors' prisons in England by 1765. The addition of any government-imposed costs in the midst of hard times was bound to be hated.

In the end, the Sugar Act was a flop. Smuggling continued to chug along at impressive levels, while revenue to the crown from the tax did not: In one year, it was estimated it cost £8,000 (roughly $1.8 million in 2019 U.S. dollars) in administrative costs to collect a paltry £2,000 (about $457,000 in 2019 U.S. currency) in duties. In 1766, Parliament reduced the tax to one penny. By that time, British officials had moved on to other mistakes.

The Stamp Act

Grenville and Parliament followed up on the Sugar Act with a law prohibiting colonies from issuing their own currency and nullified any existing colonial assembly law that approved of homegrown money. But Grenville saved his biggest blunder until just a few months before he was fired by King George III (partly for his political clumsiness and partly because the king just didn't like him, and you could still do that sort of thing if you were king).

For 70 years, residents of England had paid stamp taxes, which were fees charged for just about anything that required paper, from writing letters to getting married. British officials therefore thought it reasonable that American colonists should do the same. In March 1765, with almost no debate, Parliament approved a Stamp Act for America.

REMEMBER

The act required government-issued paper stamps, or stamped paper, to be used for everything from newspapers and playing cards to wills and liquor licenses. The act covered about 50 specific items, and the fees for each stamp or stamped document ranged from threepence to £4 (in 2019 U.S. currency, about $895) depending on the item's importance. Paying for the stamps or paper required hard currency, which was scarce in the colonies.

The Sugar Act had been bad enough from the colonists' perspective, but at least it was an indirect trade duty that would be built into the cost of products, was unseen by the consumer, and was thus considered an external tax. The Stamp Act, in contrast, was paid directly by the consumer and was the first internal tax Parliament had attempted to levy on the colonies.

The law was not set to go into effect until November 1765, which gave Americans plenty of time to raise a cataclysmic storm of protest. "They talk of revolting from Great Britain in the most familiar manner," the royal governor of Massachusetts reported to his superiors.

They did more than talk. In Boston, an action committee composed mostly of middle-class merchants and calling itself the *Loyal Nine,* and then the *Sons of Liberty,* organized the *hanging in effigy* — that is, stringing up a straw or rag representation — of Andrew Oliver, who had been appointed a stamp distributor for Massachusetts. Then they ransacked his house. Oliver resigned his post the next day, as did other stamp distribution appointees in other colonies.

In New York, the 77-year-old acting governor was warned that if he called out British troops against protestors, "you'll die a martyr to your own villainy and be hang'd." But despite the violent acts of the mobs, there were no deaths, mainly because the troops, militia, or law enforcement offered virtually no opposition.

Because the Stamp Act threatened to deeply affect the pocketbooks of printers, virtually every owner of a press in the colonies unleashed a blizzard of pamphlets, newspapers, and *broadsheets* (large pieces of paper usually printed on only one side, like a poster) excoriating the law. Perhaps for the first time in a political protest, a mass medium played a prominent role.

There were also organized boycotts of almost every British product sold in the colonies. Lambs were spared a trip to the butcher so they could eventually be sheared for their wool instead of buying it from England. Even funeral attire was altered from traditional black attire because black cloth came almost exclusively from Britain.

REMEMBER

In October, just before the act was to take effect, representatives from nine colonies met in New York City and drafted 15 formal resolutions of protest. "It is inseparably essential to the Freedom of the People," the *Stamp Act Congress* wrote, "that no Taxes be imposed on Them, but with their own consent. The resolutions had little impact on their own, but the meeting demonstrated that the colonies could compromise and cooperate with each other in matters that affected them all.

"We should all endeavor to stand upon the broad and common ground of those natural and inherent rights that we all feel and know," declared South Carolina delegate Christopher Gadsden. "There ought to be no New England men, no New Yorker known on the continent, but all of us Americans."

British officials were stunned. Of the more than £100,000 ($22.3 million in 2019 USD) in stamps and stamped paper sent to America, a grand total of £45 (about $10,000 in 2019 USD) was sold, and all of that in Georgia. Benjamin Franklin, who was living in London at the time, was summoned to Parliament. If the act were repealed, he was asked, would Americans concede that Parliament did have the authority to tax them as well as make other laws.

"No, never," Franklin replied. "They will never do it . . . no power, how great soever, can force men to change their opinions."

The British were whipped. In March 1766, Parliament repealed the act. As a face-saving measure, it also passed a *Declaratory Act* that insisted the colonies "have been, are and of right ought to be, subordinate unto and dependent upon the imperial crown and Parliament."

Jubilant colonists ignored the declaration rhetoric and celebrated with fireworks, festivals, and good sportsmanship. In New York, they unveiled a handsome statue of George III astride a noble steed. In Philadelphia, they toasted the king's birthday.

"They (Americans) are as quiet and submissive to Government as any people under the sun," wrote John Adams, adding that repeal of the act "has composed every wave of popular discord into a smooth and peaceful calm."

It didn't last long.

The Townshend Acts

In mid-1767, the British government found itself in need of money again, this time to replace revenues it lost when Parliament cut land taxes for the home folks in England. Charles Townshend devised a plan "by which revenue might be drawn from America without offence."

Townshend, the king's new chief financial minister (known as Chancellor of the Exchequer), was nearly as witty as he thought he was. He was charming, incautious — and wrong about his plan not offending Americans.

REMEMBER

The series of laws approved by Parliament imposed new duties on glass, lead, paint colors, paper, and tea. Such taxes were called *external levies* because they were paid by the importer and passed on to the consumer as part of the total cost of the good. Townshend assumed that because of this, colonists wouldn't object as they had with the *internal* Stamp Act taxes, which were paid directly by the consumer at the time of the transaction and thus much more noticeable. But colonists didn't like them anyway. Nor did they care for other aspects of the new laws.

These included using the new revenues — estimated at about £40,000 (about $8.9 million in 2019 USD) a year — to directly pay colonial governors and other officials, thus removing the "power of the purse" from colonial assemblies that had previously set the salaries for those officials. The acts also authorized the use of writs of assistance — that is, nonspecific search warrants — and transferred trials for smuggling and customs violations to nonjury courts run by the British navy.

It took a bit longer for opposition in the colonies to the acts to explode than it had after the Stamp Act, but explode it did. Boycotts were organized against British goods from sugar to ship anchors, shoes, snuff, hats, mustard, and glue.

Royal tax collectors were discouraged from performing their tasks, often by groups laying siege to their homes through the night, beating drums, blowing horns and howling like wolves. Sometimes the mobs resorted to the brutal practice of tarring and feathering the officials (see Figure 6-1).

FIGURE 6-1: British print showing colonists forcing a tarred-and-feathered tax collector to drink tea.

THE BOSTONIANS PAYING THE EXCISE-MAN OR TARRING & FEATHERING

Library of Congress

Responding to words with troops

Not all of the protests were based on economics or violence. In late 1767, a polished and successful Philadelphia lawyer, John Dickinson, penned a series of 12 anonymous essays he called "Letters from a Farmer in Pennsylvania." In a calm but eloquent voice, Dickinson gently suggested that "every government, at some time or other, falls into wrong measures (and) it is the duty of the governed to endeavor to rectify the mistakes . . . let us behave like dutiful children who have received unmerited blows from a beloved parent."

But he also laid out that the colonists' choices were to accept the British actions and become virtual slaves or express their disapproval. He cautioned against violent rebellion "until the people are fully convinced that any further submission will be destructive to their happiness." And he answered Townshend's attempt to differentiate between an external tax and an internal one with "a total denial of the power of Parliament to levy upon the colonies any tax whatever."

Dickinson's letters became a sort of bible for America patriots. They were widely circulated in newspapers and reprinted in pamphlet form. And they were also read in England (but not by Townshend, who died in September 1767), making clear the colonists were not going to accept the new laws any more than they had the old ones.

The British response was led by Wills Hill, also known as Lord Hillsborough, who had been appointed the crown's first secretary of state for the colonies. Haughty and heavy-handed, Hillsborough ordered colonial governors to dissolve their assemblies if they participated in circulating inflammatory materials concerning the acts. He ordered the governor in Massachusetts to look for people who could be tried for treason under a 16th century law still on the books and transported to London for trial.

TEA TIME

The British taxed it and made it a symbol of authority over the American colonies. The Americans dumped it in harbors (as I explain in the next chapter) and made it a totem of liberty. Mostly both sides just drank it.

But despite its status as an icon of the American Revolution, tea didn't become popular on either side of the Atlantic until well into the 17th century. In England, the first tea shop opened in 1657, but was not an overnight sensation. It grew steadily in popularity, however, after King Charles II married a Portuguese woman who adored the beverage and hence made it fashionable. In America, colonists picked up the habit from the Dutch settlers of New York, but it wasn't until 1690 that it was being sold in Boston.

One reason was the cost. A 1729 ad in the Pennsylvania Gazette offered "very good Bohea-tea" (a Chinese mountainside variety) for roughly the equivalent of $22 dollars a pound in 2019 U.S. currency. It was expensive for good reason. First, it traveled from China to England, where twice a year it was auctioned. Then it had to cross the Atlantic to the colonies. All along the way, middlemen and governments took their cuts.

By the 1770s, better shipping routes, faster ships, more favorable duties and taxes, and growing markets made it a bit more affordable and therefore more popular. Colonial women held tea parties that gave them a social outlet as taverns did for colonial men. Serving tea from silver pots into porcelain cups resting on lace and linen doilies became a status symbol, to the point that about half of the probated estates in 1770s Boston listed tea sets as assets.

Nonetheless, tea remained fairly expensive for the average American, so boycotting its use was more painful for the affluent than anyone else. To avoid being shunned, or worse, many of the better-off switched to a different drink — and never looked back: American coffee consumption soared by as much as 700 percent in the late 18th century.

Most troubling to the colonists, he also dispatched several additional regiments of British troops to Boston to quell disturbances. This last act, Benjamin Franklin said, was akin to "setting up a smith's forge in a magazine of gunpowder."

Like its Stamp Act predecessor, the Townshend Acts were abject failures when it came to generating revenues. In one year, the crown netted £295 (around $63,000 in 2019 USD) from the acts while spending an estimated £170,000 (about $36.4 million in 2019 USD) on the extra troops now stationed in America.

On March 5, 1770, Townshend's successor, Frederick North, better known as Lord North, proposed the repeal of all the duties imposed by the Townshend Acts — except the one on tea. North insisted on keeping the tea tax to demonstrate to the colonists that Britain was not relinquishing its right to rule them.

On the same day in Boston, a "massacre" was happening.

Chapter **7**

From Rabble to Rebels

After five-plus years of an almost-ceaseless war of words, Britain and America were edging closer to a much more physical confrontation. It was reaching the point where all the chips had been knocked off everyone's shoulders, all the lines drawn in the sand had been crossed, and it remained only to see who punched first or went home.

In this chapter, the chest-pounding ends, and the fighting begins.

Taking It to the Streets

The British decision to send additional troops to the streets of Boston (they arrived in October 1769) was viewed by colonists inside and outside Massachusetts as nothing less than an invasion. Parliament's earlier demands that Americans help pay for the troops to "protect" themselves — apparently from themselves — became even more galling than they had been.

The troops alarmed even colonists who had disapproved of the mob actions in the city. "Our lordly masters in Great Britain will be content with nothing less than the depreciation of American Freedom," George Washington fumed.

Three thousand miles away, some of Washington's lordly masters were confident that a prominent display of British military might be just what was needed. It was time to an end the childish behavior of what they considered a handful of *rabble-rousers*, who whipped up rum-soaked mobs for their own base purposes. "Americans are a race of convicts (who) ought to be thankful for any thing we allow them short of hanging," spouted the eminent man of letters Dr. Samuel Johnson.

Johnson and other British Americaphobes were tired of incidents like the violent protest that broke out in 1768 after customs agents in Boston seized a ship belonging to John Hancock, a wealthy merchant (and top smuggler). A crowd of 500 dragged two agents through the streets, spitting on them and pelting them with rocks.

But British officials closer to the scene had a more realistic view of what they were facing. "Tho' the People are not held in high estimation by the Troops," General Thomas Gage, commander-in-chief of the British forces in America, wrote to London, "yet they are numerous, worked up to a Fury, and not a Boston Rabble, but the Freeholders and Farmers of the country."

Gage was if anything a sensible fellow and well aware of the fact that his forces were vastly outnumbered in America and a long way from help. So no matter how contemptuous his troops were of the locals, they were functioning under basic orders to avoid trouble. In more than one case, British soldiers were sent to disperse an illegal meeting of colonists, only to be confronted with a large and defiant crowd, and then quietly retire from the scene.

But the proximity of sullen, underpaid, and bored soldiers and angry, insolent, and cocky civilians was a recipe for inevitable trouble. In January 1770, a bloody fight broke out in New York. It began after several British soldiers destroyed a *liberty pole*, a tall wooden staff with a cap on top that functioned as a symbol of colonial defiance. Several colonists were seriously injured, but there were no deaths.

A few months later, however, another confrontation at a sentry station on Boston's King Street would not turn out as lucky.

"I was soon on the ground among them"

On March 2 1770, a fight between a rope maker and a British soldier looking for part-time work escalated into several days of skirmishes between Bostonians and the *lobsterbacks*, as the soldiers were disparagingly known.

The violence peaked on March 5. According to a shoemaker named Robert Hewes, what became known to history as *the Boston Massacre* began when some soldiers bullied a barber's apprentice. A fight broke out, Hewes recalled in his memoirs, "and I was soon on the ground among them."

A group of boys then began throwing snowballs at a British sentry. A mob of about 50 gathered; a squad of seven soldiers led by Capt. Thomas Preston came to the aide of the sentry. Exactly what happened next is disputed, but before it was over, the British troops had fired on the crowd, killing five of them and wounding six more.

In the wake of the shootings, Massachusetts Lt. Gov. Thomas Hutchinson ordered the soldiers jailed, and the British commander of the forces in Boston agreed to remove his men from the streets to let things cool down. They did, even when a crowd of more than 10,000 turned out for the funeral procession of the slain men.

Nearly seven months later, the soldiers went on trial. Their defense attorneys were Josiah Quincy, a leading spokesman for the Sons of Liberty, and John Adams, an outspoken critic of the Stamp Act. Despite their political leanings, however, the two mounted a sparkling defense.

Adams in particular was masterful in selecting a jury composed of merchants who did business with the British army, while avoiding the selection of radicals who somewhat ironically shared Adams's own political views.

He also produced a surgeon as a witness who testified one of the dying men told him the soldiers had been provoked and also that the dying man didn't blame them. And in his closing arguments, Adams portrayed the mob as "most probably a motley rabble of saucy boys, negroes and mullatoes (part African), Irish teagues (derogatory term for Irish) and outlandish jack tars (sailors)."

Captain Preston was acquitted, as were six of the soldiers. Two others were convicted, but their punishment consisted of being branded on the hand rather than hanged.

The Sons of Liberty and other groups milked the incident to stir up even more anti-British sentiment. Sam Adams, a cousin of John Adams and one of the most prominent dissidents in Massachusetts, wrote a series of articles in which he described the incident as a "massacre," labeled defense witnesses as liars, and suggested without a shred of evidence that at least one of those killed had been bayoneted "a fair five inches into the head" after being shot. A Boston silversmith named Paul Revere produced, mostly for propaganda purposes, a highly exaggerated engraving of the confrontation that was widely circulated (see Figure 7-1).

But by the time of the trial, news had reached America that Parliament had repealed all of the Townshend Act duties except the one on tea. Weary of the constant tension, many colonists hoped it was a sign that things were cooling off. And they were — for about two years.

Tussling over Tea

It wasn't until 1773 that British officials committed their next blunder when it came to the American colonies — and this time they had help.

TECHNICAL STUFF

Powerful but poorly run, the mammoth British East India Company found it had 17 million pounds of excess tea on its hands. To bail out one of the nation's largest firms, the government granted the company a monopoly on the American tea market.

Under the unimaginatively named Tea Act of 1773, the company could escape paying a 30-pence-per-pound duty on tea that passed through English ports, as long as the tea kept going to America, where the duty was only 3 pence per pound — a tenth of what it was in England — and the cost of which was passed on to customers.

The company could thus drop its prices enough to undercut the costs of smuggled tea, mostly from Dutch producers, that colonists drank. (Massachusetts Gov. Thomas Hutchinson estimated as much as three-fourths of the colony's tea was contraband. "We have been so long habituated to illicit Trade," he wrote, "that people in general see no evil in it.")

The bail-out backfires

Under the Tea Act, government and company officials figured, the company could drop prices, undercut the smugglers, and offer Americans legal, good-quality tea at a reasonable cost.

But colonists were still troubled by the basic principle of having to pay *any* duty on tea to Britain and disliked the idea of a monopoly even if it had the potential to lower the cost of the pricey product.

As soon as the law went into effect, colonists began organizing efforts to prevent tea cargoes from being unloaded. They wrestled with the idea of destroying the tea — a capital offense — but decided for the time being to focus on blocking it from being taken off the ships.

To avoid trouble, several royal governors prudently allowed the tea ships that arrived to sail away without unloading. But in Massachusetts, Gov. Hutchinson balked at being pushed around. Hutchinson, who sometimes confused principle with foolish stubbornness, refused to let several ships laden with tea leave Boston Harbor, even though townspeople had blocked them from delivering their cargoes.

Under British law, the cargoes of unloaded ships in port for more than 20 days became subject to seizure by the government for disposition as government property, and Hutchinson intended to do just that under armed military protection and thus ensure its sale. The 20-day period was to end on Dec. 17, 1773.

Dunking the cargo

His plan fell one day short. On the evening of Dec. 16, a group of 100 to 150 men boarded three ships in Boston Harbor, while a crowd of 1,000 to 2,000 watched from shore. The men wore disguises as Native Americans, and not for frivolous reasons: What they were about to do was a hanging offense. Although it became known as the *Boston Tea Party*, it was not at the time regarded as much fun.

Quietly working in well-organized teams, they spent about three hours hacking open chests and dumping tea into the harbor, where, according to one eyewitness, "It piled up in the low tide like haystacks." Men in small boats beat the floating bundles with oars to ensure all the tea was thoroughly drenched.

One of the "Indians" was the shoemaker, Robert Hewes, who had been at the Boston Massacre. Hewes was chosen to lead one of the teams because of his well-known ability to command attention by whistling loudly. "We were surrounded by British armed ships," he recalled in his memoir, "but no attempt was made to resist us."

REMEMBER

In fact, both British navy and army leaders had decided that without specific orders to the contrary, and with the danger of killing innocent civilians and starting a full-scale revolt, they would not interfere. The decision was fine with Gov. Hutchinson's advisory council, and Hutchinson himself was seven miles away from the city at his estate.

None of the ships were damaged, and no one was hurt, although shoemaker Hewes reported that an Indian who tried to smuggle some tea out under his shirt was roughed up a bit by his colleagues.

News of the "tea party" reached London about a month after it occurred. King George was furious. "The die is now cast," he wrote his prime minister, Lord North. "The colonies must either submit or triumph."

On the other side of the water, John Adams used eerily similar language to describe the situation. "The dye is cast," he wrote a friend. "The people have passed the river and cast away the bridge."

"Coercive" to You; "Intolerable" to Us

In the wake of the Tea Party, the king ordered Prime Minister North, in no uncertain terms, to retaliate. It was necessary, North relayed to Parliament, "to proceed with firmness and without fear. They (the Americans) will never reform until we take measures of this kind."

REMEMBER

The "measures" to which North referred became known as the *Coercive Acts* (and later as the *Intolerable Acts*). Chief among them was an order to close Boston Harbor to all commercial shipping until the cost of the destroyed tea — about £11,000, or roughly $2 million in 2019 U.S. dollars — was repaid.

In addition, Parliament gave the Massachusetts governor the power to appoint virtually all officials in the colony, including judges and sheriffs, and gave sheriffs the power to appoint jurors. Crown officials accused of crimes such as murder and assault could choose to be tried in England rather than America. The colony's capital was moved from Boston to Salem, 17 miles away. And Thomas Hutchinson was replaced as Massachusetts's governor by General Gage, the commander-in-chief of all British forces in North America.

Another act affected all the colonies. It reaffirmed the authority of British military leaders to quarter troops anywhere they wanted — including private homes — if they deemed there were not enough local barracks available.

While not aimed at punishing the colonists, Parliament at the same time passed the *Quebec Act.* It gave conquered French subjects the right to freely practice Catholicism and maintain traditions such as nonjury trials. It also extended the Quebec province well into the Ohio River Valley. Americans were irked at the expansion of French Canadians' rights at a time when theirs were being threatened. And it was, well, "intolerable" that land they had fought to keep the French out of was being opened up to them.

Members of Parliament sympathetic to the American colonists warned that revenge would not accomplish what reasonable reform might. "Reflect how you are to govern a people, who think they ought to be free, and think they are not," said Edmund Burke, an Irish-born statesman who generally admired the Americans. "Your scheme yields no revenue; it yields nothing but discontent (and) disobedience."

Predictably, colonists reacted with disbelief and fury. The acts, said a 31-year-old Virginia lawyer named Thomas Jefferson, are "a deliberate and systematical plan of reducing us to slavery."

The colonists also began to organize, in a flurry of cooperation seldom seen before. Committees of correspondence cranked up lines of communication. Much-needed supplies of food and other items flowed in by land to Boston from as far away as South Carolina. And assemblies in several colonies, from Virginia to Rhode Island, called for the convening of "a Grand Council for America."

Congressing

In early September 1774, an extraordinary collection of American colonists gathered in Philadelphia. There were 56 of them, from all the colonies except Georgia (whose inhabitants were facing a war with Creek Indians, needed the support of British troops, and therefore didn't want to irritate government officials in London).

All of the 56 were males. About half of them were lawyers. Some, like John Dickinson of Pennsylvania, were among the wealthiest men in America. Others, like Sam Adams of Massachusetts, were so financially strapped friends had to chip in and buy him a decent set of clothes for the convention.

There were well-known figures, such as George Washington, John Adams, and Patrick Henry, and men largely unknown outside their colonies. One (Benjamin Harrison of Virginia) would be the father and great-grandfather of future U.S. presidents. Another (Stephen Crane of New Jersey) would be bayoneted to death by German mercenary soldiers during the Revolutionary War. A third (Edward Rutledge of North Carolina) would be, at the age of 26, the youngest man to sign the Declaration of Independence.

The men were delegates to what became known as the *First Continental Congress.* They had been sent by colonial assemblies to, in the words of the Massachusetts assembly, "a meeting of Committees from the several Colonies on this Continent . . . to consult upon the present state of the Colonies, and the miseries, to which they are, and must be reduced, by the operation of certain Acts of Parliament respecting America. . . ."

Getting to know each other

The first order of business was to find a suitable building in which to meet. They settled on a three-year-old structure called Carpenter's Hall, whose second floor was occupied by a public library founded by — you guessed it — Benjamin Franklin. Seated in chairs specially made for the delegates, they selected Peyton Randolph, a prominent Virginia tobacco planter, to preside over the meetings and began to acquaint themselves with each other.

The delegates' political dispositions ranged from conservatives, such as John Jay of New York and Joseph Galloway of Pennsylvania, to firebrands, such as Sam Adams of Massachusetts and Richard Gadsden of South Carolina. Their hopes for the meeting's outcome likewise ranged from a complete split with Britain to reconciliation to something in between.

But despite the differences, civility generally reigned over the proceedings, fueled in no small part by lots of fine dining and liberal drinking. George Washington wrote that he dined alone at just nine meals in the 54 days of the convention. John Adams noted in his journal that they ate "flummery (a sweet dessert), jellies, sweetmeats of 20 sorts, trifles . . . and I drank Madeira (a Portuguese wine) at a great rate, and found no inconvenience in it." His cousin Sam, however, was not as lucky: He suffered from stomach ulcers and was confined to bread and milk.

Getting down to business

The first order of business was to make it clear to British authorities that they were not immediately planning a revolution. Delegates wrote to General Gage in Boston to assure him they were trying to find "the most peaceable means for restoring American liberty."

After narrowly rejecting a conciliation plan proposed by Joseph Galloway that called for creation of an American parliament that would work with the British version, delegates drew up a *Declaration of Rights and Grievances* addressed directly to King George III. This was basically a laundry list of all the complaints America had made since passage of the Stamp Act nine years before.

They asked the king to drop the Coercive Acts. Several delegates wrote essays suggesting the colonies deal only with the king and completely ignore Parliament. More ominously, they agreed to a mutual defense pact — if one colony should be subjected to violence by British troops, the others would come to its aid.

They also endorsed a series of resolutions from Massachusetts (delivered to the convention via a Paul Revere horseback ride), known as the *Suffolk Resolves.* These called for completely ignoring the provisions of the Coercive Acts, establishing armed militias in each town, and requiring citizens to "use their utmost diligence to acquaint themselves with the art of war as soon as possible."

REMEMBER

Finally, the congress approved a total boycott of British goods, in a united resolution called *The Association.* This boycott went far beyond previous boycotts. Under it, nothing from British sources — up to and including slaves — would be imported as of Dec. 1, 1774. Furthermore, no American goods would be exported to Britain — although after protests from their delegates, rice from South Carolina and tobacco from Virginia were exempted. The export ban was delayed until the following year so "as not to injure our fellow-subjects in Great Britain, Ireland and the West Indies." Finally, British goods already in the colonies would not be bought, sold or consumed.

"We do for ourselves, and the inhabitants of the several colonies, whom we represent, firmly agree . . . to abide by the agreements," the resolution concluded. On Oct. 26, they went home, with the understanding they would reconvene in Philadelphia on May 10, 1775, if necessary. It was.

"Let It Begin Here"

It was Britain's serve in the ping-pong political battle straddling the Atlantic. Hoping to preserve peace, William Pitt, now Earl of Chatham, proposed a sweeping rollback of almost every act that had angered the Americans. But mindful of a still-furious king, the House of Lords resoundingly rejected it.

REMEMBER

Prime Minister North then offered a half-a-loaf *Conciliatory Resolution,* which said that if a colony would contribute to its own defense and pay for civil and judicial administrations within its borders, it would be exempt from paying taxes — except those necessary for the regulation of commerce. The proposal, approved by Parliament in February 1775, did not reach the colonies for several months, after the fighting had begun. It was summarily rejected when it got there anyway.

Prodded by King George, North also pushed Parliament into declaring Massachusetts to be in a state of rebellion and authorized more troops to be sent to the colonies. The so-called *Restraining Acts* limited trade between all of the British Empire and the colonies and prohibited New England fishermen from working in the cod-rich seas off Newfoundland.

Parliamentary members sympathetic to the Americans warned that Britain might be biting off more than it could chew. "You cannot furnish armies, or treasure, competent to the mighty purpose of subduing America," said Edmund Burke. "But whether France and Spain will be tame, inactive spectators of your efforts and distractions is well worthy of the consideration of your lordships."

Burke's warning was echoed by General Gage, the Massachusetts governor who was also in command of His Majesty's army in America. "If you think ten thousand men are enough," he wrote Lord North, "send twenty; if a million (pounds) is thought to be enough, give two. You will save blood and treasure in the end."

Squirreling away supplies

Meanwhile, in the colonies, efforts were being made to enforce the economic boycott — and prepare for war. To accomplish the first of these tasks, committees were appointed in every county to oversee adherence to the boycott, as well as discourage colonists from taking government jobs, particularly in Massachusetts.

Names of those who were suspected of violations were publicized, and the offenders faced social ostracism, and sometimes worse. While the occasional tarring and feathering did take place, the threat of physical violence was usually implied more than employed. Shunning by one's neighbors was usually enough. One Massachusetts man who had been appointed a councilor to the governor walked into a church service one Sunday, only to see all his fellow congregants walk out. He thereupon declined the appointment.

REMEMBER

While enforcing the boycott, the Sons of Liberty group and militia, known as *Minute Men* because they were to respond quickly to any call to arms, staged surprise raids on British supply depots and made off with arms and ammunition. They took care not to shoot, daring the British troops to fire first. The tactic followed the advice of Sam Adams: "Put your enemy in the wrong and keep him so. It is a wise maxim in politics as well as in war."

Riding with Revere

The colonists also kept a constant eye on the movements of British troops. One of their most effective spies was the son of a French immigrant who had established himself as a master silversmith in Boston. Paul Revere also made false teeth and surgical instruments — and was good on a horse.

REMEMBER

In mid–April 1775, General Gage received orders from London to arrest the colonial dissident leaders Sam Adams and John Hancock and seize any arms collected by the colonists. Gage was also directed to use force, if necessary. So on the evening of April 18, Gage ordered a force of 700 men to march from Boston to the village of Concord, about 20 miles away, arrest Adams and Hancock if they found them, and destroy a cache of arms suspected to be there.

Revere, however, got wind of the plan, and set out to warn the countryside that the British were coming. It was a harrowing trek. After crossing the Charles River at night in a small boat, he outrode British pursuers and made it to the small town of Lexington, about seven miles from Concord. There he warned Adams and Hancock.

With two other men, Thomas Dawes and Dr. Samuel Prescott, he then set out for Concord. The trio ran into a mounted British patrol. Prescott escaped by leaping his horse over a stone wall and made it to Concord, where the militia was able to hide most of the guns and ammunition.

Revere and Dawes were briefly detained, but were somewhat inexplicably released after the troops took Revere's horse. (Of the three riders, Revere is the one everyone remembers mainly because of a wildly popular 1861 poem by Henry Wadsworth Longfellow.)

"The Shot Heard 'Round the World"

At the village of Lexington, the British force was confronted by a group of about 75 militia under the command of John Parker. A farmer and veteran of the French and Indian War, Parker initially ignored the British officer's command that the Americans put down their arms. Instead, according to the later account of a man under his command, Parker replied, "Stand your ground. Don't fire unless fired upon, but if they mean to have a war, let it begin here."

REMEMBER

Outnumbered 10 to 1, Parker was in the process of changing his mind when a shot was fired — by which side is unknown — and a volley of gunfire followed. Eight of the colonists were killed and ten wounded.

The British troops then moved on to Concord, where they destroyed several cannons that had been too big to hide. By that time, however, hundreds of militia had arrived, and as the British troops began moving back toward Boston, they fired on the Americans, who returned fire.

What had been an orderly withdrawal by the British now became a somewhat disorderly retreat. "We retired for 15 miles under incessant fire," a British officer recounted, "which like a moving circle surrounded us wherever we went."

Shooting from behind rocks and inside houses, the American militia killed or wounded more than 250 of the king's soldiers, while suffering about 90 casualties themselves.

The battle was immortalized in an 1836 poem written by Ralph Waldo Emerson, called "Concord Hymn": *"By the rude bridge that arched the flood, / Their flag to April's breeze unfurled, / Here once the embattled farmers stood, / And fired the shot heard 'round the world."*

Stirring poetics aside, the long war of words between Mother Britain and her American children was over. The war of blood and death had begun.

Chapter **8**

"We Hold These Truths"

As the battle smoke cleared from the fields around the villages of Lexington and Concord, both Americans and British began trying to figure out just what had happened and, more importantly, what to do next.

In this chapter, the fighting in Massachusetts spreads to other colonies, and even into Canada. In Philadelphia, meanwhile, colonial leaders wrestle with whether to reconcile with the mother country. They name a commander-in-chief — for an army that barely exists — just in case reconciliation doesn't work out. It doesn't, so the American colonies declare independence.

"The Whites of Their Eyes"

Following its hasty retreat from the debacle at Lexington and Concord, the British army holed up in Boston. By mid-May, an estimated 15,000 American militia from Massachusetts and nearby New England colonies had hemmed in about 5,000 British troops, who had nowhere to go except through the American lines or out to sea.

The British commander, General Thomas Gage, chose to stay put, even though supplies were low and his men had to stage small raids to forage for food from the surrounding area. An American newspaper mocked: *"In days of yore the British troops/ Have taken warlike kings in battle;/ But now, alas! Their valor droops, / For Gage takes naught but harmless cattle."*

At the end of May, another 1,000 British soldiers arrived, along with three more generals: Sir William Howe, Sir Henry Clinton, and John Burgoyne. Gage ran a bluff on June 12, offering a pardon for all Americans who laid down their arms (with the notable exceptions of Sam Adams and John Hancock). "I avail myself of this last effort within the bounds of my duty to spare the effusion of blood," he wrote. No one accepted the offer, so the British generals huddled to decide their next move.

Their next move turned out to be a bad one. A few days after Gage had suggested the Americans give up, British military leaders decided to try to take some high ground on the northern edge of the city called Bunker Hill. But almost overnight, about 1,200 American militia constructed emplacements on top of the hill and another nearby rise later called Breed's Hill.

British General Lord Howe was in charge of the attack. He proved as fully capable as General Gage (whom he would soon replace as the top British commander in America) in screwing up. Howe ignored advice to attack the rebels from behind, cutting off their retreat route. Instead, he chose a full-frontal assault, which would help restore the British Army's honor, so besmirched at Lexington and Concord. As did many British commanders, Howe considered American militia as little more than "rabble in arms."

So, on June 17, after a leisurely midday meal, Howe sent 3,000 men up the hills toward the American lines. "Men you are all marksmen," the American General Israel Putnam was said to have told his troops as the British came on. "Don't one of you fire until you see the whites of their eyes."

REMEMBER

The first two assaults resulted in massive British casualties. On the third, however, the colonial forces ran out of ammunition, and after fighting hand-to-hand, as depicted in Figure 8-1, they were forced to retreat. The British had won, but at the steep cost of about one-third of their force killed or wounded. A French observer drolly remarked that two more such "victories," and the British would be out of soldiers.

"Whoever looks upon them (the Americans) as an irregular mob will find himself mistaken," British General Lord Hugh Percy ruefully remarked. "They have men among them who know very well what they are about."

In the end, the battle accomplished little. The British army remained stuck in Boston. The American militia remained a largely disorganized and undisciplined collection of volunteers who could, and did, come and go as they pleased. They remained loitering around the city's edges. They had proved they could fight, but not that they could function as an army.

FIGURE 8-1:
A mid-19th century portrayal of the Battle of Bunker Hill.

Spreading the News — and the Fighting

Almost as soon as the British troops had finished limping back into Boston after the battles at Lexington and Concord — and well before the fight at Bunker Hill — the rebellious colonials began getting news of the battles out to the rest of the colonies. Or at least their version of the news. Dr. Joseph Warren, who had fought at Concord (and was then killed at Bunker Hill), produced a leaflet for circulation by the committees of correspondence. It urged militia to be raised and turned out, "to defend our wives and children from the butchering hands of an inhuman soldiery . . . our all is at stake. Death and devastation are the certain consequences of delay."

Newspapers cranked out broadsheets with stories of the barbarism of British troops and the heroism of American patriots, under headlines such as "Bloody News" and "Bloody Butchering by the British Troops." One paper scathingly labeled the "mother country" as "a vile imposter — an old abandoned prostitute, crimsoned o'er with every abominable crime!"

News of the April 19 battles reached New York City on April 23, and Philadelphia the next day. By April 29, Williamsburg, Virginia residents were reading about it, and the residents of Charleston, South Carolina on May 8. Americans began to stir themselves.

Taking Ticonderoga and losing Canada

Even before news of the Massachusetts battles had reached the South, militia units from Connecticut and what is now Vermont were on the march — but away from Boston rather than toward it.

About 130 miles south of Montreal and 275 miles south of Quebec City, the star-shaped Fort Ticonderoga, near what is now the New York-Vermont border, controlled a key water route into Canada. Moreover, it housed a large collection of old but still serviceable cannon and other big guns.

In early May 1775, a profanely plain-spoken Vermont frontiersman named Ethan Allen and an ambitious and oily Connecticut merchant named Benedict Arnold led a force mainly composed of Allen's "Green Mountain Boys" to attack the fort. It was defended by a force of about 50 British soldiers, many of whom were old and unfit for duty elsewhere.

On May 10, the Americans took it without a shot being fired. The British commander was so surprised he was being attacked by anyone, in fact, he had to ask to whom he was surrendering. "In the name of the Great Jehovah and the Continental Congress," Allen reportedly replied.

So encouraged were Allen and Arnold (who by the way couldn't stand each other), they began making plans to keep going and conquer Canada. The hope was that the province's mostly French populace would rally to the American side. But the French Canadians had little love for either the British or the Americans and largely stayed out of the fighting.

In late June, approval for the invasion came from the Continental Congress meeting in Philadelphia. But by that time, both Allen and Arnold had been replaced as commanders by General Philip Schuyler, a plodding New Yorker who took two months to get an American force of about 1,700 troops moving.

Fortunately for the American side, Schuyler got sick and was replaced by General Richard Montgomery, an Irish expatriate and a seasoned soldier. Unfortunately, bad weather, miscommunication among militia groups, and the untimely desertion of the supply officer — who took much of the supplies with him — plagued the invasion force. The army nonetheless took Montreal without a fight and moved on to Quebec City.

On Dec. 30, 1775, the day before the enlistments of many of the troops were due to expire, the American force attacked during a snowstorm. The results were disastrous.

Several hundred Americans were killed, wounded, or captured. Montgomery was killed. Arnold, who fought bravely, was seriously wounded. And Allen had already been captured in an earlier battle and was on his way, in chains, to England. Virtually leaderless, the colonials hunkered down for the winter and then slunk back to the American side of the border the following spring.

Meanwhile, in the other direction . . .

In Virginia, Gov. John Murray, a.k.a. Lord Dunmore, was a staunch supporter of the king. In polite terms, that made him a *Loyalist,* and in derogatory terms, a *Tory.* As soon as news of the Massachusetts rebellion reached Virginia, Dunmore seized a store of militia gunpowder and had it transferred to British Navy ships off the coast of the town of Norfolk. Under threats to his life from angry Virginians, he also transferred himself to the ships.

REMEMBER

In November, Dunmore issued a proclamation that sent shudders through Southern whites: If slaves would join the fight against the rebel colonists, they would be freed. A nervous South Carolinian wrote John Adams that as many as 20,000 slaves might join Dunmore's "Ethiopian Brigade." The slave-owning George Washington warned that "Dunmore should be instantly crushed. Otherwise like a snowball rolling, his army will get size."

A month later, Dunmore was crushed, more or less, at the Battle of Great Bridge. The fight, which pitted Virginia militia against Dunmore's collection of slaves, Loyalists, and a few British regular troops, resulted in one rebel casualty and about 100 of Dunmore's army killed or wounded.

The governor subsequently retreated to the British ships, ordered the bombardment and burning of the town of Norfolk, and sailed away to New York. Most of the 800 slaves who had joined his "brigade" in return for their freedom either died in a smallpox epidemic or were sold to the West Indies.

A side-effect of Dunmore's proclamation was that some Southerners who were lukewarm about cutting ties with Britain were so shaken by the prospect of a slave uprising that they withheld overt support of the crown — and became more amenable to a colonial split with the mother country.

. . . And back in Boston

Following the fight at Bunker/Breed's Hill in June 1775, American and British forces spent most of the next eight months looking at each other through field glasses, with the occasional skirmish and smallpox outbreak thrown in. In July, the new American commander-in-chief arrived. George Washington then spent the rest of the year trying to turn the undisciplined gaggle of rebels he had inherited into something resembling an army.

REMEMBER

By the fall of 1775, Washington was anxious to attack the British in the city, but aides talked him out of it. Instead, he eventually agreed to a plan presented by a corpulent 25-year-old bookstore owner. An avid student of military engineering, Henry Knox was convinced he could move the big guns that had been captured at Fort Ticonderoga to the heights above Boston. Facing certain annihilation, the British would then have to flee the city.

Using 43 specially designed sledges pulled by oxen, Knox did what seemed impossible. Sixteen cannon, howitzers, and mortars, estimated to weigh a staggering total of 60 tons, were dragged over 300 miles of snow and ice. Knox arrived in Boston in mid-January 1776, two months after he had left for Ticonderoga. At first, the big guns were positioned too far away to do much damage.

Then a second miracle was pulled off by a machinist named Rufus Putnam, the brother of the American commander at Bunker Hill. The ground was too frozen to dig emplacements for the guns at a site closer to the British. So Putnam devised prefabricated structures that 3,000 American soldiers put into position in one night, while the British were distracted by diversionary gunfire.

When the sun rose on March 5, a distressed-but-impressed British General Howe was reported to have said, "My God, these fellows have accomplished more in one night than I could make my army do in three months."

Howe decided it was time to leave. After agreeing not to burn down Boston in return for being allowed to withdraw peaceably, Howe boarded his entire army — and about 1,000 American loyalists — and on March 17 sailed away, first to Nova Scotia and then to New York. The "rabble in arms" had won again.

Choosing to Fight, Choosing a Fighter

In May 1775, what became known as the Second Continental Congress convened in Philadelphia. Most of the 56 delegates were veterans of the previous year's congress, although there were a few notable newcomers: John Hancock, the Massachusetts merchant who was No. 1 on Britain's Most-Wanted-Rebel list; Benjamin Franklin, who had been in England all of 1774, and Thomas Jefferson of Virginia, who had not been selected as a delegate the year before.

This time they met at the Pennsylvania State House, a red-brick-faced, tall-steepled building that had opened in 1753 to serve as the colonial capitol. In later years, it would become Independence Hall, serving as host to the 1787 Constitutional Convention and seeing more than 300,000 people stream through it in 1865 to view the body of Abraham Lincoln as it made the solemn journey from Washington, D.C., to Springfield, Illinois.

Extending an olive branch

Just now, however, it was hosting what was the de facto central government of 13 rebellious colonies. How long they would stay rebellious was the first order of business. Some delegates, led by Pennsylvania's John Dickinson and New York's James Duane, wanted to take one last shot at reconciling with Britain — and threatened to walk out if the shot weren't taken.

"We find a great many bundles of weak nerves" among the delegates, wrote a disgusted John Adams, who favored "power and artillery" as the surest path to conciliation. "We are obliged to be as delicate and soft and modest and humble as possible."

REMEMBER

On July 5, Congress approved the *Olive Branch Petition*. Originally written by Jefferson, it was deemed too sharply worded by the conciliation-seeking delegates and thus rewritten by Dickinson. Addressed to George III directly, the petition repeated the colonies' complaints about the taxes and other acts of the past decade. At the same time, it assured the king that the colonies "most ardently desire the former harmony between (Britain) and these colonies may be restored." It asked the king to repeal all the offending acts, and by doing so "settle peace through every part of your dominion."

Apparently as a sop to the more hawkish delegates, Dickinson also penned a "Declaration of the Causes and Necessities of Taking up Arms." It repeated the same complaints and said the colonies would lay down their arms "when Hostilities shall cease on the part of the Aggressors."

The olive branch document was then sent off to England, accompanied by two congressional delegates. It was a wasted trip: George III refused to even read it. In fact, the week before they arrived, the king had declared all the colonies to be in a state of rebellion, and all the rebellious colonists "traitors." He also told Parliament it was time "to put a speedy end to these disorders by the most decisive exertions."

The whole effort, John Adams wrote, "gives a silly cast to our whole doings."

Picking a general

Adams's grumping aside, Congress had accomplished a few things. In mid-June, it authorized the formation of a 15,000-man *Continental Army,* as well as six companies of expert marksmen from the backwoods of Virginia, Maryland, and Pennsylvania. It followed up in October by outfitting two ships — the start of an American navy — and the following month forming two battalions of "naval infantry," or American marines.

REMEMBER

It also did a brilliant job of selecting a commander in chief for the new army, although not everyone was sure that was the case at the time. In a sense, George Washington got the job by default. Of the other potential candidates, Israel Putnam, the commander at the Battle of Bunker Hill, was thought at the age of 57 to be too old for the job. Artemas Ward, the top commander of American forces around Boston, had health problems.

Washington also had drawbacks. He had never led an army, nor anything larger than a regiment. His military experience included a couple of embarrassing defeats, although not entirely of his making. And he hadn't seen action for 15 years.

But he certainly looked the part. He was 6'2" tall and weighed a muscle-sculpted 175 pounds. He had shown up as a delegate to Congress wearing a splendid blue-and-buff Virginia militia uniform. And he made a good impression on almost everyone: "In conversation he looks you full in the face," noted one delegate. "(He) is deliberative, deferential and engaging. His demeanor is at all times composed and dignified. His movements and gestures are graceful, his walk majestic."

He had other attributes. As a longtime member of the Virginia assembly, he knew his way around politicians, a good thing for generals to know. Plus, he was extremely wealthy and willing to take the job without a salary. So on June 15, John Adams moved, and Sam Adams seconded, a motion to give Washington the post. It was unanimously approved, and he accepted with heartfelt humility.

"I am truly sensible of the high honor done me in this appointment," he told Congress, "yet I feel great distress from a consciousness that my abilities and military experience may not be equal to the extensive and important trust. However, . . . (I will) exert every power I possess in the service and for the support of the glorious cause."

In private, he tearfully told Patrick Henry he feared he had taken on an impossible task and thus forever ruined his career and reputation.

But the princes of six German states, which were still at least nominally part of the Holy Roman Empire, agreed to furnish soldiers, mostly because they needed the money. One prince was paid £100,000 (roughly $21 million in 2019 U.S. dollars). Another was paid £7 for each solider killed (three wounded men equaled one dead one) but had to replace the cost of deserters out of his own pocket.

All in all, Britain would spend an estimated £3 million (about $670 million in 2019 U.S. dollars) for about 30,000 German mercenaries. Because the majority of them came from the principality of Hesse-Cassel, they all became known as Hessians.

While a practical solution to Britain's manpower shortage, the practice was opposed by some British political leaders, who feared it would make reconciliation with America impossible. "If I were an American as I am an Englishman," William Pitt said, "while a foreign troop was in my country, I would never lay down my arms, never, never, never!"

Americans weren't crazy about it either. The long list of grievances in the Declaration of Independence about George III's conduct includes the complaint that "He is at this time transporting large Armies of foreign Mercenaries to compleat the works of death, desolation and tyranny. . .".

German soldiers were involved in nearly every major battle of the war. They were considered good fighters — and barbaric killers, who routinely bayoneted prisoners and the wounded and looted and pillaged wherever they went. Some of the reputation was earned. Some was invented by Americans for propaganda purposes and to excuse retaliation that included decapitating dead German soldiers and displaying their heads on tree stumps.

As hired guns, many of the German soldiers didn't much care who was right or wrong in the fight: "My profession and my duty demand of me to risk my life in the service of my master," a German officer wrote to a friend, "and I am ready to defend this duty."

But as the war progressed, many German soldiers became enamored of the country they were fighting in, if not for. "The houses . . . and the furnishings in them are excellent," a Hessian officer noted. "Comfort, beauty and cleanliness are readily apparent."

By the end of the war, up to 6,000 of the German troops were estimated to have deserted or chose to stay in America when the fighting stopped. Many of them settled in Pennsylvania and western New York, where a sizeable number of German immigrants had already located.

Some Hessians were encouraged by an offer from the Continental Congress of land, two pigs, and a cow if they would desert. The inducements were printed in German and stuffed in tobacco pouches sold to Hessian soldiers stationed in New York and New Jersey. It was Benjamin Franklin's idea.

Cutting the Cord

In the late spring and summer of 1776, the Continental Congress faced both a major procedural decision and a major organizational task. The decision was whether to formally and irrevocably break away from Britain. The task was to decide how to organize 13 disparate colonies into some kind of new country.

REMEMBER

On June 7, Richard Henry Lee, the son of a wealthy Virginia planter and a seasoned politician by the age of 34, proposed a resolution that declared "that these united colonies are, and of a right ought to be, free and independent states, that they are absolved from all allegiance to the British Crown, and that all political connection between them and the State of Great Britain is, and ought to be, totally dissolved."

Lee also proposed the colonies make clear that they were willing to consider allying themselves with other countries for the purposes of defending their independence and that the colonies also come up with a "plan of confederation" to govern themselves once Britain was out of the way.

"We are in the midst of a revolution," a jubilant John Adams wrote to a friend, "the most complete, unexpected and remarkable of any in the history of nations."

Adams, however, was jumping the gun. Delegates from several colonies were by no means sure they were ready to cut ties. Independence backers like Adams wanted a unanimous decision. So, after some vigorous discussion, Congress decided to postpone a final vote on Lee's resolution until July 1.

Drafting a declaration

In the meantime, a five-member committee was appointed on June 11 to draft a formal declaration, just in case. The members included John Adams; Benjamin Franklin; Connecticut judge Roger Sherman; New York lawyer Robert Livingston, and a tall red-haired Virginian who disliked public speaking and dressed as if he shopped at second-hand stores. In fact, Thomas Jefferson had been added to the committee only because Richard Henry Lee's wife was very ill and Lee had to leave Congress for a while. It was thought good politics to replace Lee with another Virginian, since the colony was the most populous.

Despite their differences in age (Franklin was 70, Livingston 30), geographic origins, and personality quirks (Franklin reportedly warned Sherman that if he didn't stop picking his teeth, Franklin was going to start blowing on his harmonica), they got along reasonably well. And despite his reticence to talk (Adams once said "during the whole time I sat with [Jefferson] in Congress, I never heard him utter three sentences together"), it fell to the Virginian to be the document's principal writer.

When Jefferson tried to decline the job, Adams gave him three good reasons he should do it. "Reason First," Adams said, "you are a Virginian and a Virginian ought to be at the head of this business. Reason Second: I am obnoxious, suspected and unpopular. You are very much otherwise. Reason Third: You can write ten times better than I can." "Well," Jefferson replied, "if you are determined, I will do as well as I can."

Jefferson sequestered himself in a second-floor room of a new brick house on the outskirts of the city. Sitting at a portable desk that he had designed himself — and swatting away the numerous horseflies that plagued him from the stable across the street — Jefferson managed to produce a draft for the other committee members to peruse (as is somewhat fancifully portrayed in Figure 8-2).

FIGURE 8-2:
A depiction of Benjamin Franklin, John Adams, and Thomas Jefferson working on the Declaration of Independence.

© Victorian Traditions/Shutterstock

They made very few suggestions, and the ones they made were masterful. "We hold these truths to be sacred and undeniable" became "We hold these truths to be self-evident." The "preservation of life and liberty and the pursuit of happiness" was tightened to "life, liberty and the pursuit of happiness."

The declaration was in large part a list of specific grievances against George III, such as taxation without consultation and the suspension of trials by jury. But its eloquent rhetorical framing elevated it far beyond a mere laundry list of gripes. (You can see for yourself in Appendix A at the back of this book.)

REMEMBER

"All men are created equal," he wrote, and all "are endowed by their Creator with certain unalienable Rights." The purpose of government was to help people secure and maintain those rights. When a government failed to do so, it was the right of the people it was supposed to serve to break away if necessary and form a new government.

Winning approval

On June 28, the committee presented about 1,600 well-chosen words to the rest of Congress. Two sections were struck. One was a criticism of the people of Britain, which delegates thought was unnecessary. The other — far more important — condemned George III as responsible for the slave trade. It was dropped after delegates from Georgia and South Carolina objected. Delegates from northern states, where much of the actual slave traders were from, did not object to the removal.

Even then, there were doubters. On July 1, a majority of the delegates from Pennsylvania and South Carolina voted no on Lee's resolution of independence, and the two delegates present from Delaware split. Anxious to present a united front, a final vote was delayed until the next day.

REMEMBER

On July 2, Caesar Rodney, a third Delaware delegate who had ridden all night through a rainstorm, arrived to break that colony's tie. Two Pennsylvania delegates who were opposed decided to abstain, putting that colony in the yes column on a 3-2 vote, and South Carolina's delegation agreed to go along with the rest for the sake of unanimity.

"The second day of July, 1776, will be the most memorable epocha in the history of America," John Adams exulted. Much to his everlasting annoyance, he was wrong again. "The Unanimous Declaration of the Thirteen United States of America," as it was formally titled, won final approval on July 4 and was made public on July 8.

America went nuts. In New York City, General Washington had the document read to his troops. They responded with three cheers and then joined a mob that toppled a two-ton statue of King George, which was later melted down and turned into ammunition. In a backwoods settlement in South Carolina, 9-year-old Andrew Jackson read it aloud, at the request of his illiterate neighbors. In a Worcester, Massachusetts tavern whose "King's Arms" nameplate had been torn down, a crowd gave 24 toasts, including a novel one that called for America's enemies to be plagued with "perpetual itching without benefit of scratching."

And back in Philadelphia, a 24-year-old bronze bell inscribed with an Old Testament verse — "Proclaim Liberty Throughout All the Land Unto All the Inhabitants thereof" — rang out in the tower of the hall in which Congress was meeting. Contrary to popular myth, the bell did not crack — it had already cracked when it was installed in 1752 and would do so again years later.

"Well gentlemen," Benjamin Franklin was said to have said, "We must now hang together, or we shall most assuredly hang separately."

A PRICELESS PIECE OF PARCHMENT

Despite a popular perception propagated by an oft-published painting, the Founding Fathers didn't all gather around a table to sign the Declaration of Independence as soon as the ink had dried. In fact, what we generally consider the definitive copy of the Declaration wasn't signed for a month. On July 19, Congress ordered the Declaration to be "engrossed" — that is, written in a large clear hand — on parchment, or untanned animal skin. It's probable, though not certain, that Timothy Matlack, a Philadelphia brewer who had great penmanship, was chosen for the task.

On Aug. 2, the handsomely written document was ready, and most of the signers gathered to do the deed. Five of the ultimate signers didn't get around to it until later (one took until 1781).

There were 500 copies printed on paper almost as soon as the Declaration was released. Called "Dunlap Broadsides" after the printer John Dunlap who produced them, they were distributed throughout the colonies. Only 26 are known to still exist, 23 of which are in various museums and public library collections and 3 in private collections.

As for the badly faded 29-3/4 x 24-1/2 piece of parchment probably penned by a Philadelphia beer maker, it resides in the Rotunda for Charters of Freedom, next to a copy of the United States Constitution and the British Magna Charta, at the National Archives in Washington, D.C.

Trying to Confederate

While hanging around to make a decision on declaring independence, Congress was also at work on forming a new government to replace the king-and-Parliament system.

After all, as Jefferson pointed out, establishing a new government "is the whole object of the present controversy; for should a bad government be instituted for us in future, it had been as well to have accepted the bad one offered to us from beyond the water, without the risk and expense of the war."

Three committees were appointed, with the Philadelphia lawyer John Dickinson in overall charge. Dickinson, who had authored the brilliant "Letters from a Farmer" essays attacking Britain's policies, had since developed cold feet about the whole revolution idea and was one of the Pennsylvania delegates who abstained from voting on the resolution of independence. Nonetheless, he worked hard to figure something out.

It took time. The *Articles of Confederation*, as the governing blueprint was called, was not approved by Congress until November 1777 (about two months after the delegates were forced to flee Philadelphia and move to York, Pennsylvania because of invading British troops).

REMEMBER

"The name of the confederacy," Dickinson wrote, "shall be the *United States of America.*" In actuality, it was more like today's UN than today's USA. The plan envisioned a loosely knit group of states, or "firm league of friendship," in which each state would function mostly on its own and come together "for their common defense, the security of their Liberties, and their mutual and general welfare."

The new federal government would have extremely limited authority. It would consist of a one-house legislature, with the delegations from each state having one vote. Nine of the 13 states had to agree on any new proposal for it to take effect. Congress could borrow money and ask the states for funds, but could not levy a tax without approval from every state.

Congress could declare war, make peace, negotiate with foreign countries and Native Americans, establish standards for weights and measures, and run an interstate postal system. There was no executive branch and no federal judiciary. Congressional delegates had term limits, and presiding over the legislative body rotated.

Individual states controlled virtually everything within their own borders. They were prohibited, however, from cutting side deals or forming splinter groups with just one or two other states and weren't supposed to negotiate treaties with foreign governments. Even so, some states were reluctant to part with any of their autonomy, and it took until 1781 for the last state, Maryland, to formally approve the Articles of Confederation.

While Congress had been crafting a federal government system, most states had formed new versions of government on their own. Most were modeled on the two-house system of Parliament, with the "lower house" having most of the power. Most had weak executive branches. Land ownership was still a requisite to vote, with the reasoning that landowners would not have a landlord dictating their votes, and they would also have a tangible stake in the welfare of the community. But most states did lower the amount of land that had to be owned to be eligible to vote.

As for women voting: When Abagail Adams suggested to her husband John that Congress "remember the ladies," John laughed it off. "We know better than to repeal our Masculine systems." To give women political power, he wrote his wife, would "compleatly subject Us to the Despotism of the Peticoat."

As tenuous as its framework was, the Articles promised to have all the stability of a soup sandwich. The system would prove highly unsatisfactory as time went by. But it was a start, and as John Adams put it, "how few of the human race have ever enjoyed an opportunity of making a government . . . for themselves or their children."

Of course, the newly christened United States of America had to win that opportunity on the battlefield before it could pass on anything to its children, and that would prove to be no easy chore.

Chapter 9

Lose Until You Win

On paper, it should have been wrapped up in about five or six months, tops. The British had a trained and seasoned army, all kinds of money to rent tens of thousands of skilled mercenary fighters, a bunch of professional military leaders, and the world's largest navy.

The Americans, on the other hand, had no army, no funds to rent one, a bunch of amateurs to lead whatever forces they could dredge up, and the world's smallest navy, as in none.

This chapter covers the hows, whens, and wheres of America's Revolutionary War. It was a war of attrition and exhaustion, took eight long years — and ended with a startling victory by the most under of underdogs.

Getting into Shape

On April 19, 1775, a 31-year-old shoemaker named Joseph Hodgkins left his wife, newborn child, and home in Ipswich, Massachusetts to join a mass of men that vaguely looked like an army and fight for a country that didn't formally exist yet.

Hodgkins had volunteered as a *minuteman* at the start of 1775, pledging to be ready with gun, 30 rounds of ammunition, knapsack, and other equipment, when and if fighting broke out. When it did, at Lexington and Concord, his colleagues elected him their second-in-command and he marched with them the 30 miles south to Boston. "The Company is well," Hodgkins wrote his wife three weeks later. "I whant to know wether you have got a paster for the Cows for I cannot tell when I shall com home." It would be four years.

The raw ingredients

What Hodgkins had joined was a collection of 15,000 to 20,000 Americans, gathered around Boston and loosely organized into militias, mostly from the New England colonies. They elected their own officers and un-elected them if they didn't like the orders they were given. Most of them had agreed to stay only until the end of 1775.

REMEMBER

Like Hodgkins, most of them had no military experience. They were tradesmen, merchants, farmers, and artisans. Many were Irish immigrants who had left the old country to escape British oppression and weren't about to subject themselves to it in their new country. By the end of the war, as many as 15 percent of the American fighting force was of African descent. A startlingly high percentage of all the men were really boys, under the age of 17. If they were older than 20, they almost certainly had wives and children.

They were armed with what they brought from home. The most common weapon was the flintlock musket. About 5 feet long and weighing 10 pounds, it could be fired and reloaded quickly. A good musket man could get off four rounds in a minute. But their range was short — maybe 60 yards — and their accuracy lamentable. Rifles — long guns with spiral grooves in the barrel's interior to make the bullet spin and thus stay on course better — were lighter, much more accurate, and had four times the range, but took longer to load.

Whatever the weapon, there was always a shortage of ammunition. Little gunpowder was manufactured in America, and so had to be imported. In mid-1775, the entire American force around Boston was reckoned to have about 10,000 pounds of gunpowder, or enough for nine cartridges per man.

The "army" also suffered from a dearth of discipline. As volunteers, they felt no need to obey orders they didn't like. When one company commander was asked how many men he led, he replied, "None. But I am commanded by 90." General Richard Montgomery complained it was impossible to command men "who carried the spirit of freedom into the field and think for themselves . . . in short, the privates are all generals."

What they lacked in military discipline, they also lacked in self-discipline. Visitors to the American encampment were variously amused and appalled by the hodge-podge of "tents" made from sailcloth, turf, driftwood, bricks, or brush. Their occupants gambled and drank prodigious amounts of rum or whatever else they could get. "Wickedness prevails very much," Lt. Hodgkins wrote home.

They also routinely relieved themselves wherever it was convenient and seldom, if ever washed, anything. They were, an observer noted, "The most wretchedly clothed, and as dirty a set of mortals as ever disgraced the name of soldier . . . they would rather let their clothes rot upon their backs than be at the trouble of cleaning 'em themselves." As a result, illnesses including typhoid fever and dysentery, as well as a catchall malady called *camp fever,* were rampant throughout the army.

None of this was lost on the British. From Boston, General Gage wrote to his superiors in London that he was "firmly persuaded there is not a man among (the Americans) capable of taking command or directing the motions of an army." As it turned out, he couldn't have been more wrong.

Enter the general

Although he forbade it among his troops, George Washington was a master at swearing when the occasion arose, and it almost certainly arose when he arrived at Boston on July 3, 1775, to take command of the American forces.

"Such a dirty, mercenary spirit pervades the whole (army)," he wrote later, "that I should not be at all surprised at any disaster that may happen . . . could I have foreseen what I have, and am likely to experience, no consideration upon earth should have induced me to accept this command."

REMEMBER

But he had accepted it, and he dutifully began whipping his army into shape, sometimes literally. Cursing, gambling, drinking, and other offenses became punishable by floggings, although Congress prudently turned down Washington's request to raise the maximum number of lashes from 39 to 500.

He ordered men to dress in accordance with their rank. Those who lacked uniforms — and that was most of them — were required to wear ribbons whose color designated their standing. He weeded out cowardly or corrupt officers and told the rest to "be easy . . . but not too familiar (with their troops), "lest you subject yourself to a want of their respect, which is necessary to support a proper command."

He also assembled his command staff. The top generals included Charles Lee, a crabby loudmouth who was nonetheless the most experienced and best military mind, having fought in the British army; Israel Putnam, the hero of Bunker/ Breed's Hill; Horatio Gates, another former British officer; Philip Schuyler, a mediocre general whose family was among the most powerful in New York; and the sickly Artemas Ward, whom Washington had relieved as the top commander.

The new boss also put together a second tier of bright and dedicated leaders. They included a young New York artillery captain named Alexander Hamilton; Henry Knox, the beefy Boston bookseller who had delivered the big guns from Fort Ticonderoga; and Nathanael Greene, an asthmatic Rhode Islander who walked with a limp and fought with intelligence and tenacity.

Holding on to the troops

One of Washington's biggest problems was keeping his men from going home. Most of the early arrivals at Boston had agreed only to stay until Jan. 1, 1776, and most of them were determined to leave, especially after spending a brutal New England winter outdoors. The Ipswich shoemaker, Joseph Hodgkins, was an exception. "I hope I & all my townsmen shall have virtue anofe to stay all winter as Volentears Before we Will leave the line with out men," he wrote his wife in late November 1775. "For our all is at stake and if we Due not exarte our selves in this glorious Cause our all is gon and we be made slaves of for Ever." (Hodgkins, who had fought bravely at Bunker Hill, would not only stay the winter, but would become an aide to Washington and fight in several major battles before returning home in 1779.)

By the beginning of 1776, Washington's army had dropped from around 17,000 to about 10,000. Rather than rely on the unreliable militias, Washington needed the regular Continental Army that Congress had promised him six months before. After another six months of dithering, Congress began offering $10 (very roughly, about $290 in 2019) to anyone who would enlist for three years. In September 1776, the offer was increased to $20, 100 acres of land, and a new suit of clothes for enlisting for the duration of the war.

The following year, Congress assigned each state a quota of soldiers to supply, which it had to fill through enlistments or a draft, if necessary. A conscription target, however, could opt out by paying a hefty fee equivalent to about $4,500 in today's dollars or find someone to go in his place (usually by offering much less than the fee).

Neither the enlistment inducements nor the draft resulted in an adequate number of "regular" troops, and the problem would plague the American army throughout the war. That meant the militias, which in the words of one officer "sometimes fought, sometimes not," would continue to be needed, even if they couldn't be relied upon in a fight.

Picking a strategy

No one ever accused George Washington of being a military genius, nor did he claim to be. (John Adams referred to him privately as Old Muttonhead.) He lost twice as many major battles as he won, in some cases because of tactical blunders on his part. In fact, his major strategic strength was in organizing retreats.

But other attributes more than made up for his deficiencies. For one thing, with his immaculate uniforms, mounted on the back of a proud white English charger, he looked the part of a general — not a trifling thing when trying to inspire untrained soldiers. He was personally brave, often at the very front of the fighting. He was an outstanding horseman. He was lucky, more than once riding inadvertently into a group of enemy soldiers and escaping injury. And he had an indomitable spirit.

REMEMBER

He also knew the only way the British could be beat was to outlast them. By keeping an army in the field, he could give the new union of 13 states time to coalesce into a nation and wear down the British will to fight. And to keep an untrained, ill-equipped army in the field meant not risking it much in battle.

"We should on all occasions avoid a general action," he told Congress in September 1776, "or put anything to the risqué unless compelled by a necessity into which we ought never be drawn."

Unfortunately, Washington didn't always listen to his own advice.

"The Fate of Unborn Millions"

After evacuating from Boston in March 1776, the British forces moved to Nova Scotia to await reinforcements. In command were the Howe brothers: Admiral Sir Richard Howe, nicknamed Black Dick for his dark complexion, was in charge of the British fleet, while General Sir William Howe was in command of the army.

Both men were competent and capable, if overly cautious, officers. Neither had a burning desire to crush the American rebellion. If anything, they preferred just bringing it to a quick end, whether through military victory or negotiations.

But just in case, they came up with a strategy to win a full-scale war. The plan was to take New York, thus cutting New England off from the rest of the colonies, and then use Rhode Island as a base to mop up the North. Once done, the British forces would take the Southern colonies easily, in part because British leaders were confident much of the Southern population was still loyal to the crown.

Washington had figured out the first British move would be at New York City and began moving his forces to defend the city in April 1776. Eventually an American army of about 19,000 was in place. Forts were built on each side of the Hudson River, and Washington divided his army into five divisions to guard various parts of the region. But neither Washington nor his top generals knew much about the area's geography, or how vulnerable it was to amphibious attacks, or how useless their defenses would prove to be.

Just about everything else that could go wrong did. Thousands of men became sick with smallpox and other diseases. Bored — and nervous — while waiting for the British to show up, the American soldiers drank, gambled, and generally goofed off when not building barricades. They were still poorly equipped; several hundred didn't even have weapons.

Washington was nervous, too, and not just because a plot to assassinate him, involving two of his own guards, had been uncovered. He had never commanded an entire army in pitched battle. "The fate of unborn millions," he wrote on July 2, "will now depend, under God, on the courage and conduct of this army."

Running from their shadows

Just a few days before Washington wrote those words, the British had shown up. There were a lot of them: 32,000 soldiers, backed by 30 warships sporting 1,200 cannon, and hundreds of support ships. It was the largest force Great Britain had ever assembled.

On July 12, several British warships sailed from the harbor up the Hudson River and past American cannons blazing away and hitting nothing. In fact, the only casualties on either side occurred when an American cannon blew up and killed its six gunners. The next day, the Howes sent a representative to Washington to offer pardons to those who would lay down their arms.

"Those who have committed no fault want no pardon," Washington replied. "We are only defending what we deem our indisputable rights."

As the weeks went by, more and more British ships and troops arrived. Finally, on Aug. 22, British forces began invading Long Island, touching off what would over the next week become the single largest battle of the Revolutionary War. It was an unmitigated disaster for the Americans. Vastly outnumbered and outgunned, many of them ran. One officer described the panic was "like electricity, it operates instantaneously . . . it is irresistible where it touches."

A furious Washington tried to stop the rout, screaming at his troops and hitting them with his cane. At one point, he was so distracted he rode within 80 yards of some Hessian soldiers and had to be hastily whisked away by his aides. "They run from their shadows," he fumed in a letter after the fight.

Beaten, those Americans not killed, wounded, or captured retreated to a fort in Brooklyn, where they waited for the British to move in for the kill. But for reasons never satisfactorily explained, Howe ordered his troops to halt. Instead, they began digging trenches to creep closer to the fort.

Washington used the time to organize a retreat. Blessed with a sudden curtain of fog that descended on the city and some adroit boat maneuvering by a Marblehead Massachusetts regiment of seamen, Washington got his remaining troops across the bay to Manhattan. The general was reportedly the last man to board a retreating boat.

Bantering over bread

While Washington hunkered down in Manhattan, trying to decide what to do next, Admiral Howe invited the Americans once again to talk about giving up. Congress sent three delegates — John Adams, Benjamin Franklin, and Edward Rutledge, a South Carolinian who at 26 was the youngest signer of the Declaration of Independence.

Over a three-hour "fine meal of good bread, cold Ham, Tongues and Mutton," washed down with red wine, Howe told the trio he could not receive them as members of Congress because the king did not recognize Congress. Adams tartly replied Howe could receive them "in any capacity he pleased except as British subjects." Howe then tried to placate them by saying he would lament America's defeat "as for the loss of a brother," to which Franklin replied, "My Lord, we will do our utmost endeavor to save your Lordship that mortification." Witty repartee concluded, they left without any semblance of a deal, and the British renewed their attack.

Crossing the Delaware — Twice

By the end of November 1776, Washington's army had been badly mauled again in a series of fights that saw him fleeing across the Delaware River into Pennsylvania with about 6,000 of his original force of 19,000. The rest had been killed, died of disease, were captured, or deserted. The British now occupied the whole of New York City and would remain there for the next seven years.

It's hard to believe, but from the American perspective, it could have been worse. Twice Howe had Washington at a point where a decisive blow could probably have smashed what was left of the American forces, captured or killed Washington himself, and ended the rebellion then and there. Twice Howe procrastinated, and Washington slipped away. Better yet, the British army decided to knock off for the winter and pulled back to New York, leaving Hessian mercenary troops to guard against Washington coming back.

Having escaped for the moment, Washington was still in a highly precarious position. Much of his remaining army's enlistments were up on Jan. 1, 1777. Without some hope, most of them would surely go. So, the Old Fox, as he had been nicknamed by a British general, decided a few days before Christmas to try a bit of melodrama.

Uncapping the pen

Washington assembled his troops and had a little pamphlet written by one of their own read to them. The writer was Thomas Paine, author of the *Common Sense* essay that had electrified America 11 months before. This time, Paine's article was the first in what would be a series of 16 pamphlets called *The American Crisis.*

"These are the times that try men's souls," he wrote. "The summer soldier and the sunshine patriot will, in this crisis, shrink from the service of their country; but he that stands it now, deserves the love and thanks of man and woman."

Paine recounted his own experiences at one of the battles lost to the British in New York and told of a Loyalist innkeeper who, with his child clinging to his leg opined, "Well, let me have peace in my day." "If there must be trouble," Paine retorted, "let it be in my day, that my child may have peace."

Paine's words struck home, stirring the remnants of the army and raising its morale above the basement into which it had sunk. It rose further when reinforcements arrived from two other American forces. And then Washington pulled a second rabbit out of his hat: He attacked.

Unsheathing the sword

On Christmas Night, 1776, Washington quietly slipped his men back across the ice-choked Delaware River, along with some cannon. At daybreak on Dec. 26, the Americans surrounded Hessian troops at the town of Trenton, New Jersey. This time, it was the Americans doing the routing. About 1,000 Hessian troops were killed, wounded, or captured. Two men who froze to death were the only fatalities on the American side. Washington's army also reaped a sizeable and much-needed cache of arms and other supplies.

A week later, Washington outmaneuvered British General Charles Cornwallis and won another battle near Princeton, New Jersey. The victories did wonders for the American army's spirits, and those of civilians as well. "The (local) inhabitants manifest very different feelings toward us from those manifested before," an American officer wrote, "and are now ready to take up arms against the British."

At least some of them were. By the spring of 1777, some of Paine's "sunshine patriots" drifted back. With his army somewhat restored, Washington promptly went back to losing battles.

Fighting for Time

The American army had begun 1776 pushing the British from Boston and ended it with a morale-boosting victory over German mercenaries in New Jersey. But in between, they had absorbed a series of fearful drubbings in New York.

So when 1777 started, Washington's troops — what there were of them after another wave of smallpox swept through the ranks— were in no condition to do much fighting. As the spring progressed, however, an infusion of arms from France and returning militia from various states gave the Americans something of an army again.

In the meantime, British leaders devised a plan that called for one force under General John Burgoyne to move south from Canada into upstate New York, while General Howe moved north to meet him from New York City. But Howe changed his mind, deciding to attack the rebel capital at Philadelphia first. No one bothered to tell Burgoyne about the change in plans, a lapse that would come back to haunt the British, big time, by the end of the year.

On Sept. 11, Washington's army moved to stop Howe's advance on Philadelphia at a place called Brandywine Creek. Once again, Washington was outstrategized by Howe and the American forces badly beaten. And once again, a brave and brilliant maneuver, this time an "orderly withdrawal" orchestrated by General Nathanael Greene, saved the army from total disaster.

Two weeks later, Howe's army entered Philadelphia, while the U.S. Congress hastily fled 100 miles to York, Pennsylvania. A week after Howe's occupation of the American capital, Washington launched a surprise attack on the Philadelphia suburb of Germantown. The Americans won the first 75 percent of the battle. Unfortunately, it was the last 25 percent that mattered. Smoke and fog — and confusion between two U.S. commanders — resulted in their troops firing on each other. Panic ensued, and, as General Anthony Wayne bitterly wrote, "We ran from victory."

Defeated but unbowed, Washington moved his troops to a small community built around an ironworks in a hilly area about 18 miles northwest of Philadelphia. It was called Valley Forge.

"Not only starved, but naked."

Washington chose Valley Forge to spend the winter of 1777–78 for political as well as strategic reasons. He was under pressure from Congress to stay close to Philadelphia with the idea of possibly launching a winter campaign to retake the capital. Strategically, the hills around the settlement also made it easier to defend the camp in case of a British attack.

REMEMBER

But a combination of factors made the choice a synonym in U.S. history for suffering. A store of supplies placed there over the summer was raided by British troops. An amazingly callous Congress did not, or would not, recognize the plight of Washington's troops: For a special Thanksgiving "feast," Congress provided for each soldier to have two ounces of rice and a teaspoon of vinegar, after which they had to listen to a sermon in the cold about what they were fighting for. Some local farmers and merchants chose to sell their goods to the British, who could pay with pounds instead of increasingly worthless Continental dollars.

"The army was now not only starved, but naked," Private Joseph Plumb Martin recalled in his memoir, published several decades after the war. "The greatest part was not only shirtless and barefoot, but destitute of all other clothing, especially blankets." Martin was lucky enough to find a piece of leather from which he fashioned a pair of moccasins; his barefooted comrades "could be tracked by their blood upon the rough frozen ground."

Clean water was in scarce supply. Meals consisted mostly of firecakes, which were nothing but flour and water fried over an open flame. "We were absolutely, literally starved," Martin wrote. "I do solemnly declare that I did not put a single morsel of victuals into my mouth for four days, except a little black birch bark . . . I saw several of the men roast their old shoes and eat them . . . (and) some of the officers killed and ate a favorite little dog."

There were some bright spots. The weather was fairly mild by New England standards. In January 1778, a group of Philadelphia women braved British sentries and smuggled oxen and 2,000 shirts out of the city to Valley Forge. And a shamed Congress eventually increased aid and put the superbly capable Nathanael Greene in charge of supplying the troops.

Even so, it was a rough winter. Of the 12,000 people who encamped at Valley Forge (roughly 600 of whom were women and children who had followed their husbands and fathers there and would not leave), about 2,000 died of disease and exposure.

"The long and great sufferings of this army is unexampled in history," wrote Washington, while praying in the snow. He may have been praying to hold onto his command. There were schemes afoot by several officers to convince Congress to oust Washington in favor of General Horatio Gates, and some receptive congressional ears were listening. Fortunately, the American commander still had enough political support to weather the storm — at least for the time being.

Turning the corner

Before he left London in early 1776, General John Burgoyne bet a pal £52 (about $11,700 in today's American currency) "that he will be home victorious from America by Christmas Day 1777."

"Gentleman Johnny," as he was known, was a member of Parliament, a gifted playwright, and a great fellow to have at parties. What he wasn't, however, was a light packer: On leaving Canada to lead his army down through New York to whip what he considered to be a collection of rag-tag rebels, Burgoyne brought along a personal baggage train that included musical instruments, a writing desk, several sets of dinnerware, and his mistress and her three young daughters.

Also along for the march were 7,200 British regulars, about 400 Indians from both America and Canada, and about 250 Loyalists. Burgoyne's force easily took Fort Ticonderoga, which had marked one of the first American victories of the war. But for some reason (maybe it was the dinnerware) Burgoyne decided that rather than travel by a well-known water route, he would cut his way through dense forest. This was made more difficult by American troops, who felled trees, destroyed bridges, and stripped the region of provisions.

It took Burgoyne's army three weeks to move 23 miles. Short on supplies and not realizing that two other British forces he was supposed to join up with were not going to show, Burgoyne pressed on. Meanwhile, an American army led by Horatio Gates was reinforced by 1,200 men under the command of Benedict Arnold, as well as 500 sharpshooters led by Daniel Morgan.

Over the course of about four weeks starting in mid-September, the two forces fought two battles near Saratoga, New York. Burgoyne's red-coated troops made easy targets for Morgan's riflemen. Despite being rewounded in the same leg he had been shot in at the Battle of Quebec, Arnold led two stirring charges. On Oct. 17, 1777, Burgoyne surrendered his remaining army of more than 5,000 men. He went home in disgrace, was stripped of his command — and needless to say, lost his bet.

REMEMBER

The Battle of Saratoga was perhaps *the* turning point of the war. The victory spurred Congress to approve the Articles of Confederation and put America on the path to a formal structure of government. It convinced France, whom American representatives had been courting for months, to formally enter the war as a U.S. ally (see Chapter 10). And it reaffirmed a growing realization among British military leaders.

"Though it was once the tone of this army to treat them in a most contemptible light," a British officer wrote home, "they are now become a formidable enemy."

BENEDICT ARNOLD

He was brave, daring, and a born leader on the battlefield. He was also ruthless, bitter, ambitious, and greedy. The former traits are mostly forgotten; the latter immortalized him as one of the most despised figures in American history. Born in Connecticut in 1741, Arnold ran away at the age of 16 to fight in the French and Indian War, but quit after less than two weeks. He then became a druggist, a bookseller, and an importer/exporter.

When the Revolutionary War began, Arnold formed a militia unit, eventually becoming a trusted aide to George Washington and a heroic, if sometimes semi-mutinous, figure in several major battles, included the turning-point battle of Saratoga. He was seriously wounded twice in the leg. He was also passed over for promotions, and it rankled him.

In 1780, Arnold began plotting with the British to turn over the key post of West Point, New York, where he was in command. The plot was thwarted when a British spy was captured with papers indicating Arnold's treachery. Arnold fled to the British army and led two brutal raids against American communities in Virginia and Connecticut. After the war, he spent the rest of his life as a pariah in England.

A footnote: At the national historical park commemorating the key Battle of Saratoga, there is a monument to Arnold. The monument is a stone boot, dedicated to "the most brilliant soldier of the Continental army" who was seriously wounded in the battle yet helped win the fight. There is, however, no name on the monument.

The War Moves On

After the debacle at Saratoga (at least from their point of view), the British made yet another half-baked peace offer. Prime Minister Lord North, who knew by now the war was unwinnable but couldn't convince the king of that, sent three representatives to America. They brought with them a pledge of no more direct taxes, the repeal of the heinous government acts of the past, and a promise to spend all the money raised by the crown in America through duties and fees, in America. No one even said no thanks.

Meanwhile, General Howe was replaced by General Sir Henry Clinton, a career military man whose father had once been colonial governor of New York. Clinton had orders to give up Philadelphia and base himself in New York. So he packed up his 18,000 men and enough equipment to fill a 12-mile-long baggage train and set off in June 1778.

Knowing the equipment and supplies would be a tempting target for Washington's army, Clinton put half his troops in front of the baggage and half behind. Sure enough, the Continental army attacked on June 28 at a place called Monmouth Courthouse, New Jersey, where Clinton was waiting for ferries to take his army to New York.

It was a blisteringly hot day. "The mouth of a heated oven seemed to me to be but a trifle hotter," noted Private Joseph Plumb Morgan, who only six months before had been freezing at Valley Forge. "It was impossible to breathe."

The all-day battle, which ended in pretty much of a draw, was notable for two things. One was that Washington was so furious that General Charles Lee had ordered a retreat at a key moment, he swore at Lee in front of the troops. "Never have I enjoyed such swearing before or since," one of Washington's aides later wrote. "Sir, on that memorable day he swore like an angel from heaven." (Lee, who had become an outspoken and second-guessing critic of Washington, was subsequently court-martialed and his military career ended.)

The other memorable thing about Monmouth was that it marked the last major battle between the two main armies. Clinton made it to New York and turned his attention away from New England and the Middle States. Washington decided New York was too formidable a target to attack and decided to wait things out until promised ships and troops from France began to show up.

Waging an ugly war in the west

At the start of the war, American negotiators had persuaded the six tribes of the powerful Iroquois Confederacy to sit out the fighting. But as the war dragged on, both British and American emissaries tried to talk the tribes into throwing in with their respective sides. (For more on the role of Native Americans during the war, see Chapter 11.)

Eventually, the British convinced three of the confederacy's tribes to join them; the Americans, two. One tribe, the Onondaga, tried to stay neutral, until attacks by American forces drove them into the British camp.

Led by a Mohawk named John Brant and an American loyalist, Col. John Butler, the British-backed tribes devastated the Wyoming Valley in Pennsylvania, as well as western New York. General Washington countered by sending 4,000 troops under General John Sullivan to "take whatever means necessary" to subdue the threat. Sullivan's men destroyed 40 Indian villages, burning vast supplies of corn and even cutting down fruit trees.

Farther south, a dashing Virginia frontiersman named George Rogers Clark led a small force into what is now Illinois, taking villages that were mostly French and lightly manned by British troops. Britain retaliated by stirring up the region's tribes. A British official, Henry Hamilton, earned the nickname Hair Buyer for the bounties he paid for American scalps.

In February 1779, Clark captured both Hamilton and a British-held fort near Vincennes, Indiana, despite being outnumbered two-to-one, and without losing a single man. The victory slowed, but did not end, the Indian wars in the area.

Fighting on the western front was vicious. Women and children were not exempted as targets. In Pennsylvania, pro-British tribes tortured prisoners to death by throwing them on beds of hot coals, sometimes while their families were forced to watch. At Fort Vincennes, Clark had four prisoners tomahawked, scalped, and their bodies thrown in the river. The executions were held in front of the besieged British as an inducement to surrender.

REMEMBER

The western battles continued to rage long after peace had been reached between British and American forces elsewhere. Soldiers saw opportunity in the new regions they fought in and were determined to settle in the area. Several states made grants of Indian lands as rewards for veterans. The resulting conflicts would last for decades.

Privateering for patriotism and profit

While Britain rented German mercenary soldiers to do some of its fighting on land, America basically rented a navy to do its fighting at sea. Building warships was enormously expensive, and trying to slug it out with the best navy in the world would have been futile.

So Congress issued what were called *Letters of Marque*. These documents basically said private ship captains — or *privateers* — could seize British ships and not be accused of piracy, as long as they obeyed certain rules, reported their seizures, and shared the loot with the American government.

By the end of the war, about 1,700 privateers had been formally commissioned, and it's reckoned scores of other American captains didn't bother getting letters. From 1,000 to 2,000 British ships were seized, carrying cargoes worth slightly more than $300 million worth of goods in today's currency. In 1777 alone, more than 2 million pounds of captured gunpowder and gunpowder ingredients were delivered to American troops.

It was a dangerous business. If captured, privateer crews were usually given a choice of joining the British Navy as virtual slaves or rotting in stinking prison ships anchored in New York Harbor. As many as 11,000 men died in such ships, the bodies often dumped in the mudflats surrounding the vessels.

Some actual U.S. Navy ships were commissioned. These were generally small coastal schooners that harassed British supply lines, especially in the West Indies. Whaleboats were used for nighttime guerilla raids on coastal outposts and lighthouses. And one ship, the *Bonhomme Richard*, made naval history.

Its captain was a 29-year-old Scot who started his career as a cabin boy and ended up a rear admiral in the Imperial Russian Navy. In between, John Paul Jones served on slave ships, killed a man in a sword fight, was accused of cruelty for flogging a crew member in the Caribbean, and eventually took up a new life in America as a U.S. naval officer (adding the name Jones to his given name to help bury his past).

In 1778, in command of a ship called the *Ranger*, Jones raided the coasts of England and Ireland and defeated a British naval vessel in ship-to-ship combat. The damage inflicted was minor, but the affrontery of a U.S. ship in British waters frightened British merchants and civilians alike.

In late September 1779, aboard his new 42-gun *Bonhomme Richard* (Poor Richard, named after Ben Franklin's popular almanac), Jones attacked the larger 50-gun *HMS Serapis* off the coast of England. The two ships endured a hurricane of cannon fire for 2 1/2 hours. At one point, the British captain asked whether Jones wanted to surrender. "I have not yet begun to fight!" Jones replied. Finally, it was the

British captain who surrendered. Jones's ship was so shot up it had to be abandoned, and Jones took command of the *Serapis*.

Like the victories at Trenton and Saratoga, the battle was a huge boost to American morale. Its impact in Britain was also felt. *"The tradesmen stand still and the merchant bemoans/ The losses he meets with from such as Paul Jones,"* a London newspaper observed.

As insurance rates for British merchant ships soared because of the losses to privateers, so did the clamor of businessmen to find a way to end the seemingly endless war with the upstart colonies. British government officials would give it one more try, in the South.

Fighting, southern style

The British had long believed that the Southern states would be easier to conquer than the rest of America. The South was home to thousands of people who remained loyal to the crown, at least in part because they were fearful slavery might be abolished if America achieved its independence.

REMEMBER

In late 1778, a large British force took the Georgia seaport of Savannah and began cementing its hold on the rest of the state. An American effort to take the city back was defeated in late 1779. And from his command headquarters in New York in 1780, British General Clinton shifted his focus south. The plan was to grab the Carolinas, then Virginia, and then move back north, supported by thousands of Southern loyalists.

By the spring, a force of about 10,000 British troops under General Sir Charles Cornwallis had moved south. In May, the British pounded the American army at Charleston, South Carolina, into one of the largest surrenders in American history. More than 5,000 soldiers under the command of General Benjamin Lincoln, along with a huge store of arms, were captured. The victory gave British commanders hope their newest strategy would work.

The Camden catastrophe

British hopes were further brightened in August. Against Washington's wishes, Congress had placed General Horatio Gates in charge of the army in the south, and it was a bad choice. Gates was thoroughly beaten at a battle near Camden, South Carolina. He had greatly overestimated the number of fighting men he had left after a bout of dysentery swept through the American forces the day before the fight. The Southern militia in the front lines ran. So did Gates, who covered 170 miles in three days on horseback before he stopped retreating. "It does admirable credit to the activity of a man at his time of life," a sarcastic Alexander Hamilton noted of Gates's retreat.

There was a silver lining to the loss, however. Gates was relieved of command and replaced by General Nathanel Greene, perhaps the best of all of Washington's subordinates. Greene adopted a hit-and-run strategy of fighting, withdrawing, harassing Cornwallis's army with guerilla raids, and stretching the British supply lines longer and thinner. "We fight, get beat, rise, and fight again," Greene wrote.

He also decided on a desperate-but-brilliant strategy that flew in the face of conventional military wisdom. He divided his army even though he was already outnumbered. Green figured it would be harder for Cornwallis to deliver a fatal blow if he had two targets at which to swing.

The cleverness of Cowpens

At the Battle of Cowpens, South Carolina, in January 1781, the Americans actually won, thanks to a clever ruse by General Daniel Morgan. Morgan capitalized on the American militias' well-earned reputation for running after a battle began. He put the militia units in the front lines, told them to fire two rounds each, and then retreat. Meanwhile, sharpshooters were to pick off all the British officers as the British, under the command of Sir Banastre Tarleton, chased the running Americans.

That was followed by another mock retreat, behind a third line of Morgan's best soldiers, who with cavalry support then attacked. The plan worked. More than 900 of the British force of 1,100 were killed or captured, against only 29 killed on the American side. The story is that when General Cornwallis heard of the defeat, he leaned so hard on his sword that it snapped.

Winning a defeat at Guilford Courthouse

Two months later, at Guilford Courthouse, North Carolina, Cornwallis won a technical victory over Greene, but a very steep cost. After a 90-minute battle, Greene ordered a retreat, after suffering only light casualties. Before the retreat, however, the American troops had killed or wounded almost a third of the British force.

Not only were the British not making headway on the battlefield, their strategy to enlist thousands of American loyalists was also a flop. "The idea of our friends (loyalists) rallying in numbers, and to any purpose, totally failed," Cornwallis wrote Clinton in late 1780.

By the summer of 1781, Cornwallis had had enough of trying to conquer the Carolinas. Instead, he moved his army to a small tobacco port in Virginia, called Yorktown.

"O God! It Is All Over!"

General Cornwallis's decision to move his army to a narrow peninsula flanked by the James and York rivers was based on the idea that he could be easily reinforced and supplied by British ships. What he did not know was that a large fleet of French warships was also converging on the site, and a sizeable force of American and French troops under Washington was moving south from New Jersey.

After the French defeated the British in a naval battle on Chesapeake Bay, Cornwallis was trapped. Washington's force of about 17,000 began a bombardment of the British fortifications in early October. On Oct. 19, 1781, Cornwallis surrendered his entire army. A bad sport to the end, Cornwallis pleaded illness and sent a subordinate to offer his sword. Washington countered by having one of his subordinates accept it, as shown in Figure 9-1.

FIGURE 9-1:
The British surrender at Yorktown. British major General O'Hara is shown handing his sword to the French General Comte de Rochambeau, standing next to General Washington.

Library of Congress

The American band played "Yankee Doodle." The British band played "The World Turned Upside Down." In London, Prime Minister Lord North moaned, "O God! It is all over!" when he heard the news.

Technically, it wasn't. Intermittent fighting continued for a while. British troops still controlled Charleston and Savannah and had 10,000 troops in New York City. They wouldn't leave for two more years, until the formal peace treaty had been ratified.

But for all intents and purposes, America's war of revolution had ended. The fight to become a country of truly united states was just beginning.

Chapter **10**

The War Abroad

"A compleat History of the American War is nearly the History of Mankind," John Adams wrote in 1783. "The History of France, Spain, Holland, England and the Neutral Powers, as well as America, are at least comprised in it."

Adams wasn't exaggerating. Although Americans tend to view the Revolutionary War as an us-versus-the-British fight, its impact, near and long term, was felt from Cuba to India.

This chapter first views the conflict from the British perspective — and how British leaders grossly mismanaged things. It also looks at the vital role France played in America achieving its independence, sees how the war affected other countries, and ends with a peace treaty that took years after the fighting ended to be approved.

From a Brit's Eye View

For much, if not most, of the 160 years prior to 1763, Britain had been engaged in one war or another, sometimes more than one at a time. But with victory in the French and Indian War, Britain had firmly established itself as the No. 1 power on earth. Its capital of London was the most populous and important city in Europe, overseeing the most far-flung holdings since the Roman Empire.

Riding herd on all that territory, of course, wasn't cheap. Britain's national debt had doubled from the beginning of the war until the end. The American colonies were beneficiaries of both the British victory and of being part of the British Empire in general.

It thus made eminent sense to British government officials that American colonists should pay part of the costs of running said empire. After all, the colonists paid a pittance in taxes, if they paid any. They were outrageous scofflaws when it came to adhering to customs regulations and rarely forked over anything close to the official rates when it came to duties and fees.

And even though there was a post-war recession, Americans had generally done pretty well economically. That was due in part to their own industry, but also because British merchants and businesses had extended generous credit, and Britain provided a ready market for American goods.

So, it was understandably a genuine mystery, at least initially, to many British officials as to why the Americans were so reticent to kick in their fair share.

"That this kingdom has the sovereign, the supreme legislative power over America, is granted. It cannot be denied; and taxation is a part of that sovereign power," said Prime Minister George Grenville in 1765. "Great Britain protects America. . . . The (British) nation has run itself into an immense debt to give them this protection; and now they are called upon to contribute a small share towards the public expense."

The real reason for rebelling

Oh, that argument about not being taxed *unless* they had representation in Parliament? That was a real head-scratcher to most Britons. In the first place, it could be argued that *all* of Parliament represented their interests as British citizens. Second, as a practical matter, it would be an exercise in futility to have a few token American members of Parliament: They would be vastly outnumbered and routinely voted down on every issue of contention between the colonies and the mother country.

REMEMBER

Finally, millions of British subjects in Britain itself paid much higher taxes than Americans, and yet had no voice in government. Only about 15 percent of English adult males had the right to vote (compared to as many as 70 percent of white adult males in America). Not only that, many Britons had no direct representation either. Because of the absurd way Parliament's seats were apportioned, for example, the town of Dunwich was represented, even though it no longer existed, while the rapidly growing industrial city of Manchester had no delegates at all.

As tax after tax was protested, repudiated, or ignored by the colonists, however, it became increasingly clear that the real issue wasn't tying taxes to representation. The real issue was that Americans were no longer interested in being governed by the British government.

"This rebellious war," King George III noted in his October 27, 1775, speech to Parliament, in which he branded the American rebels as traitors, "is manifestly carried on for the purpose of establishing an independent empire. I need not dwell upon the fatal effects of the success of such a plan."

In a later letter to his prime minister, Lord North, the king did dwell upon what he thought "the fatal effects" of American independence might be for Britain. Envisaging a "domino theory" that would be echoed by U.S. President Dwight Eisenhower 175 years later concerning Southeast Asia and communism, George III wrote that should America succeed in achieving independence, "The West Indies must follow. . . . Ireland would soon follow, and this island (Britain) reduced to itself, would be a poor island indeed."

In another letter to North, George III said, "I have no doubt but the (British) nation at large sees the conduct in America in its true light." Actually, they didn't, or if they did, they didn't care all that much about it.

"Rebellious war?" What rebellious war?

If you had asked the average Briton in 1775 for his or her opinion on the king's concern about the American colonies, the odds are very good his or her reply would have been "Huh?"

In fact, outside London, the trouble between the British government and the American colonies was of almost no interest. Most newspapers carried little about it; journals and diaries from the period rarely mentioned it. "A good murder in the west country gains far more interest than all the American news put together," a member of Parliament observed, "and is in fact far more interesting." In a letter to the *Pennsylvania Gazette*, a Londoner pointed out that "People (here) begin to entertain an Idea that America never was of Half the Consequence to us that it was generally imagined to be."

There were no mass demonstrations either for or against a war with America. Even after the fighting began, there was no surge of patriotic outrage. There was no rush of young British men to enlist in the army or navy. Women did not begin rolling bandages.

"What, in God's name, are ye all about in England?" a British officer wrote home from a Boston besieged by thousands of American rebels after the battles of Lexington and Concord. "Have ye forgot us?"

Merchants and others with financial interests in America were more alarmed at the fighting, but not because of any ideological notions about the empire's integrity: All the hubbub was bad for business. And some members of Parliament did warn of dire consequences if the king followed through with his threats to "chastise" the colonies.

"You may spread fire, sword and desolation, but that will not be government," said Charles Lennox, the Duke of Richmond. "No people can ever be made to submit to a form of government they say they will not receive."

But the king was unswayed: "I am certain any other conduct but compelling obedience would be ruinous," he wrote Lord North, " . . . therefore no consideration could bring me to swerve from the present path which I think myself duty-bound to follow." And being king still had clout.

"Farmer George" or "Royal Brute"

George III assumed the throne of Britain in 1760 after his grandfather, George II, died while sitting on the toilet. He departed the throne himself — and life in general — in 1820, completely insane. In between, the American Revolution occurred, and George III played a big role in it.

It was actually two different roles. At home, the king was generally well-liked for his "unaffected good nature." The acerbic writer Samuel Johnson, who liked hardly anyone, called George "the finest gentleman I have ever seen." Even as the war spread around the world and things began to go badly, George maintained his popularity with the British public.

In America, colonial leaders who were angered at the acts of Parliament at first went out of their way to assure the king they still were loyal subjects. They weren't angry at him, just Parliament. As full-fledged rebellion neared, however, George III became British Boogeyman No. 1. To Thomas Paine, writing in the revolutionary tract *Common Sense*, he was the "Royal Brute." To Thomas Jefferson, in writing the *Declaration of Independence*, "The history of the present King of Great Britain is a history of repeated injuries and usurpations, all having in direct object the establishment of an absolute Tyranny over these States."

Becoming British king by way of Germany

In truth, George III was both British patriot and autocratic tyrant. The fact that he was king at all was owed to the bizarre way in which Britain chose its rulers. George's great-grandfather, George I, was the ruler of the German duchy of

Hanover and second cousin to Queen Anne of Britain. Anne died childless. Since George I was her closest relative who was not a Catholic, and since Catholics were not allowed to occupy the British throne at the time, the crown fell to George I, in 1714, even though he was German, spoke very little English, and didn't like Britain.

He was succeeded in 1727 by his son, George II, who also tried to spend as much time as he could in Hanover and away from Britain. George II's son, whose name was Frederick, died before he could succeed his dad. So, Frederick's son George became king when Frederick's father George had a stroke while relieving himself and died in 1760. (Got that? This will all be on the test.)

George III was 22 when he assumed the throne. Unlike his grandfather and great-grandfather, he had been born in England and considered himself thoroughly English. That was a good thing, since he was king for almost 60 years, longer than any English monarch except Queens Victoria and Elizabeth II. "Born and educated in this country," he said in his accession speech, "I glory in the name of Britain." In fact, he never traveled outside southern England during his lifetime.

He was honest, faithful (one wife, 15 kids, no mistresses), well-educated, and keenly interested in agriculture (hence the nickname "Farmer George"), architecture, music, astronomy, and book collecting, with 65,000 of his books eventually donated to the British Museum. But George also suffered from a mental illness that greatly worsened toward the end of his life and led many to believe, falsely, that he was slow-witted. He was also stubborn to a fault, judgmental, quick to take offense, and slow to forgive a slight. "I wish nothing but good," he once said. "Therefore, anyone who does not agree with me is a traitor and a scoundrel. . . ."

As befits someone with that attitude, he planned to be a strong monarch. He looked the part, as you can see from Figure 10-1. His timing, however, was unfortunate.

As the 18th century progressed, Parliament had steadily asserted itself as the engine of state for Britain. For much of that time, the Whigs, a loosely organized political party that favored a less powerful monarchy, had been in power. The opposition party, the Tories, generally viewed kings more favorably, but had relatively little say in running the government.

REMEMBER

These characterizations are pretty general. Like modern political parties, each group had ideological schisms and sects. But that didn't negate the fact that to have a strong voice in the affairs of state, after his grandfather and great-grandfather had pretty much checked out on running things for several decades, the young King George needed to find strong and capable ministers if he hoped to be successful. Unfortunately, he didn't.

FIGURE 10-1:
A portrait of
George III by the
noted English
portraitist Joshua
Reynolds, in 1785,
the 25th year of
George's reign.

GEORGE the III.

Library of Congress

Assembling a war team

In the first eight years after George's accession, Britain went through five prime ministers and six chancellors of the exchequer (or chief finance minister.) Finally, in 1770, the king settled on Frederick, Lord North, who would fill both offices until 1782.

A heavy man, Lord North was good-natured, witty, and eager to please his king, even though he didn't want the job of prime minister, wasn't very good at it, and asked several times if he could quit, only to be told no each time by George III.

REMEMBER

So, these were the two men who oversaw the British effort in the Revolutionary War. They were eventually joined by a third, when North realized he knew nothing about military matters. Lord George Germain had been a soldier in the War of Austrian Succession and had fought well — up until the Battle of Minden, when he disobeyed a direct order to lead a cavalry charge. Germain was court-martialed in 1760 and found to be "unfit to serve His Majesty in any military Capacity whatever."

But with the accession of George III, Germain launched a career comeback. In 1765, the king added him to his council of advisers on foreign affairs. And despite the facts that just 15 years earlier he had been deemed "unfit to serve His Majesty" and had never set foot in North America, Germain in 1775 became Britain's Secretary of State for America. That meant he would be running the war. It was another bad choice.

Tallying British troubles

The British effort to bring the colonists back into the fold was hampered by a host of problems:

>> **Overconfidence:** British officials had nothing but disdain for Americans as fighting men. "Suppose the colonies do abound in men," sneered the Earl of Sandwich, who was in charge of the British Navy. "What does that signify? They are raw, undisciplined, cowardly men." It wasn't a completely inaccurate assessment in 1775, but had veered considerably from fact by 1781.

>> **No top target:** The very nature of fighting 13 loosely connected colonies meant the British could not land a mortal blow at any one key American city and cripple American war operations. During the war, the British took New York, Philadelphia (twice,) Savannah, and Charleston. They held all but Philadelphia at the end, and still lost.

>> **Lack of leadership:** The British generals ranged from okay (Henry Clinton) to awful (John Burgoyne). But even the leaders with experience didn't want to be there. Clinton was so disgusted with orders from London he asked to be recalled several times, and Gen. William Howe, who preceded Clinton as the British commander in America, had to be coerced into even serving at all.

>> **Long supply and communication lines:** "Three thousand miles of ocean lie between you and them," Parliament member Edmund Burke warned his government. "No contrivance can prevent the effect of this distance . . . seas roll, and months pass, between the order and the execution; and the want of a speedy explanation of a single point is enough to defeat the whole system."

>> **No reason to fight:** As disciplined and seasoned as the British soldier may have been, he was fighting for no compelling reason. America had not attacked the mother country, nor was it a threat to do so. It made little difference to the average trooper if America stayed part of the British Empire or went its own way. Most of them just wanted to go home. The Hessian mercenaries Britain employed were fighting only for the money, which was at best just mildly inspirational.

>> **Overdependence on Loyalists:** George III was convinced that thousands of loyal Americans had been cowed enough "to compel their acquiescence till a sufficient force shall appear to support them." While British troops were supported in some cases by Loyalists, it was never in the numbers the strategists in London had hoped for. Worse, it was not always possible to tell which Americans were loyal. As one British officer pointed out, "One of them can shout 'God Save the King!' at one moment, and shoot at you from behind a tree the next."

Yet even with all the obstacles in its path, there is little question that if Britain's overwhelming military superiority had been brought down in full force on the American rebels, their cause would have been crushed.

The Americans needed help, and they got it from some unlikely sources.

Making Friends in France

Almost as soon as the smoke cleared at Lexington and Concord, American leaders were seeking aid and allies in other countries. There were appeals to the citizens of England and Ireland to rise up, which were met with snorts of derision or big yawns. Canadians and Jamaicans were likewise not interested.

In France, however, the request fell on receptive ears. The French were still smarting over the outcome of the French and Indian War a dozen years before. Even though Americans had been on the opposing side, Britain was the real arch-rival, and French leaders were well aware of the obstacles Britain faced in trying to hold on to the rebellious colonies.

"It will be in vain for the English to multiply their forces (in America)," said Charles Gravier, comte de Vergennes, (or "count of Vergennes"), the French foreign minister. "No longer can they bring that vast continent back by force of arms."

Funneling French supplies

In the summer of 1775, a dashing and hugely popular young French playwright-inventor-musician-diplomat-spy named Pierre-Augustin Caron de Beaumarchais began looking for ways to help America. Beaumarchais was sort of the French version of Benjamin Franklin. He was best known for writing a trio of plays that included *The Marriage of Figaro* and *The Barber of Seville*, which became the books for the operas by Mozart and Rossini.

But Beaumarchais's interests ranged beyond the arts. He served as a personal spy in England for France's king, Louis XVI. He was also a romantic and an idealist and fell in love with the idea of liberating America from her British oppressor, especially after long conversations with Arthur Lee, a Virginia doctor serving as a diplomat (and spy) in London.

Beaumarchais convinced the king and Vergennes to begin secretly negotiating with America. Vergennes, who knew France was still building up its army and navy and not ready to openly confront Britain, agreed to send an agent to America. The agent assured American leaders that France had no designs on getting its former North American possessions back and that U.S. ships would be welcome at French ports.

REMEMBER

In the meantime, with the king's blessing and financial backing, Beaumarchais set up a dummy corporation that began channeling huge amounts of vitally needed supplies to America, including guns, cannon, cannon balls, and clothing. Tons of gunpowder, an exceedingly precious commodity, were sent. (It was good stuff: Much of it was made by Antoine-Laurent de Lavoisier, who would become known internationally as "the Father of Modern Chemistry.") By the end of the war, Beaumarchais' "company" would ship supplies worth more than $3 billion in 2018 currency to American forces.

Finessing France with Franklin

On its side of the water, Congress set up two secret committees in late 1775 to deal with foreign alliances. A nine-member committee was charged with making deals for arms and other supplies. A six-member committee was to run diplomatic relations with other countries. Congress also sent Silas Deane, a Connecticut businessman, to represent it in Paris. Deane was eventually joined by Dr. Lee from London — and the seemingly omnipresent Benjamin Franklin.

During his years representing America in England, Franklin had been viewed by many British officials as a bright country bumpkin. In France, however, he was the equivalent of a rock star. "His clothing was rustic, his bearing simple but dignified, his language direct, his hair unpowdered," a French aristocrat wrote. "It was as though the simplicity of the Classical World, the figure of a thinker of the time of Plato . . . had suddenly been brought by magic into our effeminate and slavish age."

Even sourpuss John Adams, who later joined the American delegation in France to negotiate peace terms, had to acknowledge Franklin's popularity. "There was scarcely a peasant or a citizen, a valet, coachman or footman, or lady's chamberlain or a scullion in the kitchen who did not consider him (Franklin) a friend to Humankind," Adams wrote. (Not everyone was so enamored. The king was unimpressed by Franklin's charm, to the point he reportedly gave out chamber pots with Franklin's likeness on the bottom.)

Prodded and cajoled by the Americans and mindful of Dr. Franklin's immense popularity with the French people, France informed Britain in June 1776 it would remain neutral in the war. That meant it would keep all its ports open to U.S. shipping, which by default included privateers. It also warned the British not to attempt to search ships in French waters.

PATRIOTS WITH ACCENTS

A lot of unemployed soldiers were in Europe at the start of the American Revolutionary War, and many of them came looking for jobs, especially if they were officers. Some of them turned out to be valuable additions: Baron Johan de Kalb, a German soldier of fortune who was an able commander and was killed at the Battle of Camden; Count Casmir Pulaski, a Polish cavalryman who was killed at the Battle of Savannah, and Baron Frederick Von Steuben, a dubiously titled nobleman and Prussian Army expert who helped Washington reorganize his army into a more efficient and disciplined fighting force and taught American soldiers what a bayonet was for.

Then there were fellows like Phillipe Charles Tronson du Coudray. A French artillery officer, du Coudray wanted to be made second in command to Washington and demanded a staff of 24, including a "designer." Amazingly, Congress agreed. Fortunately, shortly after he arrived in America, du Coudray haughtily refused to dismount from his horse while crossing a river on a ferry and drowned after the spooked animal jumped overboard.

Experiences with applicants like du Coudray made Congress leery. So when a 19-year-old wealthy French nobleman knocked on the door one evening, congressional aides declined to let him in. After he refused to go away, they reluctantly agreed to hear his demands for employment in the Continental Army. He had only one: that he be allowed to serve as a volunteer and at his own expense.

That sounded reasonable to Congress, and thus Marie-Joseph-Paul-Yves-Roch-Gilbert du Motier de Lafayette joined the American cause. Lafayette was inspired by what he viewed as a struggle for freedom from tyranny — and hopeful that an American victory would spark a similar struggle in France. He was an invaluable find. Lafayette contributed the 2018 equivalent of $200,000 of his own money to the war effort, fought valiantly at several major battles (in the first of which he was wounded), and helped bolster French support of America. Not only that, he named his first son after George Washington.

After the war, Lafayette helped smooth the sometimes-rocky relations between American and France, played a key role in the French Revolution, and remains one of America's all-time favorite Frenchmen.

But French officials pulled back on further help after the American army under General Washington was routed in the battles around New York in the late summer and fall of 1776. The American diplomats kept pressing. If France was not ready to fight alongside the newly formed United States, they suggested, it could at least extend the fledgling country formal recognition as an independent nation. French officials hesitated for months, especially after British threats to declare war on France grew louder.

REMEMBER

Then in late 1777, word came of the Americans' smashing victory at the Battle of Saratoga. French Foreign Minister Vergennes realized the rebels just might win after all, and that was a far better outcome for France than a reconciliation between American and Britain. They also recognized it as a chance for France to regain a foothold in the Americas.

The British realized it, too. They secretly approached the American diplomats in Paris and offered to negotiate peace. But it was too little, too late: When Franklin and the others set the withdrawal of all British troops from America as a condition to even begin negotiations, any hope of a deal was off.

On Feb. 6, 1778, France and the United States signed two treaties. One dealt with trade between the two countries, the other formed a "defensive alliance." France would fight for the American cause.

Britain Stands Alone

In truth, French leaders weren't all that interested in the American cause. What they really wanted was to deal the British a stinging reminder the world didn't actually revolve around London; protect and maybe expand French interests in the West Indies and India; and ensure that an Anglo-American alliance didn't form in the future that could threaten France.

As the war progressed, other countries saw the conflict as a chance to settle old grudges against Britain, or possibly pick up or reclaim some valuable colonial outposts, and took a role in the fighting. What had begun as a civil war was now a bonafide world war.

Seizing opportunity, Spanish-style

Like his French counterpart Louis XVI, Spain's King Charles III wasn't keen on helping the Americans for any idealistic reasons. Spain was Catholic, America basically Protestant. Moreover, Spain was wary of American designs on territory on either side of the Mississippi River.

After the French and Indian War, France had ceded what was referred to as the Louisiana Territory to Spain as compensation for Spain having entered the war on France's side. The area was not a moneymaker for the Spanish empire and served mainly as a buffer against the British and/or Americans getting grabby over Spanish holdings in Florida, Mexico, and what is now the U.S. Southwest.

REMEMBER

Spain had also lost territory to Britain in earlier wars that it wanted back, especially the Mediterranean islands of Minorca and Gibraltar. It also wanted to drive the British out of outposts along the lower Mississippi River. So in 1779, Spain entered the war against Britain, as an ally of France. Fearful of U.S. independence setting a bad example for its own numerous New World colonies, Spain did not formally recognize America as an independent country.

It nonetheless supplied American forces with tons of supplies, from buttons, shoes, and uniforms to guns and even 1.2 million silver pesos (about $30 million in 2018 U.S. currency) to help the American army in the South buy supplies and meet its payroll.

Irritating Indians (in India)

France had scaled back its colonial and trade aspirations in India after its defeat in the French and Indian war. But with the outbreak of the American Revolutionary War, it renewed its challenge to Britain for dominance of the huge subcontinent.

It found an ally in the kingdom of Mysore in South India. Ruled by a brilliant military tactician named Hyder Ali (he was one of the first to effectively use rockets as weapons in battle), Hyder attacked British holdings in India in 1780 and won several decisive victories. With French support, Mysore continued to fight the British into 1784.

In fact, it could be said that the last battle of the American Revolutionary War was fought in June 1783, off the coast of the Indian city of Cuddalore, between French and British ships that did not know peace treaties had already been signed in Paris. The Indian fights further strained British military resources already stretched thin by fighting in other parts of the world.

Angering other Europeans

In 1780, many other European countries had grown tired of the British navy stopping their merchant ships and searching them for supplies going to France or America. As much as 20 percent of the cargoes searched were subsequently seized by the British.

Prodded by Catherine the Great of Russia, the offended countries — Russia, Denmark-Norway, Sweden, Prussia, Austria, Portugal, and the Ottoman Empire — formed the *League of Armed Neutrality*. The countries' ships sailed in convoys to discourage the British from stopping them. While the combined naval strength of the league's members was not much of a threat to the British navy, the alliance did cause Britain to tread more carefully and made it quite clear that it could expect no empathy from the rest of Europe in its war with America.

One country that did not join the neutral nations' alliance was the Dutch Republic. That's because it was already at war with Britain. Profit-minded Dutch merchants had been selling arms and other supplies to America as early as 1774. The Dutch had also turned down a British request to lend Britain troops.

In 1779, the Dutch and Americans signed a secret treaty of alliance. But the British discovered the deal when a British ship stopped an American ship on its way to the Netherlands. On board was a copy of the treaty, along with Henry Laurens, who was a South Carolina slave trader and a U.S. envoy. Laurens was thrown in the Tower of London — the only American ever to be so treated — and Britain declared war on the Dutch. The conflicts between the two were minor, but it was yet another diversion of British military resources.

REMEMBER

In fact, by 1780, Britain found itself not only fighting the American rebels, but defending possessions in India, Africa, the Caribbean, and the Mediterranean. In America, the British commander, General Clinton, was forced to send 8,000 valuable troops from New York to garrisons in the West Indies. Worse, the British navy was compelled to keep as much as half of its fighting fleet close to home, just in case the French and Spanish decided to attack Britain itself. They did.

The War Goes Global

In late July 1778, evenly matched British and French fleets met about 100 miles off the coast of the French island of Ushant, in the first confrontation between the two countries in the American Revolutionary War. Like so many 18th century naval battles, it ended in a draw. But it had a sobering effect on British military leaders, who realized that the French navy, which had upsized and modernized its warships since the last time they had squared off with each other, was going to be a formidable foe this time.

Wine versus beer

In August 1779, the America Revolution threatened to visit the soil of Great Britain itself. Somewhere off the southern coast loomed an armada of more than 60 Spanish and French warships. Gathered in the northern French ports of Le Havre and St. Malo were 40,000 troops ready to invade.

In England, earthworks were hastily thrown up along the coast and a fort built at the port of Portsmouth. Militia camps were established, and a general call to arms was issued for what seemed the greatest threat to the mother country since the Spanish Armada, 190 years before. English newspapers tried to bolster morale, with defiant doggerel, such as

"Tho' Monsieur and Don should combine / What have true British Heroes to fear? / What are Frogs, and soup-meare and wine, / To Beef and plum-pudding and beer?"

The Spanish/French plan was to seize Britain's Isle of Wight, then attack the city of Portsmouth as a prelude to landing troops in Southern England. But the invasion never got off — make that on — the ground.

The Spanish fleet had been weeks late in rendezvousing with the French fleet. While they were waiting, the French ships ran low on supplies and were devastated by waves of scurvy, typhus, and dysentery. When the Spanish ships arrived, the diseases spread to them, killing hundreds of sailors. A last-minute change in orders confused things further. A fierce gale added to the fleet's misery.

In the end, the Great Invasion of 1779 fizzled without even a battle. The French and Spanish abandoned the plan and settled on fighting for smaller prizes.

Fighting for smaller prizes

Spain had lost the Mediterranean islands of Menorca and Gibraltar to the British in the early 1700s and wanted them back. It was successful in conquering Menorca in 1782 after a long siege, but repeated efforts to take Gibraltar failed.

It had better luck in the Americas. It repulsed British attacks on its colonies in Central America. It seized a British fort in Pensacola, Florida, and took other British outposts along the Mississippi River, including Natchez, Mobile, and Baton Rouge. By 1780, Spain controlled much of the Gulf of Mexico and helped relieve British pressure on the Southern states in America.

France was most interested in protecting and expanding its interests in the sugar-rich West Indies. The French captured the British-held Caribbean islands of St. Vincent and Grenada in 1779 and presented enough of a threat that the British actually sent more troops to the West Indies after 1778 than they did to America.

Meanwhile, in America, a whole lot of people were wondering just where all their allies were and what they were waiting for.

Waiting on the French

The first French force of any size to arrive in America came in July 1778, in the form of a naval fleet under the command of Adm. Charles Henri Hector d'Estaing. The admiral briefly thought about taking on British ships in New York harbor and then headed for Newport Rhode Island, where he was supposed to help American troops take the city.

Instead, d'Estaing decided to engage a British fleet off the coast. After a storm interfered, he then sailed to the West Indies to attack British possessions there. He came back to America in September 1779 in time to help lose an effort to take Savannah, Georgia, and then sailed back to France in semi-disgrace.

Meanwhile, a force of 7,000 French troops commanded by Gen. Jean-Baptiste Donatien de Vimeur, comte de Rochambeau, arrived in Rhode Island in 1780 — and sat there for almost a year. Rochambeau felt his army was too small, and was reluctant to leave a French fleet blockaded in Narragansett Bay by British ships.

All this inactivity and dithering alarmed American officials. "Our affairs are in a most wretched situation," wrote Daniel Jenifer, a Maryland congressman, in early 1781. "Congress is at its wits end . . . unless the French fleet and army arrive very soon, we shall in all probability be in a most deplorable situation."

REMEMBER

The French did arrive, and fairly soon after Jenifer's lament. A large fleet and 3,000 additional French troops sailed from the Caribbean in August 1781 under the command of Adm. Francois Joseph Paul, comte de Grasse. After landing its troops in Virginia, the fleet decisively whipped a British fleet in Chesapeake Bay. Then it set up a blockade off the Virginia port of Yorktown.

There it was joined by a combined force of American troops under Washington and the Rochambeau-led French troops that had been nestled for months in Rhode Island. The Washington-Rochambeau army had marched 680 miles from New York.

REMEMBER

A trapped British army under the command of Gen. Charles Cornwallis surrendered on Oct. 27, 1781. (If you count the sailors on Admiral de Grasse's ships, far more French were at Yorktown than Americans.) The American Revolutionary War was pretty much over for the Americans — but not for everyone else.

Fighting among France, Britain, Spain, and the Indian kingdom of Mysore continued for more than a year. Spain captured a large British supply convoy headed for

India; Britain won two sizeable naval battles over France in the Caribbean; and the French and Spanish failed in one more effort to dislodge the British from the island fortress of Gibraltar in the Mediterranean.

And in Paris, representatives of all the nations involved were trying to sort out a peace deal that would end the war, maximize gains, and minimize losses.

Puzzling out Peace

Even before the defeat at Yorktown, many Britons were tired of the war. Taxes had soared 30 percent since 1774. The size of both the army and navy had swelled, greatly increasing government expenses. The failure of American Loyalists to join British troops in great numbers, the staggering casualties incurred in "victories" in the South, and the global threats from Spain and France convinced many British political leaders that it was time to consider getting out of America.

Worse, there were reports that a combined French–American force was planning a massive invasion of Great Britain, with John Paul Jones leading the navy and the Marquis de Lafayette leading the army.

"Whatever puts an end to the American war will save the lives of thousands — millions of money too," said the writer Horace Walpole, echoing the sentiments of many of his countrymen.

Those countrymen, however, did *not* include King George, who insisted "the prosecution of the war can alone preserve us from a most ignominious peace," or the war minister Lord Germain, who contended "We can never continue to exist as a great and powerful nation after we have lost or renounced the (British) sovereignty of America."

As a last-ditch attempt to win some kind of reconciliation with the "colonies," Prime Minister Lord North pushed through a repeal of all the taxes and other acts America had found odious in the past two decades. But Parliament had had enough.

On Feb. 27, 1782, Parliament approved a resolution declaring that further prosecution of the war in America was at an end. It also approved a vote of no confidence in Lord North, who quit as prime minister the following month. General Clinton was replaced as the British Army's commander in chief in America by the even-keeled Sir Guy Carleton, who oversaw the removal of troops from every American city except New York.

On Dec. 5, 1782, a miserably cold day in London, George III visited the House of Lords to make a speech. To end the war, the king said in an emotion-choked whisper, "I did not hesitate to go the full length of the powers vested in me, and offer to declare them (America) free and independent states by an article inserted in the treaty of peace."

Americans in Paris

The peace treaty to which George III alluded was being drafted in Paris, as part of several simultaneous negotiations among the warring countries. Representing America was Benjamin Franklin, New York lawyer John Jay, who had been serving as the American envoy to Spain, and John Adams.

According to terms of the French-American alliance, the two countries were supposed to negotiate with Britain as a team, and Congress had instructed its representatives to be guided by the French. But there was a hitch.

Spain, France's ally, wanted to keep fighting until it had wrested Gibraltar away from Britain. To mollify its ally, the French suggested that Spain be given a vast area on both sides of the Mississippi River, which would give it control of most of present-day Illinois, Indiana, Tennessee, Kentucky, and Mississippi.

Jay, who had grown to intensely dislike the Spanish while serving as the U.S. envoy to Spain, vehemently objected. When Franklin asked in private if Jay was going to break from the wishes of Congress to be guided by France, Jay sprang from his chair. "If the instructions conflict with America's honor and dignity, I would break them like this," he shouted, and flung the pipe he had been smoking into the fireplace, shattering it.

Apparently impressed — and afflicted with the distracting agony of bladder stones — Franklin agreed to go along with Jay and Adams and cut their own deal with the British, without France. The British, who favored a better deal for American over a better deal for their ancient rivals France and Spain, were happy to oblige.

TECHNICAL STUFF

Under terms of the treaty, Britain agreed to formally recognize the United States of America as a sovereign nation — and its rights to most of the territory east of the Mississippi River. America got fishing rights off Newfoundland and Nova Scotia. Both sides had navigation rights on the Mississippi. America agreed not to further persecute those who had been loyal to the British crown during the war. Congress would "earnestly recommend" to the various states to give back property confiscated from loyalists. Both sides agreed to see that private debts were paid.

When they heard the details, the French were flabbergasted. "The British bought peace rather than made it," said French Foreign Minister Vergennes. "Their concessions exceed all that I thought possible."

Accepting the inevitability of it, however, France and Spain signed separate peace treaties with Britain on Sept. 3, 1783, the same day America signed its treaty. Eighteenth century communications, transportation, and politics being what they were, Congress did not sign off on the final version until Jan. 14, 1784 (known formally to almost no American as "*Ratification Day*"). Britain took until May 12, 1784. A war that started with a "shot heard 'round the world" in 1775 was finally officially ended with the stroke of a quill pen.

Who won?

The miraculous emergence of the United States as a nation, from a war won over a formidable foe and against long odds, was a significant victory for millions of Americans who had taken great risks, made huge sacrifices, and suffered great loss.

But the British actually did okay, too. Britain's economy weathered the war well, and the innovations in manufacturing processes that marked the Industrial Revolution continued full steam. North's eventual replacement as prime minister, William Pitt the Younger, proved to one of the ablest leaders in British history.

The most important practical value of America to Britain — as a trading partner — remained in place, as did its cultural ties with the United States. When a French diplomat prodded a British official at the treaty-signing party that America "would form the greatest empire in the world," the Brit replied "Yes, monsieur, and they will all speak English, every single one of them."

Britain's longtime foes, Spain and France, were both sharply weakened by the war and would suffer significant hangovers from it in the decades to come.

Relieved of its commitments in America, Britain turned much more of its colonial attention to what would become the crown jewel in its empire: India. General Cornwallis, for example, who had been the goat at Yorktown, became the British governor-general of India. As Jawaharlal Nehru, the first prime minister of India, wrote, "The independence of the United States of America is more or less contemporaneous with the loss of freedom in India."

Even King George eventually came around. "I was the last to consent to the separation," he told John Adams in 1785, after Adams had become the U.S. minister to Britain. "But the separation having been made and having become inevitable, I have always said, as I say now, that I would be the first to meet the friendship of the United States as an independent power."

Chapter **11**

The War at Home

America's independence was ultimately won not by the actions of a few extraordinary individuals, but by the efforts and sacrifices of hundreds of thousands of "ordinary" people. The impact of the struggle on various groups within the country, however, and their reactions to it, varied widely.

This chapter takes a closer look at how the war affected, and was affected by, women, African Americans, Native Americans, and those who stayed loyal to Britain. It also examines how greed, indifference, and political incompetence made a difficult time much more difficult for the common soldier.

Neighbor versus Neighbor

In Delaware, a mob dragged a neighbor from his home to be "humiliated in publick" by being whipped by a "lowly" African American. In Connecticut, another mob stripped a local doctor of his clothing, covered him in hog dung, and then broke the windows of his house.

"Times began to be troublesome, and people began to divide into parties," James Collins, then a 16-year-old North Carolina boy, noted in his memoirs years later. "Those that had been good friends in times past became enemies; they began to watch each other with jealous eyes, and were designated by the names of 'Whig' and 'Tory.'"

What Collins was witness to was the American civil war that raged within the larger global conflict. *Whigs* (after the British political party considered more sympathetic to the American cause) was a term used to describe those Americans who favored independence from Britain, although they often called themselves Patriots, and their foes most often called them Rebels. *Tories* (after the conservative British political party) referred to those who either remained loyal to the crown (also referred to as Loyalists) or who refused to embrace either side.

It was an ugly war. The Delaware man who was whipped happened to be a Patriot constable who was targeted by his Loyalist neighbors. The Connecticut doctor was a supporter of the king and ran afoul of his Patriot neighbors.

Whippings and beatings were by no means the worst confrontations between Americans on opposing sides. In Virginia, for example, a militia officer presided over "trials" of those not deemed patriotic enough. He resorted to hanging them so often from the large walnut tree in his backyard, his name became synonymous with such extra-legal executions. His name was Charles Lynch.

Deciding who was a Tory

For ardent Patriots such as the firebrand writer Thomas Paine, determining who was friend or foe was a straightforward process: "He that is not a supporter of the Independent States of America . . . is, in the American sense of the word, a TORY." But in reality, it wasn't that simple. Nor is it accurate to assume that Loyalists were all powdered-wig-wearing, snuff-sniffing, upper-crust aristocrats.

In fact, some Americans didn't embrace the cause of independence for dozens of reasons. True, some were indeed motivated by a wish to maintain their status quo of wealth and privilege. Others were directly affiliated with the British government in various capacities and had an obvious vested interest in the revolution failing.

But many were motivated by their own form of patriotism, to the king and Britain. Others saw themselves as sensible, moderate, and respectful of law and order. Some thought a war of rebellion wasn't necessary to work out differences between the colonies and the mother country.

Many tenant farmers of rich Patriots felt more oppressed by their landlords than they did by George III. Non-Irish Catholics feared persecution by the largely Protestant Patriots. As the war dragged on, some of the working poor were resentful of Patriot military drafts that allowed the wealthy to buy their way out of service. And some Americans didn't like being pushed around by anyone, or just wanted to be left alone.

"Many people who disapprove Independence have no other wish than to remain at peace," observed James Allen, a Philadelphia lawyer. "& (be) secure in their persons without influencing the minds of others."

Thousands — maybe as many as 80,000 at the start of the war — were religious pacifists who had come to America to avoid conflicts: Quakers, Shakers, Moravians, Mennonites, and Amish among them.

Counting Loyalists — and locating them

Just how many of the estimated 2.5 million non-Native American people living in the rebellious colonies were Loyalists is impossible to precisely determine. Historians' estimates have ranged from 20 percent to 35 percent. That doesn't include the colonies' 500,000 African American slaves, whose situation is covered in the "Tampering with the Slaves" section later in this chapter. Nor does it include thousands of Americans who strove to stay out of the war altogether.

It is safe to say, however, that the neighbor-against-neighbor conflicts were geographically widespread. Generally, the areas that had been settled the longest and had the deepest roots in self-government — Massachusetts, Connecticut, and Virginia — tended to be more for independence than newer colonies, such as the Carolinas and Georgia. The Middle States, such as Pennsylvania, which had large populations of pacifist religious groups, tended to be neutral.

REMEMBER

But exceptions and contradictions were everywhere. Wealthy people in the North might be ardent Loyalists, hoping to hold on to what they had. Their rich counterparts in the South, on the other hand, might favor independence if for no other reason than they feared British efforts to offer slaves freedom in turn for rebelling against their masters. Average Americans in urban areas, exposed to the daily bombardment of independence-minded media, might lean Patriot, while their rural brethren didn't know or care about issues like taxes on paper or duties on tea.

Ratcheting up the persecution of Tories

In the early stages of the Revolution, differences between Patriots and Loyalists generally ranged from social ostracism and bullying to beatings and vandalism. But by the time of the Declaration of Independence signing, *Tory-hunting* became a more serious pastime.

Neighbors forced neighbors to sign loyalty oaths to the cause of independence. Houses were searched to see whether their occupants were abiding by the boycotts of British goods. Longtime grudges within communities were settled, with patriotism as the excuse. And paranoia about loyalty ran so deep that at the Second

Continental Congress, some delegates, including James Madison, suspected Benjamin Franklin was a British spy.

States passed various laws to formalize ill treatment of Loyalists. Wishing good things for the king became a crime in Virginia. In Connecticut, public allegiance to the crown could get you hanged. By the end of the war, New York had proclaimed that Loyalists weren't entitled to collect legally owed debts from Patriots.

The seeming contradiction of a fight for freedom that embraced repressive civil and government actions was not lost on British newspapers, as shown in Figure 11-1. Or as a Maryland congressman mused with no little irony, "It is a strange freedom that is confined always to one side of the question."

FIGURE 11-1: Captioned "The savages let loose, or The cruel fate of the Loyalists," this British cartoon shows American "natives" murdering their Loyalist countrymen.

Library of Congress

A "Situation Truly Deplorable"

The split between Loyalist and Patriot was perhaps nowhere deeper than in the South, where it sparked acts of savagery on both sides. Longtime neighbors ambushed each other along shared paths and in towns. Weddings were interrupted, with guests — and sometimes even the groom — dragged away by a raiding party to be executed.

"The animosity between the Whigs and Tories renders their situation truly deplorable," wrote American General Nathanael Greene. "The Whigs seem determined to extirpate (wipe out) the Tories, and the Tories the Whigs. Some thousands have fallen in this way . . . and the evil ravages with more violence than ever. If a stop cannot be soon put to these massacres, the country will be depopulated in a few months more."

The Battle of Kings Mountain in North Carolina was a dismal example. Considered the largest American versus American battle of the war, it pitted Patriot and Loyalist militias of about 1,000 each. After a convincing victory, Patriot soldiers continued to fire even after the Loyalists had raised a white flag. Some of the Loyalist prisoners were hanged for treason after brief trials.

"The wives and the children of the poor Tories came in, in great numbers," wrote the young Patriot soldier James Collins. "Their husbands, fathers and brothers lay dead in heaps . . . we proceeded to bury the dead, but it was badly done . . . and the (scavenging) wolves became so plenty that it was dangerous for anyone to go about at night."

Miscounting by the British

A key part of the pathetic British military plan for fighting the war was the expectation that tens of thousands of the American Loyalists would flock enthusiastically to battle on the British side. "I never had an idea of subduing the Americans," recalled British Gen. James Robertson. "I meant to assist the good Americans to subdue the bad." The British war minister, Lord George Germain, estimated that "the Americans in the King's service are more in number than the whole of the enlisted troops in the service of the Congress."

REMEMBER

But identifying with the British side of the fight and actually fighting for it were two very different things for many American loyalists. British military leaders tended to view Loyalist militias with the same contempt they did the Patriot army.

That attitude, combined with widespread looting, burning, and raping by British troops that did not differentiate between "loyal" Americans and rebels, disillusioned many Loyalists. In addition, the British officers assigned to Loyalist militias were often second-rate. And even when American Loyalists rallied to the British army, they were left to face the wrath of their Patriot neighbors when the army moved on.

Losing and leaving

"To go or not to — is that the question?" a New York Loyalist newspaper asked as the war ended, in a play on Hamlet's famous soliloquy. "Whether 'tis best to trust the inclement sky . . . or stay among the Rebels and by our stay rouse up their keenest rage."

A whole lot of Loyalists — maybe as many as 80,000 to 100,000 — left America for Canada, Europe, or the West Indies. Most of those who did lost everything. A 70-year-old Boston clergyman who had lived for 30 years in that city recorded the abandonment of all his worldly possessions, including a library of 1,000 volumes, "a fine harpsichord," and a cow and calf.

Those who chose to stay often lost everything, too. In New York, the wife of a Loyalist fighter for the British wrote him that "I have suffered mos Every thing but death it self in your long absens," including the loss of their house and farm, seized and sold after officials told her "youre husband had forfeted his estate by joining the British Enemy."

British negotiators at the talks to end the war were mindful of the looming reprisals faced by Loyalists. They asked that Loyalist persecutions stop and that seized property be returned. American negotiators agreed to ask the individual states to comply. But the agreement was half-hearted; the states' compliance negligible. It would be years after the fighting ended before the healing between Americans was complete.

But the treatment of Loyalists during the war was clearly on the minds of those who would draw up the U.S. Constitution and Bill of Rights. Protecting the minority from the tyranny of the majority would become a key element of both documents.

"Tampering with the Slaves"

The American Revolution was drenched with deep and bitter ironies, and none was deeper or more bitter than conducting a fight for personal liberties while continuing to embrace the institution of slavery. It was a contradiction of which the Founding Fathers were well aware.

"The Plant of Liberty is of so tender a nature that it cannot thrive long in the neighborhood of slavery," warned Dr. Benjamin Rush. "Remember, the eyes of Europe are fixed upon you, to preserve an asylum for freedom in this country after the last pillars of it have fallen in every other quarter of the globe."

The Methodist minister John Allen of Maryland was blunter: "Blush ye pretended warriors for freedom! Ye trifling Patriots . . . for while you are pleading for a restoration of your charter rights, you at the same time are continuing the lawless, cruel, inhuman and abominable practice of enslaving your fellow creatures!"

But untying the knotty problem proved beyond their abilities — or desire — to do so at the risk of dissolving the shaky bonds between the states.

A stark and telling example of the contradiction — or hypocrisy — that the issue engendered was contained in the person of Thomas Jefferson. A slaveowner, Jefferson had blasted King George in the original draft of the Declaration of Independence for waging "cruel war against human nature itself, violating its most sacred rights of life & liberty in the persons of a distant people who never offended him, captivating & carrying them into slavery," and for not allowing the colonies to end the slave trade.

The section was deleted, however, at the insistence of Southern states' representatives. And two years later, as governor of Virginia, Jefferson signed a bill offering land, money, and "a healthy sound Negro" for anyone enlisting in the Virginia militia for the duration of the war. And even anti-slavery figures, such as John Adams, privately counseled that the abolition issue should be sidestepped for fear of driving Southern states out of the colonies' shaky coalition.

Fighting for freedom on the American side

The half-million African-American slaves were well aware of what the fight raging around them was all about: Of 289 slaves and former slaves who enlisted in the Connecticut militia, 23 gave surnames of Liberty, Freeman or Freedom. In applying for a military pension years after the war, Private John Grant wrote "when I saw Liberty Poles and the people all engaged for the support of freedom, I could not but like and be pleased with such things. . . ." (He did not get his pension, Congress deeming that since he was a fugitive slave at the time, he did not merit one.)

REMEMBER

That Grant and others like him fought at all for the American cause was a bone of contention among political and military leaders throughout the war. In July 1775, as soon as he took command, George Washington ordered an end to the enlistment of any more African Americans in the Continental Army. In November, he decided to discharge those already serving, after polling his command staff. None of them favored the idea of African Americans serving, whether slave or free. "The policy of our arming Slaves is in my opinion a moot point," he wrote. Washington, a slaveowner himself, was troubled by news that slaves in Jamaica had staged a bloody and ultimately failed uprising, apparently inspired by news of the American fight for independence.

Even anti-slavery advocates like John Adams were leery about the idea, although for more pragmatic political reasons than the slave-owning Washington. When a trusted aide to Washington formally proposed arming 3,000 slaves in the South with the promise of freedom for fighting the British, Adams told him, "Your Negro battalion will never do. South Carolina would run out of their Wits at the least Hint of such a Measure."

Adams's prediction was accurate. "We are much disgusted here at Congress recommending to us to arm our Slaves," South Carolina militia commander Christopher Gadsden wrote to Sam Adams. "It was received with great resentment as a dangerous and impolitic step."

But reality tempered the opposition to African Americans serving with the American forces. The simple fact was that the Americans needed every man they could get. By the end of 1775, Washington had rescinded his ban on African Americans from the army and left it up to local recruiters to use their best judgement in enlisting free — but not slave — African Americans. By the end of 1777, slaves were also allowed to enlist. In fact, some slaveowners facing their state's draft sent slaves in their place.

Washington's change of heart was spurred by another reality: The British were openly inviting slaves to join up and fight for the king — and their own freedom.

Luring slaves to the Loyalist side

As I point out in Chapter 8, the royal governor of Virginia, John Murray, Lord Dunmore, issued a proclamation in November 1775, offering freedom to every slave who agreed to enlist in what Dunmore called his "Ethiopian Brigade."

As many as 800 slaves took Dunmore up on his offer, including a 35-year-old native of the African nation of Gambia. His name was Harry Washington, and he had fled from a plantation, where he worked in the stables. The plantation was called Mount Vernon. "There is not a man among them (the slaves) here but would not leave us, if they believ'd they could make their Escape," Mount Vernon's manager, Lund Washington, wrote to his cousin, the plantation's owner George Washington.

Dunmore's proclamation sent shudders throughout the South. In "tampering with the Slaves," James Madison wrote a friend, Dunmore had hit on the Southern states' greatest weakness, "and if we shall be subdued, we shall fall like Achilles, by the hand of one that knows the secret."

Actually, the British had no intention of freeing slaves to any great degree. Dunmore's proclamation applied only to the slaves of those who supported the Rebel cause. Slaves who ran away from Loyalist masters were returned to their owners. While as many as 20,000 slaves took the opportunity to flee to British "protection" during the war, relatively few found freedom.

"Tis only changing one master for another," wrote John Cruden, a North Carolina Loyalist official who oversaw the confiscated estates of plantation owners on the American side. "Let it be clearly understood that they (slaves) are to serve the King for ever, and that those slaves who are not taken for his Majesty's service are to remain on the plantations, and perform, as usual, the labors of the field."

Those who were taken for "his Majesty's service" worked as valets for British officers, dug latrines, took care of livestock, and generally performed many of the same tasks they had as slaves. Many were abandoned when the British army moved on, and many of those died of recurring smallpox epidemics or starved to death.

In the end, perhaps as many as 5,000 African Americans served in the American forces, while perhaps 20,000 served on the British side.

Fleeing to freedom

As the war ground to an end, thousands of slaves who had fled their bondage wound up in British-held New York City, including George Washington's slave Harry. As slave owners descended on the city to claim their "property" in the summer of 1783, British clerks entered the names of 2,775 African Americans in what was called The Book of Negroes.

The slaves whose names were in the book were among, but not all of, those who had, with the aid of the British government, escaped to Canada, England, or elsewhere. Washington later ordered the book seized so that owners of slaves listed in it could petition Congress for compensation.

Harry Washington went first to Nova Scotia and then to an area in what is now the African country of Sierra Leone, established by the British as the "Province of Freedom." About 1,200 former African American slaves settled there. As if to bring the saga full-circle, Harry Washington led a rebellion against the British over unfair taxation and was eventually banished to another section of Sierra Leone.

Despite the exodus of thousands of former slaves, America actually had more people in chains at the end of the war than at the beginning, mostly because of a high birth rate among slaves. By 1807, when Congress outlawed the importation of slaves, there were more than four million already in the United States.

The contradiction of slavery and fighting for freedom did stir some states to make halting steps toward abolition. But even laws that dealt with freeing slaves were loaded with fine print and loopholes. In Connecticut, a law abolished slavery "as soon as may be, consistent with the rights of individuals (in other words, slaveowners) and the Public Safety and Welfare."

Another state law said the children of slaves born after March 1, 1784, would be free — when they reached the age of 25. The impact of that was as the slaves neared the age of 25, they were sold to other states. By the first federal census in the 1790, only Massachusetts reported no slaves within its borders.

"It always seemed a most iniquitous scheme to me," mused John Adams's wife Abigail, "to fight for ourselves for what we are robbing and plundering from those who have as good a right to freedom as we have."

"Iniquitous" as it was, however, America would raise and then drop or sidestep the issue for decades, until another bloodier and deeper civil war was waged.

"Remember the Ladies"

It is an inescapable fact that there were no "Founding Mothers," at least not in the sense the term "Founding Fathers" is used to describe the male leaders of the American Revolution. No women served in Congress, signed the Declaration of Independence, or helped draft the Articles of Confederation or U.S. Constitution.

While specifics varied from state to state and sometimes from community to community, women during this period generally had little legal standing. So tiny was their role in politics that even to suggest having a larger one was a subject of great humor — at least to men.

When Abagail Adams wrote her husband John in 1776 to "remember the ladies" while drafting the fledgling country's new government, he replied, "I cannot help but laugh. . . . Depend upon it. We know better than to repeal our Masculine systems."

To a colleague, however, John took a more serious, if just as chauvinistic, tone. Extending the right to vote too widely under the new government would open a Pandora's box of universal demands: "There will be no End to It. New Claims will arise. Women will demand a Vote."

Laboring on the home front

Women could and did enter the political arena insofar as writing letters, circulars, and tracts and helping to operate lines of communication and information. And as in all great wars, it fell to women to do everything but fight to keep things going. When Americans quit buying machine-made cloth from England, for example, American women had to make it by hand.

"I rise with the sun and all through the long day I have no time for aught but my work," wrote a Connecticut farmer's wife whose husband was off to the war. Even during family prayer time, she admitted, her mind was on "whether Polly remembered to set the sponge for the bread, or put water in the leach tub or to turn the cloth in the dyeing vat. . . ."

REMEMBER

Less specific but more important, women were expected, at least in Patriot families, to infuse the children with the spirit of representative democracy and the value of individual liberty. It was a task that historian Linda Kerber labeled "republican motherhood," and political leaders urged Revolutionary-era men to remind their spouses of its importance. "Let their husbands point out the necessity of such conduct," wrote Christopher Gadsden of South Carolina, "that it is the only thing that can save them and their children from distresses, slavery and disgrace. . .".

In addition to bearing the brunt of wartime shortages and other hardships, it also fell to women to bear the losses of men who would not come home from the fighting, as well as steeling themselves to send off their husbands and sons to war — or going themselves.

Helping near the battle front

A widowed Irish immigrant in South Carolina, Elizabeth Jackson, did both. Jackson had lost two of her three sons to the war. She nonetheless volunteered to act as a nurse for wounded Americans held on British prison ships in Charleston Harbor. After contracting cholera, she summoned her remaining 15-year-old son, who had been fighting the British since he was 12 and bore the slash marks of a British officer's sword to prove it. "Avoid quarrels if you can," Andrew Jackson recalled his mother telling him before she died, ". . . (but) if you ever have to vindicate your honor, do it calmly."

Women often served as nurses, cooks, seamstresses, and laundresses to the various militias and Continental Army. General Washington wasn't keen on the practice, since the women had to be fed precious rations. And, try as he might with repeated orders to the contrary, they often hitched rides in supply wagons, thus slowing things down. But since his own wife Martha often traveled with him, Washington did not order his commanders to ban women entirely from the army camps.

If they didn't tag along with their husbands, sons, and brothers, women might make uniforms, gather food, or perform other tasks for the troops. One group of three dozen Philadelphia residents were so persistent in raising funds for the army, a Loyalist complained "people were obliged to give them something to get rid of them." They ultimately raised the staggering modern-day equivalent of $300,000.

"Necessity," a Revolutionary War woman recalled in 1810, "taught us to make exertions which our girls of the present day know nothing of."

"O, Strange Englishmen Kill Each Other"

If there was one group destined to lose no matter how the American Revolutionary War came out, it was Native Americans. If the British won the struggle, they were no more likely to be successful in keeping the colonists from encroaching on lands promised to the tribes than they had been before the war. If the Americans won, the push west would only be accelerated. As Figure 11-2 points out, all the Indian nations could do was watch the two sides fight over land that didn't belong to them.

FIGURE 11-2:
A French engraving showing an American Patriot and Loyalist fighting over the deed to America, while a Native American looks on.

Library of Congress

"O, strange Englishmen kill each other," a baffled Seneca chief observed. "I think the world is coming to an end."

Getting pressure from both sides

At the time of the signing of the Declaration of Independence, there were an estimated 200,000 Native Americans living east of the Mississippi River, in about 85 nations. The instinct for many of the nations was to stay out of the fighting between the whites. "We are unwilling to join on either side," an Iroquois chief smoothly told the Patriot governor of Connecticut, ". . . for we love you both — Old England and New."

REMEMBER

Indian neutrality was fine for the Americans. In 1775, the First Continental Congress had sent representatives to meet with the powerful six-tribe Iroquois Confederacy, at Western Pennsylvania's Fort Pitt. The congressional delegates told the tribes that while King George was a good guy, his counselors were "proud and wicked men" who "tell us they will slip their hand into our pockets without asking." After a second meeting, the Iroquois nations agreed "not to take any part; but as it is a family affair, to sit still and see you fight it out."

But the British had a long history of dealing with the tribes. One British Indian agent, Sir William Johnson, had been so trusted by the Iroquois, he was named an honorary chief of the Six Nations. The British contended that while they wanted to protect Indian rights to their lands, the Americans were poised to invade them. "They mean to cheat you," British agent John Butler told an Iroquois delegation, "and should you be so silly as to take their advice . . . their intent is to take all your lands from you and destroy your people."

Some tribal leaders were dubious. "I now tell you that you are a mad, foolish, crazy and deceitful person," the Seneca war chief Cornplanter replied. ". . . For suppose the Americans conquer you, what would they say to us?"

But pressures mounted to forgo neutrality and side with the British. The U.S. cause wasn't helped by language in the Declaration of Independence that described Indians as "merciless savages, whose known rule of warfare is an undistinguished destruction of all ages, sexes and conditions."

In late 1775, a Mohawk leader, Thayendanegea, who dressed in English clothes and was better known by the name Joseph Brant, went to England to meet with war minister Lord Germain and enlist British logistical support and supplies. Germain was happy to oblige: "The dread the people of New England and company have of a war with the savages proves the expediency of holding that scourge over them," Germain wrote.

What neither the British nor the Americans fully grasped was that the structure of the Iroquois Confederacy was such that individual tribes, and even individual members within tribes, were free to fight on either side, or not. Americans and Britons, used to government by consensus and not pure democracy, didn't get it.

As a result, some of the Six Nations fought for the British while others fought alongside the Americans, and at least one tribe, the Onondaga, tried unsuccessfully to stay out of it.

In the South, the situation was much the same. British agents, such as the half-Creek Alexander McGillivray, convinced some tribes to fight on the British side, while other tribes tried to avoid the war or fought only when attacked by American forces who failed or refused to differentiate among the Indian nations.

For more detail on the role of Native Americans in the actual fighting, see Chapter 9.

Absorbing the aftermath

The American victory and subsequent peace treaty that the British agreed to basically hung the Native Americans out to dry. Lands that the British had once guaranteed to the tribes were given to the Americans, with no guarantees that the Americans would give any of them back. The new British prime minister, William Petty, the Earl of Shelburne, tried to put a veneer of concern on the sell-out, saying the tribes "were not abandoned to their enemies," but "they were remitted to the care of (their American) neighbors, whose interest it was as much as ours to cultivate friendship with them. . . ."

But the tribes didn't buy Shelburne's baloney. At a post-war meeting with British officials in Canada, a tribal leader said, "Pretending to give up (our) country to the Americans without our consent . . . was an Act of Cruelty and Injustice that only the Christians were capable of doing."

In the fall of 1783, tribal representatives met twice with an American delegation led by the young Frenchman Marquis de Lafayette. Lafayette had been chosen by Washington to lead the delegation because the French had historically enjoyed good relations with many of the tribes.

Lafayette, however, reminded them they had been warned not to fight Americans, and that the "great General Washington" (whom the Iroquois had named Town Destroyer for the many villages burned under his orders) had won the war, and therefore didn't have to bargain. The tribes agreed to cede sizeable tracts of land in return for promises of fair treatment in the future and profitable trade agreements. The reality turned out to be something far different — and far more tragic — for most tribes.

Money and Mutiny

As if wars weren't bad enough in themselves, it seems every conflict gives rise to a form of human pond scum known as *profiteers* — people who greedily squeeze every penny they can from supplying vital arms and supplies to troops in the field. The American Revolutionary War was no exception.

"I would to God that one of the most atrocious (of these people) of each state was hung upon a gallows," fumed George Washington. "No punishment in my opinion is too great for the man who can build his greatness upon his country's ruin."

REMEMBER

Washington's anger was well-founded. While his half-starved and raggedly clothed men huddled in the snow at Valley Forge, for example, nearby American farmers were selling their produce to the British army in Philadelphia. Boston merchants sold clothes at profit margins of more than 1,000 percent. Others bought up all they could of vital supplies to corner the markets and drive up prices even higher.

The money-making mania wasn't confined to New England, as Robert Huntsman, a Virginia doctor, noted in 1780: "The attention of the people of this state is very little taken up with the war at this time, or indeed for a year or two past . . . the greatest part of the people are entirely taken up in (financial) schemes . . . immense fortunes have been made by trade or speculation."

The speculation and profit-squeezing weren't confined to middle-class merchants or farmers. The two secret committees established by Congress to handle obtaining supplies from foreign countries were controlled by Robert Morris, a wily Philadelphia merchant. Morris took advantage of a "cost-plus" system approved by Congress in which government contracts guaranteed suppliers profits no matter what the costs of the supplies turned out to be. Morris and other committee members made sure companies in which they had financial interests got a healthy "taste" of the profits as well.

"Not worth a continental"

In their defense, farmers, merchants, and speculators argued that the high prices were defensible because the pitiable monetary system set up by Congress was so inflationary. And was it ever.

In 1775, Congress issued $2 million in paper bills of credit, with each state pledged to redeem a proportional share of the bills within seven years by imposing taxes on their residents. Another $1 million was soon issued and then another $3 million. In one year, Congress had increased the total money supply in America by

50 percent, almost none of it backed by anything other than a promise to someday make it worth something.

Worse, Congress failed to rein in the individual states' habits of issuing their own currency, which took on more value within each state than the continental dollars issued by Congress. The result was rampant inflation: In 1776, $4 in continental currency was worth $1 in gold coin. By 1780, it took $100 in continentals to get $1 in gold.

At first, patriotic fervor made it an act tantamount to treason for someone not to accept the bills Congress churned out. But as inflation soared, no one wanted the U.S. currency, and the term "not worth a continental" became widespread. And even then, most American soldiers were seldom, if ever paid anything, at least not on a regular basis.

The suffering at Morristown

As bad as the winter of 1776–77 had been at Valley Forge, the winter of 1779–80 that Washington's army spent at Morristown, New Jersey was worse. The winter saw 28 separate snowfalls, and it was so cold that nearby New York Harbor froze over. While the army of about 12,000 had built log huts at the beginning of the winter, many were without blankets, jackets, or shirts, and some without shoes.

Food was as scarce as clothing. Washington noted his troops went "5 or Six days together without bread, at other times as many days without meat, and once or twice two or three days without either. . . . We have never experienced a like extremity at any period of the war." His men were living off "every kind of horse food but hay."

Washington had resisted using his authority from Congress to seize food and supplies from civilians who refused to sell to the army for continental dollars, but now he felt he had no choice. "We begin to hate this country for its neglect of us, wrote Washington's aide, Alexander Hamilton. "The country begins to hate us for our oppression of them."

Ashamed to be an American

The bitterness of American troops ran deep. "I wish I could say I was not born an American," Lt. Col. Ebenezer Huntington wrote to his father. "I once gloried in it, but am now ashamed of it . . . I am in Rags, have lain in the Rain on the Ground for 48 hours past and only a chunk of Fresh Beef and that without Salt to dine on this day . . . no pay since last December . . . and all this for my Country (where) men who hold the Purse Strings as tho' they would Damn the World rather than part with a Dollar to the Army."

In January 1781, about 1,500 men at Morristown staged a mutiny, killing an officer and occupying college buildings at Princeton. Many of them had signed up for three-year hitches that were up. After months of being undersupplied and not being paid, they had had enough. Congress sent an emissary armed with promises, and the mutiny ended a week after it started. But other insurrections followed. A few weeks after the Morristown mutiny, troops at nearby Federal Hill mutinied. This time Washington ordered two of the leaders executed.

In June 1783, about 400 Pennsylvania militia troops marched on the U.S. capitol at Philadelphia. They surrounded the building and demanded to be paid for a war that had all but ended two years before. Washington dispatched an army of 1,500 to suppress the mutiny, and the incident ended without violence. (Although it did convince Congress to move from Philadelphia to Maryland, then New Jersey, and then New York.)

The Newburgh Conspiracy

A much more serious threat arose in March 1783, when a group of Continental Army officers at the army's winter headquarters near Newburgh, New York, decided Congress had stalled long enough in honoring promises to provide back pay and pensions. The officers threatened to either disband the army altogether — or refuse to disband the army once peace had formally been ratified with Britain. The first action would leave the nation defenseless, the second had implications of a military coup.

Washington, however, brilliantly defused the situation. First, he convinced the officers to take a few days to cool down. Then he suggested they meet to discuss things and implied he would stay away from the meeting. But as the meeting began, he strode dramatically into the room.

The general denounced the threats and asked the officers to "give one more distinguished proof of unexampled patriotism and patient virtue" and have confidence "in the purity of the intentions of Congress."

Washington begged leave to read a letter from a supportive congressman. He began to read it and then stopped. "Gentlemen, you must pardon me," he said while reaching in his pocket for a pair of reading spectacles, "for I have not only grown gray but almost blind in service to my country." Some of the officers openly wept. The crisis passed.

Why They Fought

After the Battle of Bunker Hill in 1775, a captured New Hampshire militia officer named William Scott was asked by a British doctor why he had joined the fight. Scott, who had been wounded in the knee, replied that he saw the war as an opportunity to better his lot in life. "As to the Dispute between great Britain & the colonies, I know nothing of it," Scott replied, according to the doctor's later memoirs. "Neither am I capable of judging whether it is right or wrong."

How sincere his answer was is questionable, since he may have been saying what he thought a British surgeon would want to hear. That speculation takes on more weight when you take into account what Scott did during the rest of the war: He escaped from a British prison in Nova Scotia; rejoined the American forces and was again captured; escaped again and was commissioned by General Washington to form a band of rangers; and then left the army in 1781 and joined the U.S. Navy. Then there is this: Twelve members of Scott's family, all from the tiny town of Peterborough, fought in some capacity for the American side.

Why? Some of those who fought doubtlessly did it for the purpose stated by Scott to the British doctor: to escape an otherwise inescapable future life chained to a plow or trapped in a menial laborer's job. Some, especially the young boys like 14-year-old Joseph Plumb Martin, were caught up in the romance and adventure a war promised. As he listened to the soldiers billeted at his grandparents' Connecticut farm, "Their company and conversation began to warm my courage to such a degree that I resolved at all events 'to go a'sogerin,'" he recalled years later.

It was a romantic notion quickly covered in blood. It's estimated that one of every eight soldiers on the American side died, either in battle, from disease, or as a prisoner of war. Measured as a percentage of the total American population, it was the bloodiest war in the country's history, except for the Civil War.

"Death was so frequent that it ceased to terrify," a soldier wrote after the Battle of Saratoga. "It ceased to warn, it ceased to alarm Survivors."

Ultimately, many of those who fought did so because they thought it was the only right thing to do. In his memoirs, James Collins recalled that his father Daniel came home one day in 1780, after watching an ironworks be destroyed near their North Carolina farm, and several men killed by British troops and Loyalists. It was time, Daniel said, for him to join the war.

"I have come home determined to take my gun," he said, "and when I lay it down, I lay down my life with it . . . we must submit and become slaves, or fight."

Now What?

Establishing a sound government for a new nation proves one tough task.

Some background on the men who helped create the country.

The creation of a document for the ages — the U.S. Constitution.

Chapter **12**

A Most Imperfect Union

The last major battle had been fought; the peace treaty was being hammered out; and America took its place on the globe as a new country. But it was far from being out of the woods. A new country needs a system of government, and governments, as we all know, cost money.

In this chapter, the United States struggles with staying united, flounders financially, comes up with a pretty good blueprint for all the new lands out west that it now has — and takes its first steps toward a new form of government. But first, it parts with its ablest leader.

The General Goes Home

George Washington had to wait two years after his last battle for the enemy to leave. The general had defeated the British army at Yorktown, Virginia in October 1781. But the last major British force did not depart New York City until November 1783. While waiting for the final peace terms to be hammered out in Paris, Washington spent a considerable amount of time battling with a different adversary: Congress.

The most immediate fight was over an old subject: keeping the Continental army and the state militias functioning. Despite the win at Yorktown, there existed a very real threat that major hostilities would resume.

British fleets were still in American and Caribbean waters. One of them, in fact, won a major battle in the West Indies over a French fleet in April 1782. That greatly diminished the chances of French naval aid should the British launch a new major offensive in America. The British still held the key southern port cities of Savannah and Charleston. Vicious guerilla warfare was raging in the Carolinas, with Patriot and Loyalist groups routinely committing atrocities against soldiers and civilians alike. And in England, the king and his war minister, Lord Germain, were still stubbornly insisting that the American rebels could be defeated and the colonies beaten into submission.

Keeping a fighting force ready — sort of

Recognizing all this, Washington, strove to persuade Congress and the state governments the war was not over. "To make a good peace," he reminded a congressman, "you ought to be well-prepared to carry on the war." He had little faith Congress would heed his advice. "It will (probably) lay to the states," he wrote, "to determine whether we are, early in the next campaign, to take advantage of what we have gained (at Yorktown), or whether we are as usual to let the enemy bring their reinforcements from Europe."

Washington had reason to be skeptical of congressional competence. In 1780, Congress had promised Continental Army officers half-pay pensions for life if they would stay in uniform until the war was over. It was a rash pledge for a government that was all but broke, and it soon became apparent to many officers and soldiers alike that getting paid for their service was not a government priority. The result was a series of mutinies, and even the threat of a potential military coup (see Chapter 11).

While dragging its feet on the issue of paying the army, Congress and Washington did agree to furlough most of his army in June 1783, both to lessen the threat of future mutinies or coups and to save money. By allowing the troops to go home, they would have to fend for their own food and shelter, but would be kept on call in case major fighting broke out.

Thankfully, it didn't. King George III's ardent wish to keep fighting was eventually overruled by Parliament; the British troops in the South were withdrawn; and Washington and Gen. Sir Guy Carleton, the British commander in America, reached a tacit agreement to ratchet things down while waiting for the diplomats to finish in Paris. The furloughed troops were formally discharged in November 1783, reducing the American army to a miniscule 800 soldiers.

Pitching other proposals

In addition to urging Congress to treat the army fairly, Washington made two other suggestions while waiting for the British to completely depart. The first, outlined in an essay titled *"Sentiments on a Peace Establishment,"* was for the creation of a permanent standing army. It was not a popular idea with most Americans, who feared a professional army would be a tempting tool for would-be dictators. Plus, it would be expensive to maintain.

REMEMBER

But Washington argued that "altho' a large standing Army in time of Peace hath ever been considered dangerous to the liberties of a Country, yet a few Troops, under certain circumstances, are not only safe, but indispensably necessary." He called for military posts in the West to defend American interests from foreign nations, and settlers from the Native Americans; coastal fortifications; a U.S. Navy to protect American merchant ships; and a central base at West Point New York to train officers and guard against invasion from British-governed Canada.

The second proposal was in the form of a letter Washington sent to each of the 13 state governors. In it, he recommended the states come up with a unified and centralized government. "It is indispensable to the happiness of the individual States," he wrote, "that there should be lodged somewhere, a Supreme Power to regulate and govern the general concerns of the Confederated Republic." If not, he warned, Britain would pick off the states one by one and reabsorb them into its empire.

In a private letter to his friend and former aide, the Marquis de Lafayette, Washington was more specific: America must "form a constitution that will give consistency, stability and dignity to the Union; and sufficient powers to the Great Council of the Nation for general purposes." He also called for a "Convention of the People" to draft a "Federal constitution."

REMEMBER

But Washington made it clear that he was only making suggestions, not auditioning for any role in a national government. His remarks, he said were meant "as the Legacy of One, who has ardently wished, on all occasions, to be useful to his Country," but who was retiring and would not be "taking any share in public business hereafter."

Saying goodbye

Precisely at noon on Dec. 4, 1783, George Washington entered a handsome five-story brick building at the corner of New York City's Broad and Pearl streets. The 64-year-old building housed the Fraunces Tavern, where the handful of Continental Army officers still with the commanding general had gathered to say farewell.

With his remaining troops, Washington had entered the city on Nov. 25, a bit more than seven long years since he had his army had been ignominiously driven out by the British. He had enjoyed — or endured — a round of celebratory parties and the largest fireworks display in the country's short history, courtesy of his chief artillery officer, Henry Knox. Now, he nibbled at some food, raised a glass of wine, and toasted his officers.

"With a heart full of love and gratitude, I now take leave of you," he said, fighting back tears. "I most devoutly wish that your latter days may be as prosperous and happy as your former have been glorious and honorable."

He embraced each of them and left for Annapolis, Maryland, where Congress was meeting. It took him two weeks to get there, slowed by an endless stream of events in his honor in every village and town he passed through. He visited former battlefields and was feted at dinners. The University of Pennsylvania bestowed an honorary degree. The Liberty Bell was rung, and banners unfurled declaring him "The Savior of His Country."

On Dec. 23, again precisely at noon, Washington entered the Assembly room of Maryland's new State House, still under construction. Although the room was crowded to capacity, only 20 congressmen, from seven states, were present. Congress had ignored his advice about a standing army and sent most of his troops home with little more than IOUs for their service.

But Washington rose above the pettiness. His voice choked with emotion, he said, "The great events on which my resignation depended having at length taken place, I now have the honor . . . to surrender into their (Congress) hands the trust committed to me, and to claim the indulgence of retiring from the service of my country."

He then handed a parchment copy of his commission to Congressional President Thomas Mifflin, one of his former aides, and went home to his Mount Vernon plantation.

Preserving a republic

By quietly quitting, Washington may have done as much for the future of the United States of America as he had ever done on the battlefield. He easily could have cashed in his enormous prestige, public respect, and popularity in a bid to become America's first king, or general-for-life, particularly in light of the shaky state of the confederated government at the time.

"The moderation and virtue of a single character," Thomas Jefferson observed, "probably prevented the Revolution from being closed, as most others have been, by a subversion of that liberty it was intended to establish."

The American artist John Trumbull wrote from London that when news of Washington's resignation reached Europe, it excited "the astonishment and admiration of the world. 'Tis a Conduct so novel, so inconceivable to People, who, far from giving up powers they possess, are willing to Convulse the Empire to acquire more."

Even George III was impressed. When another American artist, Benjamin West, told him Washington was really retiring, the king is said to have replied, "If he does that, he will be the greatest man in the world."

Hard Money and Morris Notes

People accept paper money printed by a government for basically two reasons. One is that they believe the currency is backed by something of widely accepted value, for which it theoretically could be exchanged, such as silver or gold. The other is that they have faith that the issuing government is sensibly run and stable enough to ensure its currency can be relied upon to purchase goods and services.

Unfortunately for Revolutionary-Era Americans, their government had no gold or silver reserves, and all the credibility of a guy selling screen doors for submarines.

Americans had ostensibly rebelled against Britain because of taxation without representation. Now they had representation without taxation. The Articles of Confederation, under which Congress functioned, gave the central government virtually no authority to impose taxes. To raise money, therefore, Congress either had to borrow it or print continental dollars that were backed by nothing of value. As more and more continentals were put into circulation, their value declined. The result was rampant inflation.

TECHNICAL STUFF

In 1780, 100 continentals were worth $1 in gold or silver. In early 1781, the ratio was 125-to-1; and by mid-1781, it was 700-to-1. Prices soared. A bushel of corn in Philadelphia cost 60 times in 1781 what it did in 1776. Merchants and shopkeepers refused to accept paper money, whether it was issued by the central government or the states. Artisans and craftsmen refused to work for anything but gold or silver coins — called *hard money* — that was usually of Spanish origin.

To quell protests and riots — one of which in Philadelphia resulted in 6 dead and 15 injured before troops broke it up — the Pennsylvania assembly abandoned paper currency altogether. Hard money or barter became virtually the only way to do business. Something needed to be done. And Congress being Congress (even in those days) it did something: It handed off the problem.

Creating a money czar

Robert Morris was one of America's wealthiest men. Born in Liverpool, England, in 1734, he came to America at the age of 13 and joined his father's successful mercantile business. By the age of 20, he had formed a partnership with Thomas Willing (who later became the first president of the First Bank of the United States), and together they created a worldwide trading company.

As a beneficiary of America being part of the British Empire, Morris was a somewhat reluctant patriot at the start of the Revolution. But he came around to the cause, eventually serving in Congress and the Pennsylvania legislature. He also developed a reputation, perhaps only partially deserved, for making sure he and his business partners profited from government contract awards and other financial decisions.

In May 1781, Morris accepted a unanimous request of Congress that he become America's one — and as it turned out, only — Superintendent of Finance. It was a job he was reluctant to take — and Congress was reluctant to create. For most of its existence, Congress had resisted giving up any of its power to executive departments. Instead, it favored setting up innumerable committees of its own members to handle things.

For his part, Morris knew what a mess he was taking on. In a letter to his friend George Washington, he said the job was "contrary to my inclination, to my judgement and to my experience," and had agreed to do it only because "the absolute necessity of a transformation of the country's finances."

Morris's acceptance had some stiff conditions, all of which Congress accepted. He had the power to hire and fire his own staff, plus oversee any government worker who handled public funds, for any reason. He supervised the government's borrowing, its role in overseas trade, and its spending. "The most trifling thing cannot be done in any department but through Mr. Morris," an underling sniffed.

Stiffing creditors and starting a bank

One of Morris's first acts was to suspend repaying any debts the government had incurred before Jan. 1, 1781, until after the war was officially over (although two of his business partners managed to get paid). He also decided not to pay the army for the time being, a decision he acknowledged was unfair and dangerous, but necessary to keep the government from going bankrupt.

And he created the Bank of North America, capitalized with $400,000 in hard money (about $8.3 million in 2019 dollars), raised by selling 1,000 shares at $400 each. It was not nearly enough, considering the government owed the modern-day equivalent of about $500 million. But Morris doubted he could raise much more and hoped the bank and his other efforts would give the government at least the appearance of getting its financial house in order.

He also borrowed from European allies. By the end of 1781, France had already given or loaned America 28 million livres (about $150 million in 2019 dollars). Through Ben Franklin and the Marquis de Lafayette, Morris squeezed out the 2019 equivalent of an additional $32 million from France. Efforts by John Adams picked up another $29 million (in 2019 currency) from private lenders in the Dutch Republic.

But Morris warned Congress there was a limit to foreign funds — and it had been reached. France, he said in early 1782, had decided "to grant us no further pecuniary aid. Spain appears to have neither the inclination nor ability to afford any, and in Holland it can only be obtained from individuals who will always require security . . . and will not lend to the United States, who, as you well know, have no security to give."

Hitting an impasse at levying an "impost"

Failing to pay bills, putting creditors and the army on hold, and begging from foreigners was not exactly a sound financial system for the American government. But Morris's efforts to get Congress to approve taxes on liquor, land, voting, slaves, and other "goods" got nowhere. A committee was appointed to study the matter and came back with a recommendation that no federal taxes be imposed until financial accounts with the various states were settled, which could take years.

In late 1781, Congress approved an $8 million ($166 million in 2019) federal budget and asked each state to kick in a proportional share of the revenues, in hard money, that was needed to fund it. The first payment was due in April 1782. Not a single state complied. By the end of the year, the government had collected just 20 percent of the $8 million.

REMEMBER

Congress did come close to doing something right financially. At the urging of Morris and a young Virginia congressman, James Madison, it approved a modest 5 percent tax on imported goods, called an *impost*. Under the Articles of Confederation, all 13 states had to approve any federal tax — and 12 of them did. But Rhode Island said no, and before Congress could convince Rhode Island to change its mind, Virginia changed *its* mind and said no. The impost was dead.

By Spring 1783, Morris was just about out of ideas. One of his last was to get the army to go home by giving each man a personally signed *Morris Note*, redeemable in six months and secured by Morris's own fortune. While the notes were certainly valid, most soldiers were broke and couldn't wait for them to mature. So they sold them to speculators for pennies on the dollar and went home bitter at the country for which they had sacrificed so much.

Morris was bitter, too. In November 1784, he quit and was succeeded by a three-member panel of congressmen who accomplished little. The financing of America's central government continued to be largely a smoke-and-mirrors affair.

If it had any value at all, in fact, it was as a shining example of how badly flawed the central government was.

A Toothless Government

America's original constitution — formally known as the *Articles of Confederation and Perpetual Union* — had been drafted hastily, debated only casually, and approved slowly. Passed by Congress in late 1777, the document took until 1781 to win ratification by all 13 states. (Figure 12-1 shows the front page of a 1778 copy of the articles.)

It was a well-intentioned effort to form a central organization that could efficiently carry out the necessary functions of government without diminishing the authority of any of the organization's member states. But it was sort of like trying to run a business with 13 bosses — all with different ideas on how to run things — and one employee. It didn't work well.

REMEMBER

The 13 articles ran the gamut from officially naming the country the United States of America to reserving to Congress the power to declare war against a foreign nation. But it couldn't even do that without the approval of 9 of the 13 states, and it took *all* of the states to approve imposing taxes to pay for wars, peace, or anything else.

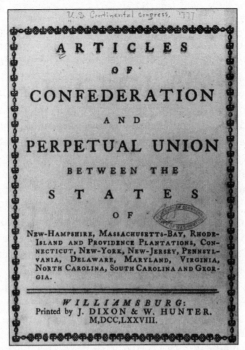

FIGURE 12-1:
The title page for a 1778 pamphlet outlining the Articles of Confederation.

"The fundamental defect (of the Articles) is a want of power in Congress," Alexander Hamilton wrote in September 1780 to James Duane, a New York politician who would become the first post-Revolution mayor of New York City. Hamilton pointed out that while Congress had done some good things, "The confederation gives the power of the purse too entirely to the state legislatures . . . (and) without certain revenues, a government can have no power; that power which holds the purse strings absolutely must rule."

Organizing the West

To be fair, in its eight years of existence, the *Congress of the Confederation* (which was its official name that no one used) managed to keep the country going, win the war, and appoint representatives who came up with a peace treaty that was extremely favorable to the United States. It also engineered a couple of nifty laws that established how America would handle the vast regions west of the original 13 states.

The first was the *Land Ordinance of 1785*. It sprang from a proposal by Thomas Jefferson to create new states from the area west of the Appalachian Mountains, north of the Ohio River, and east of the Mississippi River, generally referred to as the *Northwest Territory*. The area consisted of lands ceded by the British, as well as tracts for which several states had given up their claims.

The land would be divided into townships of 36 square miles, which would then be subdivided into 36 sections of 640 acres each. These would be sold for about $640 (about $16,600 in 2019). Each section could be further subdivided. One section in each township was to be set aside for public education, although local governments could sell part of the education parcel to raise money to build schools.

Since most people couldn't afford to buy an entire section, the act was criticized for being a bonanza for speculators and land companies. But as it turned out, there was so much land, competition among the speculators kept prices relatively reasonable. The act was also credited with encouraging an orderly settlement of the region. In addition, the requirement of setting aside land for education gave settlers a sense of investment in their new communities.

In 1787, Congress followed up the plan to divvy up the western lands with a plan to organize the area politically. The *Northwest Ordinance* established that the region was in the *public domain,* or under the supervision of the federal government. Initially, the region would be governed by five federal appointees (a governor, secretary, and three judges). When an area became populated by at least 5,000 free adult males, it would become a territory.

Residents could elect a territorial assembly, and basic "natural" rights were mandated, including the right to a trial by jury; religious tolerance; the right of *habeus corpus,* or freedom from unlawful detention; and bans on excessive fines and cruel and unusual punishment. The development of educational systems was encouraged. Slavery was prohibited, although slaves who fled to the area were required to be returned to their masters.

When a territory's population reached 60,000, it could petition Congress to become a state, with all the rights and privileges of the original 13. Eventually five states — Ohio, Indiana, Illinois, Michigan, and Wisconsin — as well as a portion of Minnesota, would be carved from the Northwest Territory.

Failing with foreigners

While it handled the question of the Western lands with surprising efficiency and cooperation, the Confederation Congress pretty much flopped at foreign relations. Its political impotence meant it had no way to get the individual states to pay the debts they owed to Great Britain and other assorted creditors. When the states refused, Britain decided it was justified in keeping a string of forts in the West on what was U.S. territory. Moreover, there was no American army in any shape to challenge them.

The country owed France and the Dutch Republic a lot of money, and that naturally frayed relations with those nations. Spain had never been a fan of the fight for U.S. independence because of the impact it might have on its American colonies. The Spanish periodically stirred up trouble between the Creek and Cherokee nations and American settlers in areas that Spain coveted, such as what is now Tennessee.

THE FRENCHMAN AND THE FARMER

You can put this story down to one of two American traits: being brave, or being rashly opportunistic. It seems that the French Gen. Comte de Rochambeau was marching his army to the seaports at Boston and Newport Rhode Island in the fall of 1782 to depart for home after helping America win its independence. On the way, he stopped for a while near Crompton, New York, about 50 miles north of New York City.

The land the French army camped on was owned by Samuel Delavan, a miller. While there, Rochambeau's troops cut down trees and chopped up some rail fences for firewood. But they also made repairs to Delavan's house and mill, built two large bread ovens they left in place, and constructed an aqueduct that provided the mill with water power.

Rochambeau was thus a bit surprised when, in the general's words, "a man respectfully walked up to me, and addressing me, stated that he was aware of the eminent services I had rendered to his country . . . but that, at the same time, he was obliged to do his duty." Turns out the man was the local sheriff, and his duty was to arrest Rochambeau for not paying for all the "damages" his troops had done to Delavan's property.

A generally polite general, Rochambeau did not order a bayonet charge on the sheriff or the miller. Instead, he suggested the law officer run along before he found himself turned over to Rochambeau's buddy, General Washington. He also ordered his aides to settle up with the miller — for an amount considerably more reasonable that what the miller had been seeking.

It's reported that Rochambeau was impressed by the Americans' insistence that no man is above the law, bemused by their greed — and amused by their *audace*. That's French for chutzpah.

True, Great Britain lifted all duties on American goods coming into Britain. But it simultaneously banned direct U.S. trade with the West Indies. That meant American products had to go all the way to Britain and pass through the hands of various middlemen before they could be sent to the Caribbean Islands, and vice versa. Individual states retaliated with tariffs against Britain, which made American manufacturers happy but angered U.S. importers.

Finally, with no U.S. navy to speak of, American merchant ships in the southern Mediterranean were easy prey for the pirate states of North Africa.

Vexing Vermont

At home, meanwhile, the 13 states constantly bickered with each other. The most serious involved New York and an upstart group of folks in Vermont. For generations, wealthy New Yorkers had claimed ownership of huge tracts of land in what they said was the western part of their state. The folks living on the land disagreed.

In 1777, led by the colorful militia leader Ethan Allen, Vermont repudiated the New Yorkers' claims, declared itself independent from Britain, and became the Vermont Republic. During the war, the Vermonters opened talks with British officials in Canada about becoming a royal province.

The British commander in chief in America, Sir Henry Clinton, asked his chief legal adviser, Judge William Smith, if Clinton had the authority to negotiate with the Vermonters on behalf of the king. Smith said no. His legal reasoning may, of course, have been influenced a bit by the fact he claimed ownership to about 100,000 acres in the area. In any event, Vermont stayed independent until 1791, when it finally became a state.

Despite mutterings about charging Allen and others with treason, in the end New York and the Confederated Congress could do nothing about it — even as Vermont nibbled away at pieces of neighboring states.

REMEMBER

The Vermont flap was by no means an isolated example of disputes Congress couldn't settle. New York imposed a tax on all vessels passing through New York Harbor to trade with New Jersey and Connecticut. Maryland and Virginia quarreled about navigation rights on the Potomac River. Connecticut charged higher duties on goods from Massachusetts than it did from Great Britain.

The United States government, such as it was, wasn't working. It was time for a change. Or as George Washington put it: ". . . according to the system of Policy the States shall adopt at this moment, they will stand or fall, and by their confirmation or lapse, it is yet to be decided whether the Revolution must ultimately be considered a blessing or a curse."

Moving toward a Fix

George Washington wanted to dig a canal, and that's how the United States Constitution was created. Okay, that's a wee bit simplistic, but bear with me, there is a link between the two.

As the Revolutionary War got further behind in America's rearview mirror, it became increasingly apparent that the Articles of Confederation weren't going to work. Even some of those who hated the idea of creating a strong central government were beginning to admit that the current system at least needed some tweaking.

Figuring out how to go about it was the tricky part. Thirteen separate state governments had to agree, not only to when and where to meet to discuss the issue, but on just how much tweaking was needed. Fortunately for America, some little, barely related things happened to get the ball rolling.

The first concerned the Potomac River, which starts in the hills of West Virginia and flows east, roughly along the border between Virginia and Maryland, before emptying into Chesapeake Bay. It also happened to be pretty close to George Washington's plantation at Mount Vernon.

Less than a year into his retirement, Washington was keen to build a canal that would make the Potomac more navigable. That would increase the value of property he owned and bring lucrative trade closer to Mount Vernon. At the same time, the states of Virginia and Maryland were trying to work out differences between them about navigation rights on the river. So, in March 1785, Washington invited delegates from the two states who were meeting in nearby Alexandria, Virginia, to come to Mount Vernon and talk things over.

They did. The meeting went so well, it branched into other topics, such as coordinating currency between the two states. In fact, it was decided to seek another meeting the following year and invite other states to participate.

Setting up Act II

In January 1786, the Virginia assembly approved a resolution asking the states to send delegates to Annapolis, Maryland, the following September to consider "the trade and commerce of the United States" and to see whether a more uniform set of rules and regulations "might be necessary to the common interests and permanent harmony" among the states.

One of those most keen on exploring the idea of a stronger central government (generally referred to as *nationalists*) was a scholarly, diminutive 34-year-old Virginian whose frail health had kept him out of the fighting during the war. Although a bit shy about public speaking, James Madison was nonetheless an adroit politician.

Because his nationalistic views were well-known and alienated him from those who opposed a powerful federal government, Madison kept a low profile during the proceedings. Instead, he got another assembly member who was not a nationalist to push the resolution.

It worked, to some degree. Five states — New York, New Jersey, Pennsylvania, Virginia, and Delaware — sent a total of 12 delegates to Annapolis. While the turnout was disheartening to the nationalists, the meeting did allow Madison to get to know one of the New York delegates with whom he shared very similar views. Alexander Hamilton had been advocating a stronger national government for years.

Pushed by Madison and Hamilton, the modest gathering at Annapolis agreed to issue a letter to all the states, written by Hamilton. It invited the states to send representatives to a meeting in Philadelphia in May 1787 "to take into consideration the situation of the United States; to devise such further provisions as shall appear to them necessary to render the Constitution of the Federal Government adequate to the exigencies of the Union." In other words, to revamp the structure created by the Articles of Confederation.

Legislatures in eight states agreed to send delegates, but five did not, which augured ill for the prospects of anything substantive being done. Then an impoverished Massachusetts farmer helped change some minds.

Shays' Rebellion

Daniel Shays went to war a Patriot and came home broke. A militia captain and veteran of the battles at Lexington, Bunker Hill, and Saratoga, Shays was called to court soon after returning home because of $12 in debts he could not pay. Shays was so destitute, in fact, he sold, for a few dollars, a ceremonial sword given him by the Marquis de Lafayette for his service.

A lot of farmers were in the same boat. Sales to U.S., French, and yes, British armies had ended with the war. The British ban on trade to the West Indies had closed one of the American farmer's most lucrative markets. Lenders and merchants, who were themselves often in debt to foreign parties, wanted to be paid for farmers' debts anyway.

The result was conflict that spilled from the legislatures and courts to the streets. There were protests and riots in New Hampshire, Vermont, Maryland, South Carolina, and Virginia. But the biggest was in Massachusetts.

Beginning in late September 1786 and lasting into early 1787, hundreds of men led by Shays and others confronted hastily formed militia groups in skirmishes that saw 4 protestors killed and 20 wounded. The protestors were eventually scattered. Two ringleaders were hanged, although Shays and 15 others condemned to death were eventually pardoned.

The "rebellion" sent shockwaves through American political leaders. "We are fast verging toward anarchy and confusion," Washington wrote Madison. "What a triumph for the advocates of despotism, to find that we are incapable of governing ourselves . . . would to God that wise measures be taken in time to avert the consequences. . . ."

How very wise they would be wasn't at all clear at the time, but the Shays insurrection convinced those reluctant to tinker with America's central government system to at last take measures to fix it.

On Feb. 21, 1787, the Confederated Congress decided it was "expedient that on the second Monday in May next a Convention of delegates who shall have been appointed by the several States be held at Philadelphia for the sole and express purpose of revising the Articles of Confederation. . . ."

They would revise the articles out of existence — and replace them with one of the most remarkable documents in the history of the world.

Chapter **13**

Who Were Those Guys?

nyone who thinks the Founding Fathers were anything more than human beings should take this into consideration: They are all currently dead. It also goes without saying that they were all flawed human beings, since, as established in the previous sentence, they were all human beings and "flawed human beings" is as big a redundancy as there is in the English language.

But were they, as a group and as individuals, extraordinary? Was America most fortunate to have them (at least most of them) at the country's inception? And just who were the Founding Fathers?

The answers to those questions are "Yes, I think so"; "Yes, I would say that's true"; and "It's both complicated and controversial." In this chapter, I tackle the third of those questions first, then lay out some generalities about the topic, and follow up with mini-profiles of ten men who played prominent roles in the American Revolution.

If you read the entire chapter, you can agree with my answers to the first two questions or take a black marker and cross them out (assuming this is your book).

Defining the Founding Fathers

Some historians think the term Founding Fathers is misleading, or insulting, or both. It's misleading, they argue, because it implies there is a finite and easily identified group of people who qualify to be called a Founding Father. It's insulting, they suggest, because it denigrates the contributions of "ordinary" people — the common soldier who fought the war, the women who kept things going at home — and ignores the situations of unrepresented and victimized segments of the era's population, such as Native Americans and African American slaves.

There is validity to such criticism. No list at the time tallied up who did and didn't contribute and therefore qualified as a Founding Father. In fact, it's doubtful anyone in the late 18th century ever used or heard the term. In addition, those to whom the term is now often applied were certainly not representative of the population of America at the time. They were all male and all white. Many, but not all, were better off financially than the average American. Some, but again, by no means all, stood to profit handsomely if a strong and stable central government could be established.

REMEMBER

But the fact remains an extraordinary group of individuals whose temperaments, backgrounds — and willingness to put in considerable effort and make considerable personal sacrifices — blended into one of those fortunate moments in U.S. history, where the nation had the right people do (mostly) the right thing at the right time.

"I know of only two occasions when the people in power did what needed to be done as well as you can imagine its being possible," the 20th century British philosopher Alfred North Whitehead observed. One, he said, was Rome under Caesar Augustus. The other was the American Revolution.

Just how it was that the right people came together at the right time became a topic for speculation almost as soon as it occurred. Washington thought the sheer difficulty of creating a new and different nation "called forth abilities which would otherwise have not perhaps been exercised." David Ramsay, a South Carolina physician who published a two-volume history of the Revolutionary War in 1789, wrote that America "*needed* the ability of all its sons, a vast expansion of the human mind speedily formed. It seemed that the war not only required, but *created* talents."

Those talents, and the varied perspectives of these Americans, complemented one another almost perfectly. There were masterful writers — Thomas Jefferson and Thomas Paine. There were liberal firebrands — Patrick Henry and Sam Adams. There were conservative contrarians — John Dickinson and John Jay. There was a resident sourpuss — John Adams — and a resident humorist — Ben Franklin.

There were masterful political intellects — James Madison and Alexander Hamilton. There was even an individual who towered over the others (literally, at 6'2") when it came to leadership — George Washington.

And if you still doubt there was anything special about the Founding Fathers, you might consider the (mostly) tongue-in-cheek observation of historian Joseph Ellis in his eloquent and thoughtful 2018 book *American Dialogue* (published by Alfred A. Knopf). Ellis notes that in 1789, American had a population of about 4 million, and its major presidential candidates were George Washington and John Adams. In 2016, with a population of 316 million from which to choose presidential candidates, the nominees were Hilary Clinton and Donald J. Trump.

Why they bothered

There was a strong feeling among political leaders at the time of *"noblesse oblige"* — the need for privileged people to act nobly and take on the obligations of leadership. As the 18th-century Irish philosopher Frances Hutchinson pointed out, because the better-off were free from having to make a living, they were "rather more than others obliged to an active life in some service to mankind. The publick has that claim on them."

Of course, the Founding Fathers weren't so completely noble or well-off that they didn't occasionally grumble about taking on the job. Washington noted that public service was expected to come "with a certain Expense and trouble without the least prospect of Gain." Jefferson complained that "public service and private misery (are) inseparably linked together."

But they were by nature generally optimistic, at least at the time. They believed that well-intentioned and capable leaders — in Madison's words, "men who possess wisdom to discern and virtue to pursue the common good of society" — would inspire confidence in government and lead people to continue to select more well-intentioned and capable leaders in the future.

There was also a confidence, bordering on arrogance, that somehow America would be different, that it would rise above the pettiness and avarice of the Old World. Tom Paine asked rhetorically if America could be happy and answered himself "as happy as she pleases; she hath a blank sheet to write upon . . . we see with other eyes; we hear with other ears; and think with other thoughts."

What they accomplished

Bucking very long odds, they won a war against the world's most powerful nation. They created the first large-scale republic in the history of the human race.

They removed the possibility of any single, powerful religious group having dominant influence over the affairs of a secular government.

They crafted a masterful document, the United States Constitution. Through it, they created an overlapping, multi-layered system, designed to prevent any one segment of government from dominance over the others, as well as balancing the rights of individual states with the overall welfare of the country as a whole. And they did it with a clear-eyed view that a nation governed by laws would do much better than a nation governed by men.

"If men were angels, no government would be necessary," Madison wryly noted. "If angels were to govern men, neither external nor internal controls on government would be necessary. In framing a government which is to be administered by men over men, the great difficulty lies in this: You must first enable the government to control the governed; and in the next place oblige it to control itself."

Kicking the Slavery Issue down the Road

The single biggest failure, particularly in hindsight, of the Founding Fathers was not coming to grips with slavery and what it portended for the country's future. Most, if not all, of them knew it was a morally wrong and indefensibly evil practice. But none of them knew or offered up a politically and economically practical solution to end it.

REMEMBER

Abolition almost certainly would have meant a dissolution of the Union, with southern states such as South Carolina and Georgia on record as threatening to go off on their own if that happened. With the ink still drying on the documents binding the states together, that might have been much easier for them to accomplish then than it was in 1861. Moreover, it would have set an early precedent for other states to pack up and leave the Union whenever they didn't like something done by the federal government.

Even if abolition had been accomplished, the question remained — as it did after the Civil War — as to how to assimilate into free society more than half a million impoverished, uneducated African Americans, who were regarded by many white Americans, both north and south, as something other than human.

Recognizing slavery as a problem

The fact is not a lot of Americans had given much thought to slavery. In the 157 years between the arrival of the first African slaves at Jamestown and the Declaration of Independence, there was no groundswell of opposition to the practice.

Slavery was generally accepted as a part of American life in all the colonies, along with indentured servitude and tenant farming.

"Prior to the great Revolution," noted John Jay, the New Yorker who would become America's first U.S. Supreme Court chief justice, "the great majority . . . of our people had been so long accustomed to the practice and convenience of having slaves that very few among them even pondered the propriety and rectitude of it."

But as talk of liberty, equality, and freedom grew, the glaring contradiction that slavery presented to such conversations became both obvious and discomfiting. More Americans began to think about the issue, and some began to take action. Benjamin Franklin, for example, helped establish America's first abolition society, in Philadelphia, while the aforementioned John Jay did likewise in New York. Both, however, continued to own slaves themselves.

Whether the conduct of Franklin and Jay indicated they were conflicted by what was a complex issue in the 1770s or merely portrays them as hypocrites, is, I think, a subjective conclusion either way. But it exemplifies the wide range of attitudes on slavery that were held by the Founding Fathers.

Some — John Adams, Alexander Hamilton, and New York's Gouverneur Morris — opposed slavery and had never owned slaves. George Washington was the only one of America's nine slave-owning presidents who freed his slaves — but only after he died.

Thomas Jefferson continually decried it as an evil institution, yet had a slave as his mistress and was convinced that as "naturally inferior" and "untrustworthy," freed slaves could never successfully integrate into American society. And Patrick Henry frankly admitted he didn't think it was worth the trouble: "I am drawn along by the general inconvenience of living without them (slaves)," he admitted. "I will not — I cannot justify it (abolition), however culpable my conduct."

Taking small anti-slavery steps

Some of the Founding Fathers, Jefferson included, hoped the problem would solve itself if slavery could be confined to the South. There it might gradually die out as the tobacco industry waned and it became too expensive to own slaves. Many Northern states, where slaves were not an integral part of the economic system, had already taken steps to gradually prohibit it. It had been banned from the vast territory covered by the Northwest Ordinance of 1787.

REMEMBER

What they did not foresee, of course, was how the invention of the cotton gin in 1793 would make cotton king of America's economy. It was a profitable-but-labor-intensive crop that was made even more profitable if producers didn't have to pay their labor. The result was an explosion in the number of slaves — from 900,000 in 1800 to 4 million in 1860 — and "slave states," from 6 in 1790 to 15 in 1860.

In the meantime, the founders nibbled at the edges of the issue. In 1794, exporting from America to sell in other countries was banned. In 1800, U.S. citizens were prohibited from engaging in the slave trade within other countries. In 1808, importation of slaves to the United States was forbidden, and in 1820, importing slaves became a capital offense.

Could the founders have done more and still kept the newly born United States of America alive and whole? Another fellow who wrestled with the same issue put it this way: "Necessity drove them so far, and farther they would not go," said Abraham Lincoln in 1854. "Thus we see, the plain unmistakable spirit of that age, towards slavery, was hostility to the principle, and toleration only by necessity."

Sorting out Signers, Framers, and Founders

A convenient sorting-out for historians as to who qualifies as a Founding Father revolves around a list of those who signed the *Continental Association,* which established a formal boycott of British goods, in 1774; the *Declaration of Independence* in 1776; the *Articles of Confederation,* which served as America's first constitution, in 1777; and the *U.S. Constitution,* in 1787.

REMEMBER

It's not a comprehensive collection. For example, neither Thomas Paine nor Patrick Henry signed any of the documents, yet both played key roles in the American Revolution. Neither did George Mason, who refused to sign the Constitution as a delegate at the constitutional convention, but is considered the "father of the Bill of Rights." Nor did Edmund Randolph, who also refused to sign the Constitution, yet is credited with helping to establish the three-branch system of the federal government and served as America's first attorney general and second secretary of state. Mason and Randolph are often included in a broader group of *framers* of the Constitution.

In fact, only one man, Roger Sherman, a Connecticut lawyer, signed all four documents, and only six signed three of the four. Of the 194 individuals who signed at least one of the documents, 104 signed only one.

HOISTING A FEW

If there was one thing many of the Founding Fathers were good at besides putting together new nations, it was bending their elbows. In other words, they drank. A lot.

John Adams, for example, reportedly started each day with a large tankard of hard cider. George Washington owned his own whiskey distillery. And Thomas Jefferson spent an estimated $10,000 on wine (that's $223,000 in 2019 dollars) during his eight years in the White House. In fact, he even had a 16-foot-deep, clay brick-lined wine cellar built next to the presidential mansion, where bottles were racked on raised platforms above a bed of ice that was replenished monthly.

When the founders gathered in groups, they also put away the sauce. There's a bill from a Philadelphia tavern for a gathering of delegates to the Constitutional Convention in 1787 for 54 bottles of Madeira (a fortified Portuguese wine); 60 bottles of claret; 8 bottles of whiskey; 22 of porter (a kind of beer); 8 of hard cider; 12 of beer; and 7 bowls of punch. It's not clear whether this was for one party, or a series of after-work get-togethers.

Not all Founding Fathers drank. Dr. Benjamin Rush, for one, frowned mightily on the habit. "A people corrupted by strong drink cannot long be a free people," he wrote in a 1790 tract entitled "An Enquiry into the Effects of Spirituous Liquors Upon the Human Body." One of the effects Rush noted was that there was often "a want of appetite for breakfast" the morning after drinking. He also traced alcohol use as a cause of tremors, liver damage, madness, and palsy. "Spirituous liquors destroy more lives than the sword," he said.

To get off the booze, Rush departed from his usual cure-all of bleeding. Instead, he recommended drinking lots of bitter tea, "or a few glasses of sound old wine every day."

Still, it is a starting point from which to compile some facts and figures:

>> Of the 145 men who lived through the period from the Continental Association's signing in 1774 and the U.S. Constitution's signing in 1787, 67 were lawyers, which probably isn't surprising. But only 9 actually made a living as a full-time politician, although many had held some political office. The rest were merchants, farmers or plantation owners, doctors, teachers, ministers, soldiers, and other occupations.

>> Of the first four American presidents, none signed both the Declaration of Independence and the Constitution. George Washington was running the army when the Declaration was signed and James Madison was not yet a member of Congress. Both signed the Constitution. When the Constitution was signed, Thomas Jefferson was serving as U.S. ambassador to France, and John Adams was the ambassador to Britain. Both signed the Declaration.

>> Six of those men who signed one or more of the four documents became U.S. Supreme Court justices; 19 became U.S. senators; and 32 became governors. Forty-eight had college degrees; 16 were born in foreign countries; 3 were later killed in duels; and 2 were lost at sea. Only 4 were lifelong bachelors.

A Brief Look at Ten Top Founders

Some of the Founding Fathers' contributions were so great and so varied that there is almost no argument they deserve the term (if the term is deserved by anyone). These men include George Washington, Thomas Jefferson, Alexander Hamilton, Benjamin Franklin, John Jay, James Madison, and John Adams. I've added three more, not because they necessarily rank higher than others, but because their contributions were in a bit different vein: Thomas Paine, Roger Sherman, and Sam Adams. So, what follows (in alphabetical order) are some factoids and tidbits about ten influential Founding Fathers — assuming you believe in such things.

John Adams

Resumé: *First U.S. vice president; second U.S. president; first U.S. minister to United Kingdom and the Netherlands; chief author of Massachusetts Constitution; chief U.S. negotiator for the 1783 Paris Peace Treaty with Great Britain; and delegate to First and Second Continental Congress.*

Massachusetts-born and raised, John Adams didn't much care if people liked him. That was a good thing, because a lot of people didn't. He was acerbic, grouchy, and sometimes mean-spirited: Listening to a general give a boring speech in Congress about a recent battle, Adams whispered to a colleague that he wished "the first ball that had been fired . . . had gone through his (the general's) head." He refused to go to the inauguration of Thomas Jefferson after Jefferson defeated him in his bid for reelection as president.

But Adams was a tireless worker for the American cause before, during, and after the Revolutionary War — and so outspoken that he was one of a handful of Americans marked for execution if the British had won the war.

Adams spent years in Europe as a U.S. envoy, separated from his beloved wife Abagail, to whom he wrote hundreds of romantic letters over their 54-year marriage. In his old age (he lived to be 90), Adams even became pen pals with Jefferson, his longtime political foe. Adams's last words before he died — on July 4, 1826 — in fact were "Jefferson survives." He was wrong, however, since Jefferson had died a few hours before.

Some John Adams miscellany: He was one of only two presidents whose son also became president. (George H.W. Bush was the other.) He once slept with Benjamin Franklin (the two had to share a bed in a filled-up New Jersey inn and had a long argument about leaving the window open). He was the first president to live in the White House (for the last four months of his one term in office). He thought the president should be addressed as "His Highness" (causing his critics to refer to the overweight Adams as "His Rotundity"). He was instrumental in forming the U.S. Marine Band and the American Academy of Arts and Sciences. And there is no monument to John Adams in Washington D.C., although one of the four buildings at the Library of Congress is named after him.

Samuel Adams

Resumé: *Governor of Massachusetts; President of Massachusetts Senate; delegate to First and Second Continental Congress; and signer of Declaration of Independence.*

Samuel Adams, shown in Figure 13-1, was a true believer. According to Dr. Benjamin Rush, Adams once told him that "if it were revealed that 999 out of 1,000 would perish in a war for liberty, he would vote for that war, rather than see his country enslaved. The survivors in such a war, though few, would propagate a nation of freemen."

With less illustrious credentials than his cousin John (see preceding section), Sam Adams is often overlooked as a key player in the American Revolution. But Adams was an early and ardent advocate of independence from Britain and was one of those men whose political and civic efforts overshadowed other aspects of life, such as making a living. Fortunately for Adams, he was, unlike his cousin, a very well-liked fellow. For example, while he was busy organizing resistance to various British acts and churning out eloquent and persuasive letters and pamphlets in favor of the Patriot cause, friends were busy rebuilding his barn and house and providing him with a wardrobe deemed suitable for a leader.

A Boston native, Adams was something of a flop at business and narrowly missed going to jail after being accused of mismanaging funds during a stint as a tax collector — by not bothering to actually collect taxes. But his efforts in such prewar groups as the Sons of Liberty and the minutemen helped keep the early flame of independence alive. After adoption of the U.S. Constitution, however, Adams's talents for rallying were not needed. When he died at the age of 81, in 1803, he had dropped from prominence.

Some Sam Adams miscellany: He was the 10th of his parents' 12 children, but only he and one sibling lived past the age of 3. He had both a bachelor's degree in law and a Master of Arts degree from Harvard. When he attended the First Continental Congress in Philadelphia, at the age of 52, it was the first time he had ever left Massachusetts. His instructions to Boston's legislative representatives on how to react to the Sugar Act in 1764 are regarded as the first written public protest to British policy in America.

Benjamin Franklin

Resumé: *First U.S. postmaster; U.S. minister to France; U.S. minister to Sweden; Speaker of Pennsylvania Assembly; President of Pennsylvania; Continental Congress representative to France; U.S. negotiator of 1783 Paris Peace Treaty with Britain.*

When at the age of 70, Benjamin Franklin was unanimously selected by Congress to represent America in France, Franklin accepted with his signature humor: "I am like the remnant of a piece of unsaleable cloth. You may have it, as the shopkeepers say, for what you please."

That's a pretty modest self-description for a man who has been labeled by eminent historians as "the First American" and "the most accomplished American of his age." With the possible exception of George Washington, Franklin was also the best-known American in the world during the 18th century. Not a bad accomplishment for a fellow who began his career as a 17-year-old runaway printer's apprentice with just two years of education and made a fortune large enough to allow him to "retire" at the age of 42.

Of course, Franklin didn't really retire. Before the Revolutionary War, Franklin served as America's eyes, ears, and voice in Britain. During the American Revolution, Franklin was primarily responsible for securing the indispensable support of France for the American cause. His editing of Jefferson's Declaration of Independence was invaluable. His humor and diplomatic skills helped smooth over tensions among his fellow founders on more than one occasion. And he was so well-loved that when he died at the age of 84, more than 20,000 people attended his funeral.

Some Franklin miscellany: His illegitimate son William was a leading Loyalist during the war, and Franklin cut him out of his will because of it. He loved swimming, invented a pair of hand paddles to use in the sport, and is an honorary member of the International Swimming Hall of Fame. Despite inventing useful objects, from bifocal glasses to the lightning rod, Franklin never patented anything, deeming the inventions gifts to the public. And responding to a call for scientific papers from a European group he considered pretentious, Franklin wrote an essay suggesting a study of how to make flatulence less odorous. He entitled it "Fart Proudly."

Alexander Hamilton

Resumé: *First U.S. secretary of the treasury; Senior Officer of the U.S. Army; delegate to Congress; chief author of the Federalist Papers; considered founder of the U.S. Coast Guard; and first Founding Father to be title subject of a smash Broadway musical.*

To suggest Alexander Hamilton wasn't your average Founding Father is to put it mildly. He was a foreign-born bastard child who became a war hero and then a lawyer, helped his chief political enemy become president, and died in a duel. Hamilton was born, out of wedlock, on the small Caribbean island of Nevis. He was orphaned at a young age, taken in by a wealthy merchant, and came to

America at the age of 15 (or 17 — it isn't clear) to attend Kings College (now Columbia University) in New York. When the war closed the college, he enlisted in the Patriot cause, rising to be a top aide to George Washington and leading a bayonet charge at the Battle of Yorktown.

Hamilton served briefly in Congress and then became a lawyer. As a delegate to the convention drafting the U.S. Constitution, Hamilton contributed little. But he was enormously valuable in helping to get it ratified by the states and by serving as the chief writer of a series of pro-Constitution newspaper essays, known as *The Federalist Papers.* He also served as Washington's treasury secretary and contributed greatly to establishing a firm financial foundation for the infant U.S. government.

Hamilton found himself in the unenviable position in the 1800 presidential election of having to choose to support Thomas Jefferson, his chief political rival, or Aaron Burr, a bitter personal enemy, whom Hamilton regarded as amoral and corrupt. Hamilton chose Jefferson — and was killed in duel with Burr in 1804, at the age of 47, or 49.

Some Hamilton miscellany: As a youth on Nevis, he wrote such a vivid newspaper account describing a hurricane that impressed businessmen sponsored his move to America. He founded the *New York Evening Post* newspaper, which is still publishing. His eldest son also died in a duel, at the same location Hamilton did. And he served as a cocounsel on the first U.S. murder trial for which there is still a record. One of his two cocounsels later became a U.S. Supreme Court justice. The other was Aaron Burr.

John Jay

Resumé: *First chief justice of the United States Supreme Court; first Secretary of Foreign Affairs; governor of New York; U.S. minister to Spain; U.S. negotiator of 1783 Paris Peace Treaty with Great Britain; and delegate to First and Second Continental Congress.*

Of all the key Founding Fathers, John Jay is probably the least well-known (see Figure 13-2). Part of the reason is that he spent less time than others in publicizing himself, partly because he was by nature quiet and reserved and partly because many of Jay's own papers and other historical documents concerning him were not made public until the first decade of the 21st century.

FIGURE 13-2:
John Jay.

CHIEF JUSTICE JOHN JAY

Library of Congress

Jay came gradually to the role of Founding Father — but when he got there, he filled it to the hilt. Born into a wealthy family of New York merchants, Jay graduated from King's College (later Columbia University) and set up a law practice in New York. While he was sympathetic early to the criticisms of British rule and served as a delegate to Congress, Jay initially favored reconciliation with the mother country over independence. But as the gap grew between the two sides, he became an ardent Patriot.

Over the course of his career, Jay served as a diplomat, a congressman, a jurist — and something of a propagandist. It was Jay who, with Alexander Hamilton and James Madison, wrote a series of newspaper essays extolling the virtues of the newly drafted U.S. Constitution, which became known as the *Federalist Papers*. Although an unwavering conservative, Jay was valued by leaders across the political spectrum for his intelligence, integrity, and willingness to take the heat for unpopular decisions.

Some John Jay miscellany: During the Revolutionary War, he handled a group of spies and informants so successfully that the CIA's website calls Jay "the first national-level American counterintelligence chief." He was elected governor of New York while in England negotiating a new peace treaty with Great Britain in 1795. But when he returned to America, the treaty was so widely criticized that Jay joked he could have traveled from Boston to Philadelphia at night, guided only by the lights of himself being burned in effigy. And despite having a long and varied career in public service, he managed to squeeze in 28 years of retirement before dying in 1829 at the age of 83.

Thomas Jefferson

Resumé: *Third U.S. president; second U.S. vice-president; first U.S. secretary of state; U.S. minister to France; Governor of Virginia; chief author of the Declaration of Independence; founder of University of Virginia; and delegate to First and Second Continental Congress.*

President John F. Kennedy once hosted a White House dinner with a guest list so impressive that he quipped it was the most impressive group of genius and talent to gather there "since Thomas Jefferson dined alone."

But Jefferson, shown in Figure 13-3, was not only multitalented; he was a bundle of contradictions. He hated slavery, but owned slaves; regarded African Americans as inferior, but had an African-American mistress; preached frugality but died deeply in debt; and believed in sticking closely to the Constitution but bent it to the breaking point at a crucial time in his presidency.

FIGURE 13-3:
Thomas
Jefferson.

Library of Congress

"He possessed a genius of the first order," noted Dr. Benjamin Rush. "It was universal in its objects. He was not less distinguished for his political, than his mathematical and philosophical knowledge."

The son of a wealthy Virginia plantation owner, Jefferson went to the College of William and Mary and became a lawyer, several times representing slaves seeking freedom through the courts. He authored a landmark Virginia law guaranteeing religious freedom (although he despised organized religion). As a member of Congress, Jefferson was chosen to write the Declaration of Independence. He missed the drafting of the U.S. Constitution because he was serving as U.S. minister to France, but sent crates of books to James Madison to aid Madison's research into drafting the document.

Some Jefferson miscellany: He was an obsessive recordkeeper at his Monticello estate, down to how many peas would fill a pint (about 2,500). He was an amateur inventor, paleontologist, and architect. He had a pet mockingbird, named Dick, who would sometimes sit on his shoulder or sing along while Jefferson played the violin. He often dressed like he shopped at rummage sales. Continually in debt, he sold his personal book collection to the fledgling Library of Congress. And he loved ice cream and macaroni and had his own recipes for making them. Presumably not together.

James Madison

Resumé: *Fourth U.S. president (and also the shortest); U.S. secretary of state; member of Congress; member of Virginia legislature; considered chief architect of the U.S. Constitution; and coauthor of The Federalist Papers.*

It was easy to underestimate James Madison, and people did (see Figure 13-4). A Massachusetts politician said Madison was "a little too much of a book politician and too timid." A journalist remarked, "There appears to be a mixture of timidity in his disposition." Alexander Hamilton suggested he "was very little acquainted with the world." It was also easy to understand why people viewed Madison in that light. He was slight, frail, and shy and an awkward public speaker. But while it was easy to underestimate Madison, it was also a mistake.

Perhaps none of the Founding Fathers put as much effort into preparing for the job of, well, founding, than did Madison. For months before the convention to draft a new U.S. constitution, he spent days and weeks reading dozens of books, making lists of the pros and cons of virtually every republican form of government that had ever existed. As a result, in the words of fellow convention delegate William Pierce of Virginia, "In the management of every great question he took the lead . . . From a spirit of industry and application which he possesses in a most eminent degree, he always comes forward the best-informed Man of any point in debate."

Born in Virginia to a wealthy tobacco planter, Madison was a sickly child. He was a Princeton University graduate, but was one of the rare founders who never had a job outside politics. His quiet, bookish personality actually served him well in an era where hammy theatrics by politicians often irritated rather than convinced. Madison, according to Pierce, had "a remarkable sweet temper. He is easy and unreserved among his acquaintance, and has a most agreeable style of conversation."

Some Madison miscellany: Like Jefferson, he was very fond of ice cream. His wife's favorite flavor was "oyster." He once suggested America hire the Portuguese navy to protect U.S. ships from pirates as cheaper than having its own navy. He was proficient in both ancient Latin and Greek. British troops ate a dinner prepared for him when they captured the White House during the War of 1812. His last words were reportedly, "I talk better lying down."

Thomas Paine

Resumé: *Journalist, political theorist, and propagandist.*

Thomas Paine, shown in Figure 13-5, signed no momentous documents, cast votes on no significant proposals, won no military battles, and held no political office, elected or appointed. He had no formal training as a writer, philosopher, or political scientist. In fact, he was pretty much a failure at almost everything he tried. But Thomas Paine qualifies as a Founding Father all the same.

FIGURE 13-5: Thomas Paine.

Library of Congress

Paine's essays, *Common Sense* and *The Crisis*, electrified Americans at a time when many of them were wary of separating from Great Britain and weary of a political conflict they could not fathom had anything to do with them. His direct, simple, and yet passionate writing style was hugely popular and widely credited with providing an easily understandable explanation of what the American Revolution was all about. "I never tire of reading Tom Paine," an admirer named Abraham Lincoln said, a half century later.

That's high praise for an English-born fellow who once lost a job as a tax collector because he left his post to appear before Parliament — to lobby for higher pay for tax collectors. Other jobs at which Paine failed included making corset stays, running a store, and teaching school. As a congressional secretary, he publicly accused American diplomat Silas Deane of war-profiteering — and let slip that France was secretly aiding the U.S. cause. For that he received two beatings from Deane's supporters — and lost his job.

Paine left America for Europe in 1787. There, he wrote a brilliant tract, *The Rights of Man*, supporting the French Revolution. The French lionized him, right up until the revolution turned into the Reign of Terror, whereupon he was imprisoned and narrowly escaped the guillotine. In his later years, he bitterly and publicly criticized George Washington and others who he said had failed to support him. He died, almost friendless, in New York in 1809. (See Chapter 20 for what happened to him after he died.)

Some Paine miscellany: He advocated a form of social security as early as 1795. He was widely scorned in the late 19th century as an atheist (although Mark Twain praised him). And to show there were no hard feelings, a 2002 BBC poll ranked him No. 34 among the 100 greatest Britons of all time.

Roger Sherman

Resumé: *U.S. senator; member of Congress; first mayor of New Haven, Ct.; only signer of all "Big Four" American historical documents; lawyer, professor of religion; and cobbler.*

For a Founding Father most people have never heard of, Roger Sherman got a lot done in his 72 years of life. He made shoes. He became a lawyer, with a formal education that stopped at grammar school. He served as a mayor, a judge, and a member of both houses of Congress, along with teaching religion at Yale University. And he still had time to have 15 children.

Born in Massachusetts in 1721, Sherman moved to Connecticut in 1743. An avid reader with a natural aptitude for math, he gave up shoemaking to become surveyor for New Haven County and gravitated to politics. After passing the bar and becoming a lawyer, Sherman served as a Connecticut delegate to nearly every major convention and conference in America. He is the only person to have signed the Continental Association (the formal boycott of British goods), the Declaration of Independence, the Articles of Confederation, and the U.S. Constitution.

But Sherman did more than just sign things. At the constitutional convention, for example, Sherman was an extremely active delegate, making or seconding 160 motions on the proposed plan (compared to James Madison's 177). Sherman was a key player in crafting major components of the document, including establishing the structure of the legislative branch and banning the issuance of paper money without a solid backing of gold or silver.

At 66, Sherman was second in age only to Ben Franklin at the convention. That may explain why one of his colleagues described him as "awkward, unmeaning and unaccountably strange in his manner." Thomas Jefferson, on the other hand, said Sherman "never said a foolish thing in his life."

Some Sherman miscellany: He was one of five men selected to draft the Declaration of Independence. One of his descendants, Henry L. Stimson, served in the cabinets of four different presidents. Another, Archibald Cox, was a federal special prosecutor and helped topple Richard Nixon from the presidency.

George Washington

Resumé: *First U.S. president; Commander-in-chief of Continental Army; president of Constitutional Convention; member of Second Continental Congress; "Father of His Country;" and guy on the one-dollar bill.*

George Washington has become such a mythical figure in U.S. history that it's understandable to think his importance is overrated. Trust me, it isn't. Along with Abraham Lincoln and perhaps Franklin D. Roosevelt, Washington is an American leader whose presence at a key period in the nation's history may well have made all the difference between having a successful result and a far more problematic one.

Defining just who Washington was as a human being has been wrestled with by historians and writers as far back as his lifetime. His education was scant, but he became a graceful writer and was apt enough at math to become a talented surveyor. Before he was 16, he had memorized 116 maxims on how to behave correctly in public ("don't puff out your cheeks," "don't rub your hands together"), and he religiously adhered to them — except when his fearsome temper erupted into a volcanic eruption of swearing. He bowed, rather than shook hands, but was so charming with women that they sometimes literally swooned in his presence. He kept his powdered hair (no wig) neatly coiffed and seldom smiled because of his terrible teeth.

He was so obsessed with correctness that he would sometimes laboriously recopy even a casual letter if he deemed it had too many mistakes in it. He declined offers to go to France and be honored because he did not speak French and was embarrassed at having to rely on an interpreter.

Maybe members of the Adams family said it best. "He is polite with dignity, affable without formality, distant without haughtiness, grave without austerity; modest, wise and good," said John Adams's wife Abagail. "More than all, and above all," said Adams's grandson, Charles Frances, Sr., "Washington was master of himself."

Washington miscellany: His dentures were not made of wood, as legend has it, but from metal alloy, hippopotamus ivory — and human teeth, quite likely at least some of which were purchased from slaves.

Chapter **14**

"We the People"

Suppose you took your beat-up 2005 pickup truck in to the shop for an oil change and maybe a new set of tires. And suppose when you went to pick it up, they handed you the keys to a brand-new electric prototype SUV. Would you be excited, angry, apprehensive, or cautiously optimistic?

Well, that's a little how America must've felt in the summer of 1787. Fifty-five men went into a brick building in Philadelphia to fine-tune a beat-up set of rules for running the country and came out with an untested blueprint for a brand-new form of government.

This chapter goes inside the building (something 1787 Americans couldn't do) to see how the "Founding Framers" came up with the U.S. Constitution.

Straggling into Philadelphia

George Washington didn't want to go. His rheumatism was acting up. His teeth hurt. He had pumpkins and turnips to plant and lots of other work to oversee at his Mt. Vernon plantation. He had already turned down an invitation to a meeting of former Army officers in Philadelphia, and he didn't want to hurt anyone's feelings by attending the constitutional convention that would be going on at the same time.

True, he vigorously supported the idea of overhauling America's government. "A thorough reform of the present system is indispensable," he wrote James Madison, adding that the convention needed to "probe the defects of the (current) constitution to the bottom, and provide radical cures. . . ."

But Washington had officially — and very publicly — retired at the end of the Revolutionary War, and he didn't want to be viewed as "unretiring." At 55, he wanted to spend his remaining years at his beloved Mt. Vernon. "Gliding down the stream of life in tranquil retirement is so much the will of my soul," he wrote a friend, "that nothing this side of Elysium (the afterlife) can be placed in competition with it."

He also had more earthly reasons: He wasn't sure it would be worth the effort. "Much is expected by some" from the convention, he wrote Thomas Jefferson, "but little by others — and nothing by a few." Washington also was not crazy about getting involved in what would certainly be a controversial situation that could damage his lofty and hard-earned reputation.

REMEMBER

But *nationalists* — advocates of radically changing the sputtering federal system created by the Articles of Confederation — were counting on Washington. Support from the most popular man in America was vital. "I am fervent in my Wishes that it may comport with the Line of Life you have marked out for yourself, to favor your country with your counsel on such an important & single occasion," New York's John Jay wrote to Washington.

Finally, in late March 1787, Washington agreed to once again "favor" his country. On May 9, accompanied by three slaves who served as his valets and coachmen, he set off on the 150-mile trip to the City of Brotherly Love. It took him five days, including a full day wasted while waiting for a flooded river to subside enough for his coach to cross.

James Madison was already in Philly. Unlike Washington, he was so excited about the convention's potential he had arrived ten days before its scheduled May 14 starting date. The diminutive Virginian had spent months reading everything he could get his hands on regarding the successes and failures of nearly every representative government the world had ever known. He had also drafted a lofty plan for reconstituting the American constitution.

Other delegates, chosen by their state's legislatures, gradually trickled in, but so slowly that the convention didn't get started until May 25, when there were finally representatives from 7 of the 13 states present. One reason for the delay was the winter, and spring had been unusually cold and wet, making already-difficult travel even more difficult. Another was that at least some of the delegates had a pretty good idea what they were letting themselves in for. (In fact, 18 delegates so dreaded the prospect or were so opposed to the idea that they never showed up at all.)

With a population of about 40,000, Philadelphia was America's largest city. It had a bustling port on the Delaware River. It was neatly, if somewhat unexcitingly, laid out in neatly intersecting blocks, with rows of brick and wood houses that European visitors sometimes complained were boring in their sameness. It afforded great shopping opportunities — Washington bought a gold watch chain and a four-volume English translation of *Don Quixote*. And like most late-18th century big cities, it stank.

"The streets and alleys reeked of garbage, manure and night-soil," one visitor noted, while another sardonically wrote that "dead dogs, cats, fowls and the offal of the market are among the cleanest articles to be found." While off-putting to humans, massive swarms of black flies, horse flies, and blue bottle flies found the city's aroma irresistible.

Rental housing was in short supply and expensive, and some delegates had to double up in boarding houses or in small, stifling rooms above the city's numerous taverns. The weather was mostly hot, interspersed with torrential thunderstorms that lowered temperatures but raised humidity to nearly unbearable levels. "It is quite the most miserable place I have ever been in," a New England delegate complained in a letter to his wife, "or hope to be."

Summing up the delegates

Thomas Jefferson called the 55 men who did convene in Philadelphia "an assembly of demigods," and while they were hardly that, they also weren't average Americans. They were generally better educated, wealthier, and more widely traveled than their fellow citizens.

Many knew each other from serving together in various congresses, legislatures, or the Continental Army. At a time when most people rarely traveled more than a few miles from their farm or town, the delegates were generally far more familiar with people and issues in other parts of the country than the average American.

Of the 55 delegates, 34 were lawyers or judges, so they weren't strangers to legal arguments. Nineteen had served as military officers; seven were or had been governors; and two were college presidents. Forty had served in various congresses or legislatures, and therefore had experience in trying to sway opinion through speeches. There were merchants, farmers, manufacturers, physicians, a minister, and a former ship captain.

They averaged about 42 years of age, from 26-year-old Jonathan Dayton of New Jersey to Philadelphia's own 81-year-old Benjamin Franklin, who was so afflicted with gout and kidney stones he had to be transported in a sedan chair by four brawny inmates, on loan from the prison across the street from the Pennsylvania State House, where the delegates were meeting.

At least 19, and perhaps as many as 25, of the delegates owned slaves. A dozen or so held sizeable amounts of government securities that would be almost worthless without a strong central government — and quite valuable with one. Only three could be said to come from "humble" origins: Alexander Hamilton, an immigrant from a small Caribbean island; Benjamin Franklin, a soap maker's son; and Roger Sherman, whose first job was as a shoemaker.

Some of the delegates were well-liked, such as Connecticut's Sherman. Some were almost universally disliked, such as Elbridge Gerry of Massachusetts, whom a fellow delegate described as "a Grumbletonian . . . objecting to everything he did not propose himself." Two — Franklin and Washington — were indeed as close to demigods as there were in America.

Not all the Founding Fathers were in attendance. Jefferson was in Paris as the U.S. minister to France. John Adams was in London as the U.S. minister to the United Kingdom. John Jay was too busy as America's foreign minister to attend. Sam Adams was sick and had not been selected as a delegate. Patrick Henry, an ardent apostle of states' rights, said he "smelt a rat in Philadelphia" and wanted no part of forming a strong federal government.

Not even all the states showed up. Rhode Island, so historically contrary that it was often referred to as Rogues Island, refused to take part. New Hampshire's delegation didn't arrive until mid-July. And two of New York's three delegates got angry and went home early, leaving only Alexander Hamilton to unofficially represent the state, since without a quorum of its delegates, New York had no vote. In fact, it was rare during the 17 weeks of the convention that more than 30 delegates were together at the same time.

Still, it was a pretty impressive group, and it engendered high hopes. "A union of abilities in so distinguished a body of men," noted the *New Hampshire Gazette,* "among whom will be a FRANKLIN and a WASHINGTON, cannot but produce the most salutary measures."

Getting down to business

The first thing on the agenda was probably the easiest: picking a convention president. The unanimous choice was Washington, who accepted with his usual protests that he was not suitable for the task, but would do his best. He then assumed his post behind a desk, on a slightly raised platform that made him tower above the rest even more than his height already did.

From his perch on the platform, Washington looked out on a 1,600-sq.-ft., high-ceilinged chamber known as the East Room in the Pennsylvania State House. It was the same room in which the Declaration of Independence had been signed

11 years before. Each state's delegates were seated together in handsome Windsor chairs, behind 13 tables (except Madison, who had grabbed a seat at a desk in the front of the room, from where he could be sure to hear every speaker).

REMEMBER

Two key rules were agreed upon early. One was the need for secrecy. Without a lid on the proceedings, the delegates feared, they would not be able to freely speak their minds — or change them later. It was, as Virginia representative George Mason put it, "a necessary precaution to prevent misrepresentations or mistakes; there being a material difference between the appearance of a subject in its first crude and undigested shape, and after it shall have been properly matured and arranged."

The secrecy policy meant the room's windows and doors remained closed at all times to discourage eavesdroppers and spies. That must have done wonders for the atmosphere of a chamber filled with two or three dozen sweating adult males in an era when neither air conditioning nor "casual clothes Fridays" existed.

Fortunately, delegates generally met "only" five hours a day, six days a week, although more hours were spent in various committees. These included — and I am not making these names up — the Committee of Style, the Committee of Detail, the Committee of 11, and the Committee of Postponed Parts.

KEEP YOUR NOTES TO YOURSELF

A telling example of how much awe George Washington inspired in his peers was told by William Pierce, a Georgia delegate to the Constitutional Convention. It seems that someone dropped a page of his notes on the floor during a convention session, and the page was picked up and given to Washington.

"Gentlemen," Washington sternly addressed the delegates at the session's close, "I am sorry to find that some one member of this body has been so neglectful of the secrets of the convention as to drop in the State House a copy of their procedures, which by accident was picked up and delivered to me this morning. I must entreat gentlemen to be more careful," he continued, "lest our premature speculations disturb the public repose by getting into the newspapers. I know not whose paper it is, but there it is," and tossing it down on the table, added "let him who owns it, take it." He then left the room, according to Pierce, "with a dignity so severe that every person seemed alarmed."

Apparently, no one wanted his own notes enough to risk earning Washington's disapproval, for no one ever claimed them.

Delegates were allowed to take notes, and Madison took advantage of this to exhaustively chronicle what went on. In fact, much of what historians believe went on at the convention comes from Madison's voluminous notes. Well afterwards, he dutifully checked with some of the speakers to ensure he was quoting them accurately. So seriously did he take the secrecy issue, however, that he promised not to publish his notes until after the last delegate was dead. That turned out to be him, in 1836, at the age of 85. Madison's notes were not published until 1840.

The second rule delegates quickly agreed to was that nothing was off the table for discussion. Even if issues had been decided, they could be opened again. And they were, repeatedly. Alliances shifted, minds changed, and problems that had seemingly been solved became unsolved.

Tackling the Big Three

With the rules in place, the convention promptly decided to completely ignore the purpose for which it had convened. The Confederation Congress (created under the Articles of Confederation) had given delegates specific instructions: The Philadelphia assemblage was only to fine-tune the existing articles of government that had been drafted a decade before (see Chapter 8).

The Congress's instructions were followed — right up until the first speaker after the convention rules had been established. Virginia Gov. Edmund Randolph, a burly 34-year-old "with a most harmonious voice," who would become America's first attorney general, began by thanking the drafters of the Articles of Confederation, "who had done all that Patriots could do, in the then-infancy of the science of constitution and confederacy making."

REMEMBER

Then he started what would be a months-long process of dismantling their work. Though there were dozens of nuances and details to be worked out, most of the debate centered on three issues. The first was creating a national legislature that equitably reflected the varied — and sometimes conflicting — interests of the individual states, big and small, North and South. The second was dealing with the bitterly divisive and nationally embarrassing horror that was slavery. The third was how to pick a president.

WARNING

AUTHOR'S ALERT: Before I get into the complexities of drafting the U.S. Constitution, I should note that the framers often used the terms *National Legislature*, *supreme and inferior tribunals*, and *Executive* to identify the three branches of government. I've used the more familiar *Congress*, *judiciary*, and *president* for clarity and simplification. Also, I've compressed or altered the timelines on various issues a bit, because they tended, confusingly, to pop up, disappear, and then pop up again during the convention — or occur simultaneously. Carry on.

Creating a New Kind of Congress

Under the Articles of Confederation, the federal Congress was a one-house organization in which each state cast one vote. That meant delegates from each state had to confer and hold a vote within the delegation. What the majority decided was how the state would stand on each issue. Nine of the 13 states had to agree for any legislation to pass. New amendments could not be added to the Articles without unanimous approval from all the states. Congress had no authority to levy taxes without approval of every state's legislature. There was no executive branch and no federal judiciary.

Presenting the Virginia Plan

Randolph smoothly pointed out all the defects of the Articles-spawned government. Then he surprised many of the delegates by unveiling a series of 15 resolutions that became labeled the *Virginia Plan*. Actually, the plan was chiefly the brainchild of James Madison. But because he was so well-known as an ardent nationalist — and was a poor speaker and generally regarded as something of nerd — Madison had handed it off to be presented by the better-liked Randolph.

Under the plan, Congress would have two houses. The lower house (what became the House of Representatives) would be elected directly by the voters. Seats in the lower house would be apportioned according to the populations of each state, meaning the most populous states — Virginia, Pennsylvania, and Massachusetts — would get the lion's share of representation. Each member of Congress would cast his own vote, regardless of what the rest of his state's delegation did.

The other congressional house (which became the Senate) would be elected by the lower house, which meant the bigger states would also have the most say in selecting senators, because the bigger states would have more members in the lower house.

Congress would also pick the president and the federal judiciary. In turn, the president and judiciary would form a Council of Revision that could veto congressional acts. But Congress could re-pass them. Congress would also have the power to veto any state law it deemed in conflict with federal law, and state and local officials would have to take oaths agreeing to uphold and support the federal government.

Needless to say, delegates from small states, as well as states' rights advocates, were not overly enthusiastic about Madison's convoluted plan.

One delegate asked Randolph if he "meant to abolish the state governments altogether." The Delaware delegation announced they had been specifically instructed by their state legislature to consider no plan that deviated from each state having only one vote in Congress.

Countering with the New Jersey Plan

Led by acid-tongued William Paterson, a New Jersey delegate who was that state's attorney general, the small states countered with their own plan. After sarcastically suggesting that the small-state/big-state problem might be solved by cutting up the Union like a cake, into 13 equal-sized portions, Paterson outlined a federal government that looked a lot like the Articles of Confederation version.

Congress would gain the power to regulate foreign and interstate trade, but still have no taxing authority. A president would be chosen by Congress for a one-year term, but could be removed from office if a majority of state governors asked. A national judiciary would be established, and federal court decisions would trump state courts. Congress would have only one house; each state would get one vote; and it would take a minimum of nine states to accomplish anything.

Big state delegates were as outraged at the New Jersey Plan as small state delegates had been about the Virginia Plan. "All authority (is) derived from the people (and) equal numbers of people ought to have equal numbers of representatives," thundered Pennsylvania delegate James Wilson, a Scottish immigrant who was to become a U.S. Supreme Court justice (and ultimately a debt-ridden fugitive; see Chapter 20). "Are not the citizens of Pennsylvania equal to those of New Jersey? Does it require 150 of the former to balance 50 of the latter? I say no! It is unjust. I will never confederate on this plan."

A side order of Hamilton

Alexander Hamilton liked neither plan, suggesting they were both "pork . . . with a little change of sauce." Instead, he spoke at length — some estimates are for about six hours — and eloquently on his own vision of government.

The British government, he said, was the best in the world. America should have a president for life, selected by Congress. States were nuisances, and if allowed to function at all, should be regarded by the federal government as counties were by the states. Political power should reside in the hands of the rich and educated, because they were best suited to handle it.

It was one of the biggest mistakes of his career. One delegate described it as being "praised by everybody" and "supported by none." To even suggest there was something good about British government, or propose a presidency that would essentially be a substitute monarchy, was absurd to most of the delegates, and the speech permanently damaged Hamilton's reputation.

Compromising with Connecticut's plan

Weeks passed with little progress, and as temperatures rose, so did tempers. At one point, Benjamin Franklin suggested that it might help to start each session with a prayer. Hamilton, however, objected to bringing God into the debates. Another delegate pointed out there was no money to hire ministers for the task, so the proposal was dropped.

But the delegates were generally intelligent, reasonable, well-intentioned — and sick of arguing. In late June, they came up with a compromise that became known as the *Connecticut Plan* because two of its biggest supporters were delegates from that state, Roger Sherman and Oliver Ellsworth.

Ellsworth, a lawyer whose eloquent speeches sometimes ran so long he acquired the nickname Endless Ellsworth, suggested the convention was trying too hard to come up with a perfect solution that would please everyone. "We are razing the foundations of the building," he said, "when we need only to repair the roof."

REMEMBER

Under the final version of the Connecticut proposal (which the ever-diplomatic Ben Franklin helped craft), the lower house of Congress would be elected directly by voters and would have sole authority over bills to spend money. The number of representatives from each state would be determined by the state's population. At first the ratio was one representative for every 40,000 residents, but in the last hours of the convention, it was lowered to one for every 30,000. (Side note: This was the only issue on which George Washington spoke. He was in favor of it.) In the upper house, each state would have two representatives, selected by the states' legislatures.

The proposal was narrowly approved on a 5-4 vote, with New York abstaining because Hamilton was the only delegate from that state still at the convention and thus couldn't vote. And, of course, Rhode Island wasn't there at all.

To round out the creation of Congress, the convention gave the legislative branch the authority to declare war, levy taxes, oversee interstate and foreign commerce, borrow and coin money, oversee the postal system, and create federal courts below the Supreme Court.

Getting Congress organized, however, was just one of the problems. It also had to be decided who got to serve in Congress and who got to vote.

Deciding who runs and who votes

It's easy to forget that *democracy* — the idea that every person has an equal voice and the opinion held by the majority was the opinion that would rule — was something of a dirty word to many of the Founding Fathers. It implied a governmental system in which the "tyranny of the majority" would ultimately squash the rights of individuals to pursue their own destinies. As Ben Franklin put it, "Democracy is two wolves and a lamb voting on what to have for lunch. Liberty is a well-armed lamb contesting the vote!"

So it's not surprising that some convention delegates wanted to ensure that the new U.S. government wasn't wide open to "rule by the mob." To that end, they proposed various restrictions on who could serve in public office and who could vote for them.

South Carolina delegate Charles Pinckney, for example, wanted to require that members of Congress and the federal judiciary have at least $50,000 (about $1.3 million in 2019 dollars) to ensure they would be "independent and respectable" and above the temptation to be corrupted.

The proposal was defeated after Ben Franklin pointed out that "possession of property (often) increases the desire of more property" and added that "some of the greatest rogues I was ever acquainted with were the richest rogues."

Delegates did, however, impose requirements that to run for the House of Representatives, a candidate had to have resided in the United States for seven years and to run for the Senate nine years.

Deciding who could vote was also a sticky issue. Gouverneur Morris, the wealthy son of an aristocratic New York family who was representing Pennsylvania at the convention, wanted to restrict the vote only to *freeholders*, or those who owned property.

"Give the votes to people who have no property," he warned, "and they will sell them to the rich." Someday, he added, "this country will abound with merchants and manufacturers who will receive their bread from their employers." Would these people "be faithful and secure guardians of liberty?"

Once again, it was Franklin, the son of a humble soap maker, who defused the issue. Too weak to deliver his own remarks, he gave a long speech against the freeholders-only proposal through the voice of fellow Pennsylvania delegate

James Wilson. "It is of grave consequence," Franklin said, "that we should not depress the virtue and public spirit of our common people."

Other delegates also argued that since each state already had its own widely varying voter eligibility requirements, it should be left to the states to decide who could vote in federal elections. That view prevailed.

Sidestepping Slavery

Yet another element to be decided was figuring out how to apportion the seats in what would be the House of Representatives. And it was here that the ugly elephant in the room — slavery — reared its huge head.

None of the states had sent their delegates to the convention with specific instructions on how to deal with the issue. Only one state in 1787, Massachusetts, had banned slavery, and that was through a court decision. Four other states — New Hampshire, Pennsylvania, Connecticut, and Rhode Island — had enacted "gradual manumission" laws that were designed to eventually free the children of slaves.

The views of the individual delegates varied widely, from those who defended the "peculiar institution" on historical and biblical grounds, to those who regarded it as one of man's darkest and most evil practices. Even slaveowners were conflicted. "There is no man living who wishes more sincerely than I do, to see a plan adopted for the abolition of (slavery)," George Washington had written the year before the convention.

REMEMBER

The wide range of views, the varying depths of feeling about slavery, the economic ramifications — and the very real threat that the issue would not only prevent drafting a new constitution but split the new nation apart — resulted in two compromises at the convention. Both would help finalize a new plan for the American government, preserve the Union, and postpone the country's day of reckoning over slavery.

Three-fifths of a human

The first of the Faustian bargains on slavery involved gaining Southern states' support of the plan to allocate seats in what would be the House of Representatives according to each state's population. Under a proposal pushed chiefly by Pennsylvania delegate James Wilson and South Carolina's John Rutledge, in return for Southern support of allocating House seats by state populations, slaves would be partially counted as part of the population.

House seats would thus be allocated "in proportion to the whole number of white and other free Citizens & inhabitants . . . and three-fifths of all other persons not comprehended in the foregoing description, except Indians not paying taxes. . . ." In other words, each slave was to be considered as 60 percent of a human being for purposes of deciding how their masters would be represented in the new U.S. government.

From a purely political standpoint, it was a bad deal for states without large numbers of slaves. When the first federal census was conducted in 1790, for example, New Hampshire was found to have 140,000 free residents and was thus entitled to four seats in the House of Representatives. South Carolina had a population of only 100,000 free residents, but because it also had 100,000 slaves, it was entitled to six seats. Massachusetts, which at the time also included what became the state of Maine, had a larger population of free citizens than Virginia, but was allocated five fewer seats in Congress.

As a matter of logic, it was nonsensical. "Upon what principal is it that the slaves shall be counted in the representation?" Pennsylvania delegate Gouverneur Morris asked rhetorically. "Are they men? Then make them citizens and let them vote. Are they property? The houses in this city (Philadelphia) are worth more than all the wretched slaves which cover the rice swamps of South Carolina."

Morris was just getting warmed up. "The admission of slaves into representation," he said, "when fairly explained, comes to this: That the inhabitants of Georgia and South Carolina who go to the coast of Africa, and in defiance of the most sacred laws of humanity, tears his fellow creatures from their dearest connection and damns them to the most cruel bondage, shall have more votes in a government institution for the protection of the rights of mankind than the citizens of Pennsylvania or New Jersey, who view with a laudable horror so nefarious a practice."

The Southern response was weak. South Carolina delegate Charles Pinckney cited that past republics, such as Greece and Rome, had slaves. "If slavery be wrong," he said, "it is justified by the example of all the world . . . in all ages, one half of mankind have been slaves."

In the end, political expediency carried the day. The proposal passed 9–2, with only New Jersey and Delaware voting no.

Trading taxes for slave importing

The second slavery-related compromise involved the twin issues of whether Congress should have the power to tax goods imported into America and whether the slave trade — which was considered even more immoral and horrifying than slavery itself — should be abolished.

Northern states, which had growing manufacturing interests, favored the taxation of foreign products, to lessen competition with home-grown goods. Southern states produced little other than agricultural goods and therefore didn't like the idea of adding a tax to the cost of the imported items they relied on. The South thus favored a requirement that two-thirds of the states had to approve any duties on imports and exports.

At the same time, many Northern delegates, and a few from the South, wanted to bring an end to the importation of more slaves into the country, if they couldn't end slavery altogether. That was a deal-breaker for several of the Southern states.

"If the convention thinks that North Carolina, South Carolina and Georgia will ever agree to the plan, unless their right to import slaves be untouched," warned South Carolina delegate John Rutledge, "the expectation is in vain. The people of those states will never be such fools as to give up so important an interest."

John Dickinson of Delaware was one of the few men in the room who had been associated with slavery and was free of hypocrisy on the issue. He had inherited 37 slaves and not only freed them, but posted cash bonds to ensure they would not be a burden on the state. To him, it was "inadmissible with every principle of honor . . . that the importation of slaves should be authorized" by the new constitution.

But honor and principles again took a back seat to political pragmatism. A ban on the slave trade might push the Southern states to not only walk out on the constitutional convention, but out of the union. "Great as the evil is," shrugged Madison, "a dismemberment of the Union would be worse."

REMEMBER

In the end, the convention agreed, on a 7–4 vote, to delay an end to the slave trade until 1808. In return, Southern states dropped their demand for a two-thirds approval on imposing import-export duties.

In a clumsy attempt to camouflage the deal and keep the actual words "slaves" and "slavery" completely out of the new constitution, the delegates worded the deal thusly: "The migration or importation of such persons as any of the states now existing shall think proper to admit shall not be prohibited by the Congress prior to the year one thousand eight hundred and eight."

But they did impose an import tax of $10 for each such "migrating" person.

Picking a President

Compared to dealing with an issue like slavery, setting up a system to select a chief executive would seem to have been relatively simple. It wasn't. There were no models to follow from any other country. As on nearly every other issue, the big-state/small-state, North/South splits had to be reckoned with.

And because it was put off for serious discussion until the end of the convention, it suffered from delegate exhaustion. Or as Madison more delicately put it, the subject "was not exempt from a degree of the hurrying influence produced by fatigue and impatience."

Who the American president was going to be was a foregone conclusion. All during the debates on the issue, delegates chose their words more carefully than on other subjects, knowing they were talking about an office that would be occupied first by the tall man at the front of the room.

"Many of the members cast their eyes toward General Washington and shaped their ideas of the powers to be given to a president by their opinions of his virtue," noted South Carolina delegate Pierce Butler. "So the man, who by his patriotism and virtue contributed largely to the emancipation of his country may be the innocent means of its being, when he is laid low, oppressed" by giving the presidency too much power.

The delegates discarded an idea to have an "executive council," in favor of a one-man show, although they eventually added the office of vice president, whose only two duties were to preside over the Senate and be ready to step in if the president died or was otherwise incapacitated.

They also agreed to an impeachment process in which the president could be indicted by the House and tried by the Senate for bribery, treason, and any other "high crimes and misdemeanors" he committed, although just what that covered was left vague. "Shall any man be above justice?" rhetorically asked delegate George Mason of Virginia. "Above all, shall that man be above it who can commit the most extreme injustice?"

Almost everything else about the presidency, however, was argued about. Over and over. James Wilson of Pennsylvania noted that delegates were "perplexed with no part of this (constitution drafting) plan so much as with the mode of choosing a President."

There were different ideas for the length of presidential terms, ranging from 1 year to 20 years. There were proposals to have the president elected by Congress, by the state legislatures, and by the states' governors. It was suggested that each state submit a "favorite son" candidate and then have Congress pick from the group.

REMEMBER

A motion to have the president elected directly by voters was shot down on a 9–1 vote, mostly because the smaller states feared no one from their states would ever be elected. Lacking any nationwide media, only a very small handful of candidates — such as Washington — would be known throughout the country. That meant candidates from the most populous states would have a clear advantage.

Finally, in early September, the delegates agreed on a plan. The president had to be born in America. He (no one dreamed it could be a "she") had to be at least 35 years old. He could run for as many four-year terms as he could stand. He would have the powers to make treaties, make recommendations to Congress, serve as commander-in-chief of the military, and appoint ambassadors, federal judges, and other officers, subject to Senate approval. He could also veto congressional acts, subject to congressional overrides.

REMEMBER

The presidential election process delegates adopted brought to mind the old adage that an elephant is a mouse designed by a committee. Each state would have *electors,* chosen by whatever method the state's legislature agreed on, and equal in number to the state's representatives in the House and Senate. Each elector would vote for two candidates, one of whom had to be from outside the elector's state. Congress would then count the votes of this *Electoral College.*

The candidate who got the most votes would be president; the candidate who got the second-most vice president. In the event no candidate got a majority of the votes, the House of Representatives would decide the outcome.

As you can see in Chapters 16 and 17, after the unanimous and uncontested election and reelection of George Washington, the system would turn out to work about as well as a hair dryer in the shower.

Cleaning up and Signing Off

While the Big Three issues of creating Congress, dealing with slavery, and setting up a way to pick presidents dominated the convention, there were a host of other details also worked out. These ranged from setting a minimum age for members of Congress (25 in the House, 30 in the Senate) to spelling out the oath new presidents must take on assuming the office.

There was debate over whether to have a standing army. Quarrelsome delegate Elbridge Gerry proposed that the army's maximum size be limited to no more than 2,000 or 3,000. But after Washington muttered — loud enough to be heard — that it should therefore be made unconstitutional for any country to attack America with a larger force, Gerry's proposal was shelved.

Preambling the Constitution

In the waning days of the meeting, it was also thought a good idea to put a polished preamble on the document. The job was given to Gouverneur Morris of Pennsylvania. And as James Madison put it, "A better choice could not have been made, as the performance of the task proved."

ANYONE SEEN THE CONSTITUTION AROUND HERE?

For a pretty important document, the U.S. Constitution wasn't exactly handled with kid gloves for its first 100 years or so. The official Constitution's four pages were penned on parchment by Jacob Shallus, a Pennsylvania legislative clerk. Shallus was paid $30 (about $815 in 2019) and given two days to copy the 4,543 words.

When he was done, the constitutional convention's secretary, Maj. William Jackson, took it to the Confederation Congress in New York. It moved back to Philadelphia when Congress shifted itself there in 1789 and then on to the new town of Washington D.C. when Congress moved again in 1800. There, it resided at the Treasury Department and then on to the War Department. In 1814, as the British Army was busy burning down most of the American capital during the War of 1812, three quick-thinking clerks stuffed the Constitution in a sack and took it for safe-keeping to a grist mill in Virginia.

What happened to it after that is a little hazy, although it did surface in 1846, when a book publisher had access to it for research. It fell out of sight again until 1883, when John Franklin Jameson, a founding father of the history profession in America, discovered the document folded up in a tin box on a closet floor, in a new D.C. building that housed the State, War, and Navy departments. A decade or so later, State Department officials placed it between two glass plates and locked it in a basement safe. Finally, in 1924, the Constitution was put on public display at the Library of Congress. But its odyssey wasn't over.

During World War II, it was moved for safety to the Fort Knox military base in Kentucky (where they keep all the gold). And in 1952, after some restoration and preservation work, it was moved — under heavy military guard — to the National Archives. There it resides in the Rotunda for Charters of Freedom, next to the Declaration of Independence and the British Magna Charta.

At least it was there the last time I checked. . . .

In 52 extremely well-chosen words, Morris eloquently distilled the essence of America's new government:

"We the People of the United States, in Order to form a more perfect Union, establish Justice, insure domestic Tranquility, provide for the common defence, promote the general Welfare, and secure the Blessings of Liberty to ourselves and our Posterity, do ordain and establish this Constitution for the United States of America."

Morris, who was known for his sparkling wit and his wooden leg (the result of a carriage accident), spoke more often than any other delegate during the convention (173 times) and was chiefly responsible for trimming the final document down to the four parchment pages it ultimately occupied.

REMEMBER

So it was altogether fitting that he also was chosen to write two other documents. One was a resolution outlining the delegates' recommendation to the Confederation Congress that the constitution be considered for ratification by conventions "chosen in each state by the people," and not the states' legislatures.

The second was a letter to Congress explaining that the proposed constitution was the result of trying to accommodate the "difference(s) among the several states as to their situation, extent, habits and particular interests."

Watching the sun rise

It had been a long, hard process. Through the last days of the convention, there were more arguments and more issues raised. Some delegates wanted a commitment that a second convention would be called to fix the problems unfixed by the current meeting. Others wanted a Bill of Rights included, spelling out specific safeguards for individuals and delineating the powers of government entrusted in the states.

REMEMBER

Weary at the end of a grueling summer and convincing themselves that a Bill or Rights wasn't necessary, all the state delegations rejected the proposal. It would turn out to be a major political blunder that would threaten to prevent the document they had worked so hard on from ever taking effect. But by mid-September, most delegates felt they had done the best they could do.

On the morning of Monday, Sept. 17, 1787, Benjamin Franklin rose unsteadily to his feet in the East Room of the Pennsylvania State House and handed a speech to his colleague James Wilson to read for him.

"I confess that there are several parts of this Constitution which I do not at present approve," Franklin said, through Wilson. ". . . (but) I agree to this Constitution, with all its faults, if they are such."

Franklin observed that it would be impossible to create a perfect document, because "when you assemble a number of men to have the advantage of their joint wisdom, you inevitably assemble with those men all their prejudices, their passions, their errors of opinion, their local interests, and their selfish views. . . . It therefore astonishes me, sir, to find this system approaching so near to perfection as it does. . . . Thus I consent, Sir, to this Constitution, because I expect no better, and because I am not sure, that it is not the best."

After Franklin's remarks, a few more last-minute suggestions were made, including one that Washington be entrusted with the convention's journals and records and they be kept private, because "a bad use would be made of them by those who would wish to prevent the adoption of the Constitution." Washington agreed to guard them.

Finally, 39 of the delegates lined up to sign the document. Washington signed first. Hamilton signed as an individual, since his state of New York lacked a quorum. Three of the delegates who had participated extensively in the convention refused to sign: Elbridge Gerry of Massachusetts; George Mason of Virginia; and Edmund Randolph, also of Virginia. Gerry and Randolph were miffed that the document did not include a Bill of Rights, Mason that it did not end the slave trade.

As the last members were signing, Franklin got in the last words. Noting the painted half-sun carved into the top of Washington's chair, he said he had often stared at it during the proceedings "without being able to tell whether it was rising or setting: but now at length, I have the happiness to know, that it is a rising and not a setting sun."

Others were more cautiously optimistic. "That it is the best which human wisdom could devise, I mean not to assert," Pennsylvania delegate Thomas Fitzsimmons wrote to a friend, "but I trust it will be found consistent with the principles of liberty and calculated to unite and bind together the members of a great country."

Now all they had to do was convince the great country's members.

Chapter **15**

Selling It

When they were done shaking other people's hands — or wringing their own — the framers of the new U.S. Constitution faced the equally onerous task of persuading Americans to support it.

This chapter covers how they pulled it off. A new Congress is seated, a laundry list of rights is proposed and approved, and the Father of his Country takes his seat at the head of the table.

Convincing Congress

Like any parent, James Madison was anxious to protect his newborn child. So once the constitutional convention in Philadelphia was over in mid-September 1787, the Father of the Constitution hurried to what was then the American capital in New York City rather than home to Virginia.

The fledgling Constitution was now in the hands of the Confederation Congress, the legislative body created by the Articles of Confederation. It was Congress that had directed the Philadelphia convention to improve the Articles, *not* throw them out and replace them. Madison suspected foes of the new document would try to torpedo it, and he was right.

Madison's fellow Virginian, Richard Henry Lee, categorized the Constitution as scarcely more important than a report from a committee. He pointed out that convention delegates had blatantly ignored the instructions they had been given by Congress to improve, not rebuild, the Articles. (In fact, Congress briefly considered a formal censure of convention delegates, before deciding such a move would be meaningless.)

Lee also unsuccessfully proposed that the ten members of Congress who were also convention delegates be barred from Congress's consideration of the matter. That included Madison. And Lee pushed for allowing Congress to tinker with the Constitution before sending it on to the states for ratification. "To insist that it should go as it is without amendments is like presenting a hungry man 50 dishes and insisting he should eat all or none," Lee said.

But Madison countered that the responsibility to craft a new governmental system had been assigned to the convention, not Congress. "A circumstance distinguishes this report from others," he argued. "The Convention was not appointed by Congress, but by the people from whom Congress derive their power." It therefore should be sent, as is, to the states.

REMEMBER

After three days of debate, it was decided to follow the recommendation that had been made by the constitutional convention. The document would be sent to the states. Voters in each state would elect delegates to ratification conventions. If 9 of the 13 states' conventions approved it, the Constitution would take effect. Congress also decided to send it along without officially endorsing it or opposing it.

Waging a War of Words

Shortly after Congress sent the proposed Constitution on to the states, Philadelphia businessman Pelatiah Webster — sometimes referred to as America's first true economist — used the term *Federalist* to describe those who favored the document, including himself. The term caught on, and those who opposed the new set of rules naturally became *Anti-Federalists*.

There were plenty of big names on both sides of the fight. Opponents included Patrick Henry, Sam Adams, New York Gov. George Clinton, the quarrelsome congressmen Elbridge Gerry and Richard Henry Lee, and a 30-year-old Revolutionary War hero named James Monroe. (He's the one holding the flag in the famous painting of Washington crossing the Delaware. He was also the fifth U.S. president.)

But the Federalist team was even brighter. It included Madison, Alexander Hamilton, John Jay, and John Marshall, a 32-year-old Virginian who had served with Washington at Valley Forge and was making something of a name for himself in Virginia legal circles.

Plus, the Federalist side had the two biggest aces in the deck — Ben Franklin and General Washington himself. One of the most popular pro-Constitution campaign pieces was a calendar for 1788. On the cover was a Federal Chariot being pulled by 13 people to represent the states. Riding in the chariot — presumably to victory — were Franklin and Washington.

What followed over the next year or so was one of the biggest blizzards of political arguing in pre-electronic-media U.S. history. Paper was cheap, opinions were abundant, and long and passionate speeches were popular (at least with the speakers).

Newspapers were filled with essays and letters for and against the Constitution. Often, they were signed with pseudonyms such as Fabius, Cato, Landholder, or Roderick Razor. Among the most widely circulated were by three men who signed them Publius.

REMEMBER

Between October 1787 and August 1788, Publius published 85 articles and essays, first in New York newspapers and then throughout the country. All but five were written by Madison and Hamilton, with Jay contributing the rest. The pieces were soon collected in book form and published under the title *The Federalist*, which became known in the 20th century as *The Federalist Papers*.

There is no question that in the 200-plus years since they were written, *The Federalist Papers* have become a widely used tool — or weapon — in judicial and political arguments over just what the Founding Fathers had in mind when they drafted the Constitution and established the U.S. government.

Washington, who along with Thomas Jefferson and a few others, knew the true identities of Publius, recognized how impactful the essays would be someday. "When the transient circumstances and fugitive performances which attend the (present) crisis shall have disappeared," he wrote Hamilton, "that work will merit the notice of Posterity." At the time, however, they were basically just one more collection in an ocean of perspectives.

Federalists championed the new Constitution and the governmental system it outlined as a practical and flexible melding of individual liberty and representative democracy. It was what James Wilson of Pennsylvania called "the true chain between the people and those to whom they entrust the administration of the government."

But Anti-Federalists argued that the government established by the new Constitution was nothing less than a betrayal of the American Revolution. The war, they contended, had been fought to end a system where people from far away, with no knowledge or concern about local or regional issues, made laws arbitrarily — and without consulting those who had to live under them. The new system was just a mirror image of the old one.

REMEMBER

Their most effective argument was that while it outlined the structure and powers of the central government, it failed to specifically list the rights of individuals that would be guaranteed. It also weakened the authority of the individual states. Adding a list of specific rights, said Virginia's Richard Henry Lee, would "secure the minority against the usurpation and tyranny of the majority." The Anti-Federalists insisted a second constitutional convention was needed, at the very least, to consider such a list.

Hamilton countered that the Constitution itself was "founded upon the power of the people, and executed by their immediate representatives and servants . . . the people surrender nothing, and as they retain everything, they have no need of particular reservations" of specific rights. And Madison suggested that the new Congress to be created by the new Constitution could come up with a list of rights, although in his view it wasn't necessary.

And, of course, this being politics, there was a fair amount of name-calling. Federalists labeled Anti-Federalists as "malignant, ignorant and short-sighted triflers." George Mason of Virginia, one of the three convention delegates who had refused to sign the Constitution, referred to his former convention colleagues as "coxcombs" (vain and conceited dandies), "intriguing office-seekers," and "fools and knaves."

Convincing the Conventions

James Madison wanted to get out of the gate fast. He and his fellow Federalists had to win the approval of 9 of the 13 states considering the new constitution. The Anti-Federalists only had to win in 5 states to block it from taking effect. They were sure they already had one state in the bag, because Rhode Island was so opposed, it hadn't even sent a delegation to the constitutional convention. In addition, there were ample signs that North Carolina was also going to vote down ratification.

The Federalists were therefore desperate to establish some momentum by winning in the first states to vote, thus putting more pressure to ratify on indecisive states down the road.

The first one was easy. Like most of the small states, Delaware figured the little-guy protections built into the proposed Constitution — particularly getting the same two seats in the Senate as the big states — was as good a deal as it could expect. On Dec. 7, 1787, Delaware's ratifying convention unanimously approved the document.

Pushing it through Pennsylvania

Somewhat surprisingly, a big state was next. Pennsylvania was the third-most populous state, trailing only Virginia and Massachusetts. James Wilson, the immigrant lawyer who had been a constitutional convention delegate, gave the Federalists an early boost when he delivered a brilliant address that became known as the *State House Speech* in early October and was reprinted in newspapers around the country by the Federalists.

Speaking with a Scottish burr that one listener described as "charming and poetical," Wilson neatly set up each major objection to the Constitution and then knocked it down. (It should be noted that Wilson himself was knocked down: Twice he was beaten up in altercations with Anti-Federalists.)

"I will confess, indeed, that I am not a blind admirer of this plan of government, and that there are some parts of it which, if my wish had prevailed, would certainly have been altered," he summed up. "But when I reflect how widely men differ in their opinions, and that every man . . . has an equal pretension to assert his own, I am satisfied that anything nearer to perfection could not have been accomplished. . . . I am bold to assert that it is the best form of government which has ever been offered to the world."

It also didn't hurt that the Federalists were strongest in and around Philadelphia, the most populous part of the state. Neither did some strong-arm tactics on the part of Constitution supporters. To prevent the state's legislature from establishing a quorum so that it could elect delegates to the ratifying convention, some Anti-Federalist lawmakers attempted to hide in various taverns and attics. But several were found and dragged forcibly to the State House so that delegates could be elected. On Dec. 12, in the same building the Constitution had been drafted, the Pennsylvania ratifying convention voted 46–23 in favor of it.

Picking up some small states

Pennsylvania was followed within a month by Federalist victories in New Jersey, Georgia, and Connecticut, all considered small states. That gave the pro-Constitutionalists five in a row and helped level the playing field for the remaining states.

Up next was another populous state, Massachusetts. The decision promised to be a close one. Anti-Federalists had blanketed the state with well-written pamphlets and newspaper essays. Two of the most prominent political leaders, Sam Adams and John Hancock, had withheld their support of the new Constitution. And the Bay State's citizens had elected a whopping 370 delegates to its convention, which meant it took forever just to call the roll.

REMEMBER

The meeting dragged on for nearly a month. Finally, a compromise was reached: The Constitution would be ratified, but with the condition that when the first new Congress met, it would add specific rights to the document. That stipulation brought Adams and Hancock aboard, and the convention voted 187–168 to ratify. The idea of *conditional ratification* caught on, and several other states also attached the add-the-rights proviso to their approval.

A week after Massachusetts voted in early February 1788, the New Hampshire convention convened. As in Pennsylvania, the Federalists played political hardball. When they discovered they didn't have the votes to ratify, they hastily rammed through a motion to adjourn and come back later. Before they came back, Maryland and South Carolina had ratified, meaning the Constitution was one state away from being adopted. But it could prove to be a hollow victory.

Battling among the Heavyweights

The New Hampshire convention reconvened in June 1788. This time, the Federalists pulled together enough votes (57–46) on June 21 to ratify, by adopting the Massachusetts condition of Congress adding specific rights to the Constitution. That made nine states, the majority specified for adoption.

REMEMBER

But there was nothing in the Constitution to force any state that chose to reject the new government to join, even if most of the other states had done so. Without the consent of the most populous state, Virginia, and financially formidable New York, the "United States of America" would be a somewhat laughable title for the country.

"Mounted on alligators"

The Virginia convention began in early June, with both sides boasting a star-studded lineup of delegates. The Federalists were led by James Madison, John Marshall, and Gov. Edmund Randolph, who had refused to sign the Constitution in Philadelphia but had changed his mind and now supported it. The Anti-Federalists featured Patrick Henry, James Monroe, and George Mason, who had also refused to sign the Constitution and still opposed it.

Madison and Henry were the principal speakers, and at first glance it seemed a mismatch. Henry was a rhetorical flame-thrower, who could read a grocery list and make it sound inspirational. Madison was about as inspiring as elevator music. On more than one occasion, the secretary who recorded the proceedings noted that Madison "spoke too low to be understood." But as John Marshall put it, while Henry had the power to persuade, Madison had the power to convince.

Henry attacked the first three words of the Constitution, contending that "we the people" negated, or at least greatly lessened, the liberty of the individual states. Madison countered that dependence on the states was the very thing that made the Articles of Confederation a toothless document, "whereas this (Constitution) is derived from the superior powers of the people."

Henry turned to sarcasm. Among the so-called "mighty dangers which await us if we reject the Constitution," he said, were that "the Carolinians, from the south, mounted on alligators, I presume, are to come and destroy our cornfields and eat up our little children." Madison calmly and methodically cited governments in other countries — Germany, Switzerland, Holland — that had failed to work effectively as a loose confederation of states.

After three weeks of debate, the Virginians voted 89–79 to ratify, with the recommendation that "subsequent amendments" be added by Congress.

Conquering New York

New York's convention began two weeks after Virginia's, and going in, the Federalist cause looked hopeless. One estimate put the number of Anti-Federalist delegates at 46, compared to only 19 Federalists. But several factors helped turn the tide in favor of ratification.

One was Alexander Hamilton. While he had been almost a nonentity at the constitutional convention, Hamilton summoned all his considerable charm, eloquence, and intellect at the ratifying convention. As James Wilson had done in Pennsylvania, Hamilton systematically deflated each of the major arguments raised by the Anti-Federalists.

He also pointed out that the Articles of Confederation had been hastily created under the pressures of the war for independence. The new Constitution had been drafted after several years of experience with what worked and what didn't work in running the country.

"The proposed Constitution affords a genuine specimen of representative and republican government," he said, ". . . it will answer, in an eminent degree, all the beneficial purposes of society."

New York's delegates were also swayed by the news that New Hampshire and Virginia had already provided the ninth and tenth votes for ratifying. That left New York the choice of joining up or being isolated. Sobered by that thought, and mollified by the assurance a Bill of Rights would soon be established, delegates narrowly (30–27) approved ratification on July 26.

Scooping up the holdouts

New York's approval made 11 states in favor of the Constitution — and left North Carolina and Rhode Island out on a limb. Both grudgingly, and belatedly, joined the Union; North Carolina in November 1789 and Rhode Island in May 1790.

The Confederation Congress, meanwhile, had on Sept. 13 1788, already formally recognized the Constitution as the new law of the land. In the space of about 17 months, America had adopted a new system of government — with a torrent of heated debate and a trickle of bloodshed (although there were a few fist-fights).

Most Anti-Federalists, in fact, took their political lumps with good grace. Massachusetts's Elbridge Gerry, for example, said he felt honor-bound to work within the new system. To do otherwise, he wrote, "would be to sow the seeds of Civil war & to lay the foundation of a military tyranny." Patrick Henry was reportedly asked after losing the Virginia convention fight what to do next. "Go home and sleep," he replied, "and turn up at the next election."

Setting up House (and Senate)

On the cold and rainy morning of March 4, 1789, New York City welcomed the first U.S. Congress under the new Constitution. Cannon were fired, flags raised, bells rung. "A general joy pervaded the whole city on the great, important and memorable event," one newspaper noted.

Unfortunately, only 13 congressmen were on hand to be welcomed. Bad weather and unreliable modes of transportation contributed to the absences. A 220-mile coach ride from Boston to New York, for example, could take four 18-hour days, even under fair skies. Travel by ship was subject to delays due to loading and unloading cargoes, unfavorable winds or bureaucratic hassles in dealing with port authorities. And in some cases, the newly elected representatives were just in no hurry to get to work.

"The public will forget the Government before it is born," moaned the punctual Massachusetts Rep. Fisher Ames in a letter to a friend. Ames, who had defeated the venerable Sam Adams for the congressional seat, was one of many of the new congressmen who were lawyers. More than 25 had been officers in the Revolutionary War, and many had previously served in various state and federal legislative bodies.

The first House of Representatives had 59 members (which rose to 65 when North Carolina and Rhode Island got around to ratifying the Constitution). The initial class of 22 senators would increase to 26. But a quorum of the House wouldn't show up until April 1, and the Senate wouldn't get started until April 6.

When it finally got started, one of the new Congress's first orders of business was to consider ways to get out of New York. Members didn't mind their chambers at 26 Wall Street. The former city hall had been newly remodeled and renamed Federal Hall. Designed by the French engineer Pierre Charles L'Enfant, who would later lay out the new U.S. capital city of Washington, D.C., the building featured Tuscan columns and Doric pillars. There was also a handsome balcony overlooking Wall Street, decorated with the sculptured relief of a giant eagle, holding 13 arrows.

But New York City, in the words of one delegate, was comprised of "streets badly paved, very dirty & narrow, as well as crooked & filled up with a Strange Variety of wood, Stone & Brick Houses, & full of Hogs and mud."

Plus, New York was expensive. Some congressmen were already grousing about the paltry $6 a day (about $175 in 2019 dollars) they were receiving in pay. And some senators were sniffing that whatever House members were paid, they should get more.

Whether senators were worth more was hard to judge, however, since while House sessions were open to the press and public, the Senate chose to meet in secrecy.

Building a Bill of Rights

James Madison was eager to construct a Bill of Rights. It wasn't that he thought the country actually needed a list of specific safeguards to protect individuals and states from the central government.

In fact, he believed it was meaningless. "A mere demarcation on parchment of the constitutional limits of the several departments," he had written in *The Federalist Papers*, "is not a sufficient guard against those encroachments which lead to a tyrannical concentration of all the powers of government in the same hands."

But Madison recognized the overwhelming popularity of the idea. In ratifying the Constitution, the state conventions had come up with more than 200 suggestions for "rights" to be added to the document by the first Congress. So Madison had run for a seat in the new House of Representatives. His opponent was James Monroe, in a district specially drawn by Anti-Federalists to include concentrations of Monroe supporters. Madison won anyway. (There was no personal animosity between the two candidates, who sometimes shared a coach on their way to debates.)

In Congress, Madison wanted to ensure that whatever list of rights that was approved did not materially detract from the document to which he had become so fervently attached. To that end, he announced about a month after Congress got started that he would be bringing a list of amendments for the new Constitution to the House floor on May 25.

But the House yawned and ignored the issue in favor of dealing with more pressing problems, such as raising money for the new government. On June 8, Madison tried again. He argued that quickly drafting a Bill of Rights would help bring the two holdout states of North Carolina and Rhode Island into the Union and it would lessen the fears of many who were still leery of the new Constitution and the powers of the federal government.

"It will be a desirable thing to extinguish from the bosom of every member of the community," Madison somewhat floridly put it, "any apprehensions that there are those among their countrymen who wish to deprive them of the liberty for which they valiantly fought and honorably bled."

But the House consensus was that it was too soon to take up the issue. "Our Constitution, sir, is like a vessel just launched and lying at the wharf," said Rep. James Jackson of Georgia. "She is untried. . .. It is not known how she will answer her helm, or lay her course."

Heating up the House

On July 21, Madison tried again. This time the House agreed to send the proposal to an 11-member committee, with each state having 1 representative. The committee came back in mid-August with a list of 17 amendments.

Congress had wanted to go home at the beginning of August. Now it was stuck, debating an issue too big to kick into the next session or handle cavalierly. New York was suffering a heat wave severe enough to cause some fatalities. Tempers grew short and arguments long.

Madison proposed revising the Constitution's eloquent and memorable preamble with bureaucratic language that faintly echoed the Declaration of Independence. Fortunately, the idea was shot down. There was a long debate over whether the proposed amendment concerning militias and the right to keep and bear arms should include a provision specifically exempting from military service men who objected to fighting on religious grounds. It was also rejected. Then there was the issue of just where to put the amendments.

Madison favored inserting them in the body of the Constitution. But some members, led by Roger Sherman of Connecticut, argued that doing so would expose the document that had been ratified by the people to tinkering by the state legislatures that would have to approve any changes.

"We ought not to interweave our propositions into the work itself, because it will be destructive of the whole fabric," Sherman argued. "We might as well endeavor to mix brass, iron, and clay. . . .. The Constitution is the act of the people, and ought to remain entire. But the amendments will be the act of the state governments."

Rep. Elbridge Gerry of Massachusetts — who a fellow representative said "manifested such an illiberal and ugly disposition . . . that I believe no man has fewer friends" — didn't endear himself by suggesting the House go through, one by one, all 200-plus amendments that had been suggested by the states. Needless to say, that idea fizzled.

Anti-Federalists decried the amendments themselves. They were, they claimed, mere window-dressing that fell far short of overhauling the federal government system and restoring significant power to the states. "They are not those solid and substantial amendments which the people expect," said South Carolina Rep. Aedanus Burke. "They are little better than whip-syllabub, frothy and full of wind, formed only to please the palate."

Finally, on Aug. 24, the 17 proposed amendments were sent to the Senate. "We have at last so far got through the wearisome business of amendments," Rep. Benjamin Goodhue of Massachusetts wrote to a friend, "to the great joy of I believe every member of the House."

Meeting behind closed doors, the Senate went over the amendments, changed some and cut others. Twelve were sent back to the House. A six-member conference committee made a few tweaks, and the package of a dozen amendments was sent to the state legislatures on Sept. 28.

Ratifying rights turns out to be easy

Compared to the furor over ratifying the Constitution, approval of the Bill of Rights went fairly smoothly. All but two received the requisite approval of three-fourths of the states by the end of 1791.

The two amendments that failed to pass dealt with establishing populations for House districts, and a ban on congressional salary hikes taking effect during the session they were approved. (The pay hike amendment was finally approved by enough states — in 1992 — and became the 27th amendment.) For the ten that made it, see Appendix B at the back of this book.

It should be pointed out there were a few bumps in the road to ratification. Georgia's legislature didn't see the need for a Bill of Rights and rejected it. Both houses of the Massachusetts and Connecticut legislatures approved the amendments, but somehow failed to reconcile their votes with the other house or report them on time.

But it would all work out — eventually. Georgia reconsidered, and the other two states finally got their acts together. All three formally approved the Bill of Rights in time for the sesquicentennial celebration of the document's adoption by Congress — in 1939.

Hail to the Chief

While the new Congress was getting settled in, the new president was making his way to New York. George Washington had been elected unanimously when members of the constitutionally created Electoral College cast all 69 of their first-place votes for him. John Adams was named as second choice by 34 and thus became vice president. Adams was followed by John Jay with 9. Nine other men split up the remaining 26 votes. There was no popular vote tallied, since five states had their legislatures name the electors.

The outcome was not exactly a big surprise to anyone, including Washington. As early as the end of the constitutional convention in September 1787, Alexander Hamilton had told Washington that it was "indispensable you should lend yourself to the first operation (of the executive office). It is of little use to have introduced a system if the weightiest influence is not given its firmest establishment at the outset."

For his part, Washington was looking forward to the new job with all the enthusiasm of a patient awaiting a colonoscopy. "My movement to the Chair of Government will be accompanied by feelings not unlike those of a culprit who is going to the place of his execution," the president-elect confided to his friend Henry Knox.

Washington's movement to his inauguration in New York took a week. It was one long parade, with crowds of more than 10,000 in Wilmington, Delaware, and Baltimore turning out to catch a glimpse of him. In Philadelphia, the crowd was twice that size, as riding a white stallion he passed under a triumphal arch. A 50-foot barge, manned by 13 white-smocked sailors, rowed him across the Hudson River from New Jersey into New York City.

The inauguration itself took place on April 30, on the balcony of Federal Hall, where Congress was meeting. Washington decided to take the oath of office with his hand on a Bible, so the ceremony was delayed a few minutes while a search was made for a copy of the book.

In his inaugural address, the new president spoke in a quiet voice about his own deficiencies, announced he would not be taking any salary while in the job, and promised to do his best.

Then he endured hours of celebration, including a giant fireworks display, before starting his carriage ride to a small mansion that had been rented for the chief executive on Cherry Street. But the crowds were so big, the carriage could make no headway.

So the new president got out and walked the rest of the way home.

4

A Nation's Baby Steps

America sets up its presidency and the U.S. Supreme Court.

Newborn political parties duke it out for control.

The American Revolution goes global in its impact.

Chapter **16**

Branching Out

Given that there were lots of legislators among the framers of the Constitution, it's not surprising that the branch of government it best defined was the legislative branch. Fleshing out the duties and powers of the other two branches — the executive and judicial — took a little more imagination for the folks who first occupied those offices.

In this chapter, the structures of those two branches are put together. In addition, Alexander Hamilton builds a federal financial system, and America's two-party political system is born. Oh yeah, and there's a fight over whiskey.

"I Walk on Untrodden Ground"

This is how strange and unfamiliar George Washington's new job was: No one knew just how to address him. John Adams, who was Washington's vice president and aspired to someday be No. 1 himself, wanted something lofty: "His Elective Majesty"; "His Mightiness," or even "His Highness, the President of the United States and Protector of Their Liberties."

In an unusual burst of common sense, the House and Senate decided on the simple and direct "George Washington, President of the United States." That was fine with Washington, who preferred just "Mr. President."

Washington's preference reflected his wish to establish the presidency as an office that people respected, but did not worship. He winced when a supporter wrote to him, "You are now a king, under a different name, and I am well-satisfied that sovereign prerogatives have in no age or country been more honorably obtained." Washington did not want to be a king and correctly assumed that most Americans did not want him to be one either.

REMEMBER

But figuring out what to call the president was just the start. The Constitution was pretty vague about what the office's range of duties were or how far its powers and authority extended. There was in fact more in the document about how to remove a president from office than what he was supposed to do in it.

"I walk on untrodden ground," Washington often said. It was a sentiment echoed by Washington's fellow Virginian, James Madison, who had emerged as the new president's top adviser in Congress. When it came to fleshing out the executive branch, Madison noted, "We are in a wilderness, without a single footstep to guide us."

Taking it slowly

Washington prudently took it slowly during the first months of his presidency. It was more than four months after taking office, for example, before he sent his first nominee for a cabinet post to the Senate for confirmation. (There was no hurry: The Constitution did not require, or even mention, a cabinet, although it did say the president could ask for written opinions from the heads of various government departments.)

One thing Washington knew he wanted from the outset was a way to avoid being plagued by a constant stream of visitors and appointments. He established a system of Tuesday afternoon receptions, called "levees," at which he would endure an hour of small talk with government officials, foreign delegates, and other visitors to the presidential residence.

He did not enjoy it. Dressed in a black velvet coat, yellow gloves, black satin breeches and wearing a ceremonial sword, Washington would bow stiffly — he did not shake hands — and become something of, in the words of one visitor, "a frozen ghost." His demeanor was deliberate. "It is best to be silent," he counseled a grandson, "for there is nothing more certain than it is at all times more easy to make enemies than friends."

Washington and his wife Martha also hosted Friday evening receptions and Thursday dinners — and Washington apparently did not have much fun at these either. "The president seemed to bear in his countenance a settled aspect of melancholy," noted Sen. William Maclay of Pennsylvania, after attending a dinner.

"At every interval (between courses) . . . he played on the table with a knife and fork, like a drumstick."

One reason Washington may have been melancholy was the fact that he was doing something he didn't want to do — and being attacked for it anyway. Critics claimed the levees and dinners smacked of "foreign pomp." Sen. Maclay called them "a feature of royalty" and "certainly anti-republican." (The acerbic senator apparently didn't find them so repugnant, however, that he passed up a free meal with the president.)

While the attacks on Washington putting on monarchal airs were generally unfair, the chief executive did like to travel in style. He had pledged to visit every state during his time in office, and he made two extensive trips around the country — in a $950 ($25,000 in 2019 currency) white coach, pulled by six white horses who were rubbed with paste to make them gleam.

On arriving at the outskirts of a town, the president knew how to make an entrance. Washington would leave the carriage and mount one of two white chargers that accompanied him, sitting astride a gold-lined saddle with a leopard-skin seat.

If Washington needed a lesson in humility, he got one on his only visit to Congress. A few months after taking office, the president decided he wanted advice on a treaty he was negotiating with several Native American tribes in the South. Heeding the constitutional provision that he seek "the Advice and Consent" of the Senate, Washington visited that body.

His visit, however, degenerated into a long, loud argument over procedure, including a decision to send the issue to a committee and have the president appear before it. Washington was infuriated. "This defeats every purpose of my being here," he fumed, before stalking out, according to one observer, "with a discontented Air . . . of sullen dignity." He did not come back.

Picking a cabinet

If Washington wasn't blessed with the gift of gab, he was a gifted listener. Lacking genius, he relied on good judgment. He gathered opinions from people who knew a lot and picked the ones that made the most sense to him.

"Perhaps the strongest feature in his character was prudence," Thomas Jefferson recalled, "never acting until every circumstance, every consideration, was maturely weighed . . . (and) once decided, going through with his purpose whatever obstacles opposed." For once, Jefferson and Alexander Hamilton agreed on something. "He consulted much, pondered much, resolved slowly, resolved surely," Hamilton said of Washington.

Of course to listen, the president needed someone to listen to, and so Washington went about assembling a team to not only offer counsel, but implement policies. In September 1789, Washington announced his first cabinet pick, naming Hamilton as his treasury secretary.

Hamilton was not Washington's first choice. He had tried to convince Robert Morris, the Philadelphia businessman who had kept the government's finances afloat during the Revolutionary War, to take the job.

But Morris was in deep personal financial trouble and declined (settling for a U.S. Senate seat instead). Morris recommended Hamilton, who had served as one of Washington's top aides during the war but had fallen out with the president over mostly trivial matters. "He knows everything, sir," Morris said of Hamilton. "To a mind like his, nothing comes amiss."

Hamilton didn't want the job, in large part because the $3,500 annual salary (about $100,500 in 2019 dollars) would mean a substantial pay cut from the money he could make as a sought-after New York lawyer. But he took it anyway. "I conceived myself to be under an obligation to lend my aid towards putting the machine in motion," he explained.

For his secretary of state, Washington sought out Jefferson, who also wasn't keen on the offer. Jefferson liked his current job as U.S. minister to France. Plus, he wasn't exactly sure what the secretary of state was supposed to do. But after Washington got James Madison to persuade him to take the job — and after Madison explained the post dealt with foreign affairs and not administrative and clerical duties — Jefferson agreed. "I must be troublesome to you till I know better the ground on which I am to be placed," Jefferson cautioned Madison.

To round out his cabinet, Washington selected his old friend and former chief artillery general, Henry Knox, to be secretary of war. Virginia Gov. Edmund Randolph was chosen to be attorney general, although the job was considered part-time and functioned more as the president's legal adviser than its later role as head of the Justice Department.

REMEMBER

Unlike many of his successors, Washington didn't care for cabinet meetings, preferring to meet with his department heads individually so they would feel freer to speak their minds. He also liked to hear from his advisers on a range of subjects, not just those for which they were responsible, or in which they were considered experts.

On the rare occasions they did meet as a group, the cabinet gathered at Washington's home. One government official who was seldom invited was Vice President Adams. Other than presiding over the Senate, the vice president had nothing much to do. The dearth of duties rankled Adams, who described the job as "the most insignificant office that ever the invention of man contrived."

Actually, Adams may have come closer to becoming president far sooner than anyone anticipated. In mid-June 1789, just a few months after taking office, Washington developed what was described as "a malignant carbuncle" on his left thigh. A Dr. Samuel Bard diagnosed the problem as "anthrax," a term that at the time did not mean the bacterial disease associated with livestock or modern-day terrorist threats. He also determined the growth was on the verge of becoming gangrenous.

With the aid of his 73-year-old physician father, Dr. Bard surgically removed the growth — without benefit of anesthesia. Washington's recovery took more than a month. Although it's unclear just how ill he was, it was nonetheless a sobering reminder how important Washington was in holding the still wobbly federal government together.

"The alarm is now over," Madison understated a bit coldly. "(But) his death at the present moment would have brought on another crisis in our affairs."

Ordering the Courts

If the Constitution said relatively little about setting up the executive branch of government, it said even less about how to put together the judicial branch: There would be "one supreme Court," which would serve only to hear appeals of most cases — except on issues involving representatives of other countries or where a state or states were plaintiffs or defendants.

Under the Supreme Court would be "inferior Courts as the Congress may from time to time ordain and establish. The Judges, both of the supreme and inferior Courts, shall hold their Offices during good Behavior." And they would get paid for their efforts. That's pretty much it.

After some squabbling about which legislative house should take up the matter first, the Senate began deliberations to "ordain and establish" a federal judiciary in July 1789. The effort's chief shepherd was Sen. Oliver Ellsworth of Connecticut, a talkative but able lawyer and one of the key players in the drafting of the Constitution. "This vile bill is a child of his," the caustic Pennsylvania Sen. William Maclay noted, "and he defends it with the care of a parent, even with wrath and anger."

TECHNICAL STUFF

While Maclay and a few others opposed the plan as infringing on the authority of state courts, the Judiciary Act of 1789 rather easily passed both houses and was signed into law by Washington in September 1789. Under the act, the Supreme Court would consist of six justices — a number that would move up and down several times before settling on nine members in 1869. (President Franklin

Roosevelt would try to "pack" the high court in 1937 with an additional six justices sympathetic to his "New Deal" policies, but Congress shot down his proposal to amend the Constitution.)

Below the Supreme Court were three circuit courts, which consisted of two Supreme Court justices who traveled "the circuits" twice a year to hear cases. Below the circuit courts were district courts, whose jurisdictions roughly followed state lines.

The three-layer system is essentially the same as the modern federal system, although the circuit-riding Supreme Court justices have been replaced by 13 appellate courts and the district courts expanded to 94, with additional specialty courts to hear bankruptcy cases, claims against the federal government, and international trade cases.

"The weakest branch"

The Constitution's framers took most of their cues for forming a judicial branch of government from the British system. Lacking a written constitution, British judges constantly modified *common law* — law formed by customs, social norms, and earlier court decisions rather than specific written codes — as the need arose. But America *did* have a written constitution, and the framers apparently didn't give much thought as to how the judiciary might function with a document from which other written codes would grow.

REMEMBER

What they did intend was that the judiciary would be the weakest of the three government branches. "The executive holds the sword," Alexander Hamilton wrote in *The Federalist Papers*, "the legislative the purse . . . the judiciary, on the contrary, has no influence over either the sword or the purse, no direction either of the strength or the wealth of the society; and can take no active resolution whatever." In other words, all federal judges were supposed to do is judge. "The judiciary," Hamilton wrote, "is beyond comparison the weakest of the three departments of power."

That's certainly how things started. The nation's highest court first convened on the second floor of an old stone building called the Merchants' Exchange, in what is now the Financial District of New York City. On its first day, only three of the six justices showed up. Without a quorum, the court went home. Even when it did meet, justices heard relatively few cases. When in 1800 the federal government moved to its new setting in Washington, D.C., no one had thought to find a place for the Supremes. They were forced to meet in a small first-floor room of the Capitol that had served as a Senate clerk's office.

Being named a Supreme Court chief justice was deemed no great honor either. Washington's first choice, John Jay, resigned after being elected governor of New York and declined an offer to resume the job five years later, saying the court lacked "energy, weight and dignity."

Jay's replacement, South Carolina's John Rutledge, was ousted by the Senate (see the nearby sidebar to find out why). Chief Justice No. 3 was Oliver Ellsworth, the Connecticut senator chiefly responsible for organizing the federal judiciary. Ellsworth quit the court after becoming ill while doing double duty as a U.S. envoy to France. But the fourth chief justice stuck around — and had a major impact on the course of American history.

THE INJUDICIOUS JUSTICE

If ever there was Supreme Court justice who lacked judicial temperament, it was John Rutledge. A South Carolinian by birth, Rutledge was a former governor of the state and played a key role in the drafting of the U.S. Constitution. In 1790, he was appointed by George Washington as an associate justice on the first U.S. Supreme Court. Just 15 months later, however, Rutledge quit to become chief justice on the South Carolina Supreme Court.

He changed his mind again in June 1795 and asked Washington to appoint him the U.S. Supreme Court's chief justice, after John Jay announced his resignation from the post. Washington agreed, naming Rutledge to the job while Congress was in recess. While waiting for his appointment to come through, however, Rutledge publicly attacked a treaty Washington's administration had worked out with Great Britain, exclaiming that he "had rather the President should die" than sign the treaty.

Needless to say, this did not sit well with Washington or supporters of the treaty. When the Senate reconvened in the fall, it refused to confirm Rutledge's appointment, the first rejection of a Supreme Court nominee and the only time in U.S. history an "interim" appointee to the court has been rejected. Then things got worse for Rutledge. Ten days after the Senate rejected his appointment, he attempted suicide by walking into a river near his home in Charleston.

Rutledge, who owned slaves and as a lawyer had defended the rights of owners to abuse their "property," was rescued by two slaves "while he cursed and abused them," according to a witness. Rutledge lived quietly — and reportedly more sanely — for five more years before dying in 1800 at the age of 60.

Laying down the law

The three U.S. Supreme Court chief justices chosen by George Washington lasted in the job for a total of about 11 years. The only chief justice chosen by Washington's successor as president, John Adams, lasted more than 34.

"My gift of John Marshall to the people of the United States was the proudest act of my life," Adams would later write.

Adams's "gift" was a tall, handsome Virginian, whose unruly brown hair and rumpled clothes somehow left the impression of a comfortable-but-unmade bed (see Figure 16-1). Born in a log cabin in 1755, Marshall was a second cousin to Thomas Jefferson. After the Revolutionary War, in which he served with Washington at Valley Forge, Marshall studied law, eventually opening a successful legal practice in Richmond.

FIGURE 16-1: John Marshall, fourth chief justice of the U.S. Supreme Court.

Library of Congress

He also became active in politics, helping to win Virginia's ratification of the Constitution, serving as a U.S. diplomat in France, and winning a seat in the House of Representatives. In 1800, Adams selected Marshall to be his secretary of state and then appointed him to the Supreme Court a month before Adams left office.

REMEMBER

Prior to the 45-year-old Marshall's appointment, the nation's highest court had issued fewer than 70 rulings, most of them relatively minor. Before his death in 1835, the court would issue more than 1,000 decisions, about half of which would be written by Marshall. But none of them were as significant as an 1803 ruling that involved a Maryland businessman, some sour-grapes politics — and a clerical goof by Marshall himself.

Marbury v. Madison

After losing the 1800 presidential election to Thomas Jefferson, the incumbent president John Adams proved to be a poor sport. In the last days before he left office, Adams appointed 58 federal circuit judges and justices of the peace, all of whom were political allies. (The last-minute appointees were derisively dubbed the midnight judges.)

But the Secretary of State's office screwed up and failed to deliver several of the commissions before Adams's term was up. The secretary of state, by the way, was John Marshall, who was serving in both that office and as chief justice. Marshall's replacement as secretary of state was James Madison, who refused to deliver the judicial commissions.

One of those appointees was a banker and Maryland political power-broker named William Marbury. After failing to get the Senate to act on their behalf, Marbury and three others petitioned the Supreme Court to order Madison to hand over the commissions. By that time, what was a minor issue in the first place was moot. Marbury's term as a justice of the peace had already more than half expired, and Congress had eliminated the position anyway.

The court's February 1803 decision, however, was anything but minor or moot. In a unanimous decision, written by Marshall, the court ruled that Marbury's appointment was legal. But — and this is the important part — the law under which he could petition the Supreme Court to order the executive branch to honor it was unconstitutional, because it gave powers to the Court that Congress did not have authority to grant.

"It is emphatically the province and duty of the Judicial Department to say what the law is," Marshall wrote, adding "that a law repugnant to the constitution is void, and that courts, as well as other departments, are bound by that instrument."

REMEMBER

The court's decision helped establish two major precedents. One was that of *judicial review* — the authority of courts to invalidate legislative and executive branch acts that judges decide are in violation of the Constitution. The second was the doctrine of *separation of powers* — that all three branches of the federal government are co-equal, and none can claim precedence or authority over the others except in areas clearly delineated by the Constitution.

Not everyone was pleased by the decision. Thomas Jefferson, for one, called it a "twistification." "The opinion which gives to the judiciary the right to decide what laws are constitutional and what not," he complained, ". . . (will) make the judiciary a despotic branch."

Jefferson's complaint has been regularly repeated in the 200-plus years since the court's decision, and the legitimacy of Marshall's ruling questioned — but the impacts of the decision have endured.

Taxes and Logrolling

As clumsy as Alexander Hamilton could be when it came to pure politics, he was brilliantly adroit at transforming his ideas into reality. He was also undeniably a hard worker. On Sept. 11, 1789, for example, while the Senate was confirming his appointment as America's first treasury secretary, the 34-year-old Hamilton was already busy securing a $50,000 loan for the federal government (about $1.4 million in 2019) from the Bank of New York.

REMEMBER

A few months after taking office, Hamilton issued a detailed document called *Report on Public Credit*. In it, he proposed to fully pay off the government's $53.9 million debt (roughly $1.5 billion in 2019), about a quarter of which was owed to foreign creditors. Not only that, he proposed that future creditors always have first call on government revenues. A sound credit rating, he argued, was vital for establishing a stable financial system and earning international respect for the young country's economic practices — and attracting international investments to America.

Hamilton didn't stop there. He urged that the federal government assume another $25 million ($687 million in 2019 currency) in debts owed by the individual states, mostly from the Revolutionary War. His public argument for federal assumption of state debts was that the war had been everybody's responsibility, and thus the war debts belonged to the nation. Privately, he was counting on the fact that if creditors were being paid by the federal government rather than the states, they would be more inclined to make future loans to the central government and invest in federal bonds.

To raise money, Hamilton recommended a combination of tariffs on imported goods and the imposition of *excise taxes* — taxes charged directly on those who made the products rather than on those bought them. He also proposed redeeming government bonds at interest rates lower than had been promised when the bonds were issued, as a condition of getting them redeemed at all.

Finally, Hamilton suggested there was nothing wrong with a national debt — in fact, it was the best way to keep the economy moving — as long as the government had a method in place to pay it down. It should be, he said, "A fundamental maxim" that "the creation of debt should always be accompanied with the means of extinguishment." He proposed what was called a *sinking fund,* which were reserves set aside to regularly pay down 5 percent of the debt until it was gone.

Stirring up the storm

Not surprisingly, Hamilton's plan sparked a firestorm of protest, led by his former ally, James Madison. "I go on the principle that a public debt is a public curse," Madison said. One of his objections was that some states, such as Maryland and his own Virginia, had dutifully paid their war debts. It was unfair, he said, for those states to bear part of the obligation for paying off the foot-dragging likes of Massachusetts and South Carolina.

Worse for Madison and other opponents, the nation's debts were being paid to the wrong people. Many war veterans had been paid with government IOUs. Desperate for cash, they had sold them for pennies on the dollar to speculators. Now the speculators would be able to redeem them for close to their face value. These speculators, wrote Thomas Jefferson, were "fraudulent purchasers of this paper. . . . Immense sums were thus filched from the poor and ignorant. . . ." But Hamilton argued that the IOU-buyers had themselves taken a big risk in buying securities that were next to worthless at the time. They were entitled to be compensated for that risk.

Finally, Hamilton was accused of what amounted to "insider trading" by snatching up government securities with the expectation they would become much more valuable if his plan was approved by Congress. There is evidence that more than a few members of Congress profited from such actions. Hamilton's assistant secretary, William Duer, quit after being exposed as a speculator — and eventually died in a debtors' prison. But there was no evidence Hamilton profited from his proposals. As the nearby sidebar shows, however, establishing his innocence came at a great personal cost.

IT WAS LUST, NOT GREED

In 1797, Alexander Hamilton was publicly accused of having conspired, while he was Treasury secretary, with a notorious speculator named James Reynolds to profit from Hamilton's proposals to finance the federal government. But Hamilton had a novel — if embarrassing — defense. His relationship, he said in a widely published newspaper account, was not with Reynolds, but with Reynold's wife, Maria. Hamilton confessed he had had a long affair with Maria Reynolds and that Reynolds had blackmailed him over it.

"The truth was I dreaded extremely a disclosure," Hamilton wrote, "and was willing to make large sacrifices (i.e., thousands of dollars in blackmail payments) to avoid it. . . . This confession is made not without a blush. The public . . . will I trust excuse the confession. The necessity of it to my defense against a more heinous charge (of speculation) could alone have extracted from me so painful an indecorum."

The "dinner table bargain"

After several months of debate, Hamilton's plan was narrowly defeated in the House of Representatives. But while tact was not one of Hamilton's strengths, he did understand the political stratagem of *logrolling*. Named after a frontier custom of neighbors getting together to help move massive timbers into place for log cabins, logrolling in politics was basically just trading an aye for an aye.

One night in July 1790, over dinner at the boarding house where Thomas Jefferson was staying, Hamilton, Jefferson, and James Madison worked out a deal. In return for the two Virginians enlisting support from Southern congressmen for Hamilton's finance plan, Hamilton would lend his support to siting a proposed federal district in the South. The "dinner table bargain" resulted in a financial system for America — and the 100-square-mile District of Columbia. Situated on the banks of the Potomac River next to Virginia and Maryland, the district opened for government business in late 1800.

Warring over whiskey

Hamilton wasn't done. In December 1790, he proposed a seven-cent-per-gallon tax on whiskey and other "hard spirits," to be paid directly by the distillers rather than the consumers. Congress approved the proposal. America's liquor producers — of which there were many — were dismayed, particularly since their product often sold for as little as 25 cents a gallon.

Consumers were also irked, since the tax would naturally be passed on to them in the form of higher prices. And whiskey was so popular and so ubiquitous in rural areas that it was often used as a form of currency. Plus, distilling whiskey was often the cheapest way for farmers to market some of their surplus corn crops.

By 1794, anger reached a fever pitch in western Pennsylvania. Tax collectors were roughed up when they tried to collect the tax. In July, when law enforcement officials tried to summon 60 tax scofflaws to court, a full-scale insurrection broke loose. The chief tax collector's house was burned, and a U.S. soldier was killed.

After Pennsylvania's governor refused to act, a furious President Washington, egged on by Hamilton, declared the rioters traitors and called out militias from four states to subdue the insurrectionists. The resulting army of more than 12,000 — larger than any force Washington had ever commanded during the Revolutionary War — scattered the rebels. Three protestors were killed and about 20 arrested. But only two were convicted, and they were subsequently pardoned by the president.

While short-lived, the federal government's response to the *Whiskey Rebellion* was notable in that it served notice the government was willing to take significant steps to enforce federal laws. It also demonstrated that the federal government under the new Constitution was a vast improvement over the Articles-of-Confederation government that had failed to cope with the similar Shays' Rebellion in 1786–87.

Bickering over banks

A day after he proposed the whiskey tax, Hamilton unveiled a plan for a Bank of the United States. The proposal called for a bank chartered for 21 years, with a main office in Philadelphia and eight branches around the country. It would be overseen by a 25-man board. It would be capitalized with $10 million ($275 million in 2019 currency). The federal government would hold a fifth of the bank's stock and be its main depositor. The rest of the stock would be available to the public (which snapped it up in less than two hours when it went on sale).

Hamilton argued the back was necessary to ensure a large and flexible money supply for the federal government as well as the general economy. But opponents, led by Madison and Jefferson, countered that its benefits accrued mainly to wealthy businessmen in the North and East, at the expense of rural areas in the South and West. Moreover, they said, it was unconstitutional.

After Congress easily approved creation of the bank, Jefferson, as secretary of state, urged Washington to issue his first veto. Jefferson contended that Hamilton overreached when he said the constitutional clause giving Congress the power "to make all Laws which shall be necessary and proper" for running the federal government included starting a bank. Hamilton, Jefferson argued, was substituting "convenient" for "necessary." "To take a single step beyond the boundaries (of "necessary"), Jefferson wrote, "is to take possession of a boundless field of power" by Congress.

But Hamilton persuaded the president to take a "broader" view of the Constitution's wording — and Washington signed the bill. "Congress may go home," Pennsylvania Sen. William Maclay sarcastically noted. "Mr. Hamilton is all powerful, and fails in nothing he attempts."

Planting partisan seeds

Sarcasm aside, there was truth in McClay's observation. Hamilton had become second only to Washington in terms of influence over the federal government. His department included more than half of all federal workers, and extended to overseeing such far-flung agencies as the Post Office. He even dabbled in foreign affairs (much to Secretary of State Jefferson's annoyance).

And his fiscal policies worked. In 1791, the federal debt was estimated at $197 ($5,300 in 2019 dollars) per American. In 1804, it had dropped to $140 ($3,000), and by 1811, to $49 ($946). America's credit was good enough that when it needed to borrow heavily in 1803 to finance the purchase of the vast Louisiana Territory, it was easily accomplished.

Moreover, the U.S. economy prospered, mainly by avoiding direct involvement in the wars between France and Britain, and profiting through trade with both sides. The nation's population was booming, land remained relatively cheap, particularly in the West, and industries developed. Even Jefferson had to admit that "in general our affairs are proceeding in a trend of unparalleled prosperity . . . there is not a nation under the sun enjoying more present prosperity, nor with more in prospect."

But the arguments over establishing a financial system also reflected a growing split in fundamental philosophies of economics and government. The split gradually coalesced into two camps — and the makings of America's partisan political system.

"Daily Pitted . . . Like Two Cocks"

Thomas Jefferson and Alexander Hamilton both had red hair, and both were terrible when it came to personal finances — and there their similarities ended.

Jefferson was tall (6'2") and lanky, a careless dresser who moved with an easy, athletic grace (he had once been considered, after Washington, the best horseman in Virginia). He intensely disliked public speaking: As president, his two inaugural addresses were described as being "only partly audible," and all of his State of the Union addresses were delivered to Congress on paper, and not in person. And his personal interests tended to be solitary pursuits, such as designing beds for his beloved plantation home of Monticello.

At 5'7", Hamilton was about average height for men of his time and slender. He was fastidious in his clothing and grooming. His appearance belied the physical courage he had demonstrated on the battlefield. Although he fretted constantly over upcoming events and challenges, he was very fond of the sound of his own voice and loved the limelight in social settings.

Their backgrounds were equally dissimilar. Jefferson had been born into, and remained part of, Virginia's plantation aristocracy. Despite his avowed hatred of slavery, he was a slaveowner throughout his adult life. Hamilton was born out of wedlock on a Caribbean island, emigrated as a teenager to New York, and thus felt no great allegiance to a particular state or way of life. He was a loud voice for the abolition of slavery.

Given their different backgrounds and temperaments, it's not surprising they developed sharply opposing views on politics and government. As Jefferson recalled in an 1810 letter to a friend, "Hamilton & myself were daily pitted in (Washington's) cabinet like two cocks."

Parting into parties

For many of the Founding Fathers, the term "political parties" was enough to trigger shivers of revulsion. Formal organizations built around a formal set of principles and a specific political philosophy — and that expected their members to vote and unwaveringly support those principles and that philosophy — seemed to spit in the face of personal liberty and independent thought. Parties also elevated winning elections over doing the right thing.

"If I could not go to heaven but with a (political) party," Jefferson declared, "I would not go at all." Then he formed a political party. In May 1791, under the guise of what they called a "botanical excursion," Jefferson and James Madison took a trip to New York. There they met with New York politicians Robert Livingston and Aaron Burr to lay the foundation of what would become known as the *Democratic-Republicans Party* and then just *Republicans.*

They also convinced the poet Phillip Freneau to start a newspaper. *The National Gazette* became a frequent critic of Washington's administration and acted as a counter to the *Gazette of the United States,* edited by John Fenno, a staunch supporter of Hamilton and Hamilton's allies, who appropriated the name *Federalists.*

The establishment of Freneau's newspaper (which was subsidized by Jefferson giving Freneau an undemanding job as a translator for the State Department) coupled with the alliance of convenience between the Virginia and New York politicians were key steps in defining the opposition party to the dominant Federalists.

Choosing up sides

In general, Federalists favored a strong central government that would prime and protect the nation's economic engine. They were leery of extending political power to "common" Americans — "Those who own the country," sniffed John Jay, "ought to govern it." They liked tariffs that protected U.S. manufacturers, weren't averse to limits on public speech and press freedoms, and leaned toward efficiency and order over public debate and personal liberties. The Constitution was viewed as an elastic document, whose interpretation should be dependent on contemporary circumstances.

Republicans were okay with a strong national government when it came to foreign affairs, but wanted it to take a passive role in domestic affairs. They favored cheaper foreign products over protective tariffs and were generally more tolerant of free speech and a free press. "Our liberty cannot be guarded but by the freedom of the press," Jefferson wrote. And Republicans saw the Constitution as a document that specifically limited the authority of the federal government: Any power not spelled out in it belonged to the states.

It's overly simplistic to suggest that yesterday's Federalists are today's Republican Party and yesterday's Republicans are today's Democratic Party. Hamilton, for example, supported big federal government programs while modern Republicans generally don't. Jefferson wanted to minimize government, which doesn't square with modern Democratic support of the New Deal, the War on Poverty, or the Affordable Health Care Act. But the emergence and dominance of two major parties certainly foreshadowed the two-party system America has stuck with through most of its political history.

Saying Goodbye — Again

Washington hated the whole thing. He hated the constant arguing between Hamilton and Jefferson, which would drive both of them out of his cabinet. "I will frankly and solemnly declare that I believe the views of both of you are pure and well-meant," he said in vainly trying to keep the peace.

He hated the idea of formalized political parties. "I believe it will be difficult, if not impractible," he warned, "to manage the reins of government . . . if, instead of laying our shoulders to the machine after measures are decided on, one pulls this way and another that . . . it must inevitably be torn asunder."

And he hated the idea of a second term. Washington had every intention of stepping aside in 1793. But Hamilton, Jefferson, and almost everyone else talked him into it, mostly with the argument that the government was still too young for him to retire. So in the 1792 election, Washington was once again unanimously selected by the Electoral College as president. Adams was reelected vice-president, although the Republicans did mount a challenge to Adams through the candidacy of New York Gov. George Clinton.

The decision to serve a second term was one Washington came to regret. At the age of 60, his health was not good. The public's near-worship of him had begun to wane. As the political combat between the two parties accelerated, Washington was often attacked as a "would-be king" by Republican newspapers who viciously (but accurately) viewed him leaning toward the Federalist side of things.

While he impatiently waited for the last few months of his term to be over, Washington drafted a farewell address (with a great deal of help from Hamilton). Delivered publicly via a Philadelphia newspaper, the address contained three main themes: America must always keep the Constitution and the Union above the goals and desires of political parties. It must keep clear of "foreign entanglements." And it must be a nation of high morals.

On March 4, 1797, he attended the inaugural ball for his successor, John Adams. According to Adams, Washington muttered beneath his breath, "Ay! I am fairly out and you are fairly in! See which of us will be the happiest."

Then "the Father of His Country" went home — this time for good.

Chapter **17**

The Toddler's Transition

With the departure of George Washington from the national scene, any illusion that America's new system of government would somehow learn to function without partisan politics quickly disappeared.

In this chapter, Washington's immediate successor is chosen; there's an informal war with France; the First Amendment is briefly trampled on; and a "peaceful revolution" takes place — all in the space of about five years.

Electing Adams

The unanimous election and reelection of Washington as president concealed some significant flaws in the system the Founding Framers set up in the Constitution for choosing chief executives. And, as they usually do, the flaws inevitably began to bubble to the surface.

The Constitution provided that each state would choose *electors*, via whatever method the state's legislature decided on. The number of electors for each state would equal the number of the state's seats in the House of Representatives and the U.S. Senate. Each elector would vote for two candidates, one of whom had to be from outside the elector's state. Congress would then count the votes of this *Electoral College.*

The candidate with the most votes would be president; the candidate with the second-most would be vice president. In the event no one got a majority of the votes, the House of Representatives would decide the outcome.

Leaving it up to each state to determine how to choose its electors created a multi-horned beast. In the 1796 election, 6 of the 16 states (Vermont, Kentucky, and Tennessee had joined the original 13 by then) chose their presidential electors by a public vote; 7 left it up to their legislatures; and 3 used a mixed system of popular vote and legislative choices.

The Founding Framers had envisioned that however they were chosen, electors would be relied on to consider the various presidential candidates and make wise and independent choices. But that vision hadn't factored in the rise of sharply divided and competitive political parties. Voters (or legislators) didn't want electors exercising their own judgment. As one Federalist official put it about his support for an elector, "I chose him to act, not think."

Lining up the "tickets"

As America's political system polarized into two major parties, the members of each soon realized the way to win elections was to unite behind particular candidates. So, in 1796, the Democratic-Republicans (often shortened to "Republicans") backed Thomas Jefferson for president, with U.S. Senator Aaron Burr for vice president. Burr was a sleazy-but-skilled New York political boss and a detested personal enemy of Alexander Hamilton. The Federalists countered with John Adams for president and Thomas Pinckney, a South Carolina war hero, former governor, and diplomat, as vice president.

But the process of selecting party-candidate "tickets" was informal, meaning electors were free to name other people. And some of them did, which would prove to have significant consequences.

Neither Jefferson nor Adams actively campaigned, since to do so was considered unseemly. "I am determined to be a silent spectator of the silly and wicked game," Adams declared. But that doesn't mean there weren't campaigns. Surrogates delivered stump speeches. All kinds of social gatherings — barn-raisings, quilting-bees, weekly town markets, even weddings — were turned into political events.

A key weapon in each side's political arsenal was the country's highly partisan newspapers. The papers regularly printed praise of the candidates they supported — and even more regularly ripped into the opposition. Republicans were "fire-eating salamanders" and "poison-sucking toads," according to one Federalist paper. A Republican journal opined that Federalists were "monarchal lick-spittles" and "womanish hypocrites."

The level of vitriol troubled Jefferson. "You and I have seen warm disputes and high political passions," he wrote to a friend. "But gentlemen of different politics would then speak to each other . . . it is not so now. Men who have been intimate all their lives cross the street to avoid meeting, and turn their heads another way lest they should be obliged to touch their hats." But, it should be noted, it did not trouble him enough to rein in the nasty attacks mounted on his behalf by Republican newspapers and pamphleteers.

Hamilton schemes behind the scenes

Alexander Hamilton never ran for president, probably because he knew he was too controversial, and possibly because he knew he was not a particularly skilled politician. Not being a candidate himself, however, didn't mean he couldn't meddle in presidential campaigns. Hamilton had resigned as Treasury secretary in early 1795 to return to his law practice in New York, where he soon became the city's most prominent attorney. But he hadn't given up his desire to play a major role in determining how America would be run.

Trouble was, he intensely disliked both of the top two 1796 presidential candidates. Hamilton considered Thomas Jefferson "a contemptible hypocrite" for espousing democratic ideals and love for the common man, while at the same time being part of the South's slave-owning, plantation aristocracy. "All . . . must give way to the great object of excluding Jefferson" from the presidency, he wrote a friend.

At the same time, he loathed his fellow Federalist, John Adams. Hamilton thought Adams suffered from a number of serious character defects that included "disgusting egotism," "distempered jealousy," and "ungovernable indiscretion."

(For the record, both Adams and Jefferson disliked Hamilton as much as he disliked them. Adams once called him the "bastard brat of a Scotch pedlar" and considered him "as great a hypocrite as any in the United States." Jefferson regarded Hamilton as "not only a monarchist, but [in favor of] a monarchy based on corruption.")

REMEMBER

Faced with the unpalatable choice between supporting Jefferson or Adams, Hamilton came up with a scheme designed to defeat them both. He privately urged all the Federalist electors in each state to cast their votes for Adams and Pinckney. But he also quietly urged the Republican electors from South Carolina to split their votes — one for their party's candidate, Jefferson, and one for Pinckney, their home-state guy. If it worked, Pinckney would pick up the same number of Federalist votes as Adams, plus a few Republican votes, which would be enough to make him president.

Hamilton's strategy worked in South Carolina — and failed elsewhere. Some Federalist electors in New Hampshire, Maryland, Massachusetts, Connecticut, and Rhode Island split their votes between Adams and other Federalist politicians. As a result, Adams was elected with 71 electoral votes — but Jefferson, with 68, came in second and Pinckney third, with 59. That meant the Republican Jefferson became vice president under the Federalist Adams.

It was a politically awkward arrangement — and it took eight years to fix it. In 1804, the 12th Amendment to the Constitution was ratified. It changed the presidential election system so that electors voted for only one candidate for president and only one for vice president. (In case you're wondering, the first ten constitutional amendments are the *Bill of Rights*; the 11th, ratified in 1792, banned federal courts from hearing certain lawsuits brought against states.)

Adams and Jefferson were *frenemies* — personally civil toward each other but diametrically opposed in their political philosophies. Adams worried that the legislative branch of the government had too much power, Jefferson fretted that the executive branch was too powerful.

Adams saw the Constitution as a sort of referee in what he thought was an inevitable struggle between the privileged few and the needy many. "Equal laws can never be expected," he wrote. "They (laws) will either be made by (the many) to plunder the few who are rich, or by (the rich), to fleece the many who are poor." Jefferson put his faith in the common man gravitating toward doing the right thing through consensus. "The will of the majority," he wrote, "of every society, is the only sure guardian of the rights of man."

Jefferson, who had spent the years since he left Washington's cabinet tending to his plantation at Monticello — and his constant personal financial problems — was apparently content with his second-place finish. Even before the election, he had written James Madison that if he and Adams finished in a tie, he would step aside. "He (Adams) has always been my senior from the commencement of our public life . . . (and) this circumstance ought to give him the preference." Besides, Jefferson knew that trying to be the first successor to Washington — and with war clouds looming on the horizon — would make Adams's job no picnic. "This is certainly not a moment to covet the helm," he said.

Trying to Avoid Foreign Entanglements

One of the bits of advice Washington doled out in his Farewell Address was that when it came to dealing with other countries, the United States, whenever possible, should mind its own business.

"The great rule of conduct for us in regard to foreign nations is in extending our commercial relations, (and) to have with them as little political connection as possible," he warned. "So far as we have already formed engagements, let them be fulfilled with perfect good faith. Here let us stop. . . . Why, by interweaving our destiny with that of any part of Europe, entangle our peace and prosperity in the toils of European ambition, rivalship, interest, humor or caprice?"

It was advice Washington had tried hard to follow himself during his second term, as France and Britain once again descended into long years of bloody conflict, and many Americans lined up to root for one side or the other.

Revolting developments in France

Triggered by a host of elements that ranged from the price of bread to a tax system left over from the Middle Ages, a revolution began in France in 1789. While it started as a relatively peaceful transition from an absolute monarchy to a modified republic, the *French Revolution* soon degenerated into an internal bloodbath known as the *Reign of Terror*. Thousands of people were beheaded, often on transparently flimsy charges they opposed the revolution.

The turmoil spilled over into the rest of Europe, and in early 1793 — ten days after the French monarch Louis XVI took a one-way trip to the guillotine — France declared war on Britain.

REMEMBER

Americans were divided in their sympathies — and antipathies — toward the two combatants. Jefferson, and Republicans in general, tended to support the French. While he decried the horrific excesses, Jefferson nonetheless defended the revolution itself. "My own affections have been deeply wounded by some of the martyrs to the cause, but rather than it should have failed, I would have seen half the earth desolated," he wrote to a friend. "Were there but an Adam & Eve left in every country and left free, it would be better than as it now is."

Hamilton and the Federalists, on the other hand, were appalled by what Hamilton called "a state of things which annihilates the foundations of social order and true liberty. . . .. The French Revolution is a political convulsion that in a great or less degree shakes the whole civilized world."

As Treasury secretary, Hamilton also saw an important pragmatic reason for supporting Britain in its war against France. Almost 90 percent of the U.S. government's revenue came from customs duties — and about 75 percent of that came from duties on imported goods from Britain. In short, it made more financial sense for America to support the British than the French.

Bickering with Britain

In April 1793, President Washington issued a *Proclamation of Neutrality,* in which the United States declared itself officially on the sidelines in the European conflict, and warned Americans to stay out of it as individuals.

But as a practical matter, Washington knew it was in America's interests to settle some issues with Britain that had been lingering since the end of the Revolutionary War. Britain still controlled eight forts on the U.S. western frontier. Both countries had failed to follow through on war-related debts they had agreed to pay. Some British ports were still closed to U.S. goods.

And the British navy had stepped up its infuriating practice of stopping U.S. ships on the high seas to seize cargoes it deemed were bound for France, or kidnap American sailors for service in British ships — a practice known as *impressment.*

Anxious to cool down growing American anger at the British, particularly over the ship seizures and impressments, Washington sent U.S. Supreme Court Chief Justice John Jay to London in early 1794, with instructions to work out a deal. Jay's only real bargaining chip was a threat that America would join the neutral nations Denmark and Sweden in military action against Britain, if it didn't stop its maritime predations. But Hamilton privately alerted the British that America really had no plans to do anything of the sort.

REMEMBER

As a result, Jay succeeded in obtaining only half a diplomatic loaf. Britain agreed to abandon its forts on American soil and open some of its ports in the Caribbean to U.S. trade. Both sides agreed to submit issues concerning war debts, U.S.-Canada border disputes, and British seizure of the U.S. ships to arbitration by neutral parties.

The issue of impressment, however, was left unresolved. That, along with evidence the British had supplied arms and advisers to Native American tribes battling U.S. troops in present-day Ohio, infuriated many Americans. A wall near Jay's home in New York City was painted with the words "Damn John Jay! Damn everyone that won't damn John Jay! Damn everyone that won't put up lights in the windows and sit up all night damning John Jay!"

Despite the anger, and Washington's own private misgivings about the treaty, the Federalist-controlled Senate ratified the deal in June 1795 on a 20–10 vote, the bare two-thirds majority it needed. Ratification eased friction between the United States and Britain.

It also helped the United States reach accommodation with Spain on several issues. Fearing a new U.S.-British alliance might threaten its interests in the Americas, Spain agreed in October 1795 to give Americans navigation rights on the Mississippi River, as well as ceding disputed territory in what is now part of Georgia and

Mississippi. But the Jay Treaty deepened the division between Federalists and Republicans — and greatly irritated France.

The "XYZ Affair"

"No man who ever held the office of president would congratulate a friend on obtaining it," John Adams wrote to his son John Quincy, sometime after Adams began his tenure in the job. (The warning apparently fell on deaf ears, since John Quincy Adams would become America's sixth president.) Indeed, Adams's time as president was dominated by a single vexing issue: trying to avoid a war with France.

The ratification of the Jay Treaty with Britain had angered the five-member *Directory*, which had taken over running things in France. French officials saw the treaty as nothing less than an Anglo-American alliance and subsequently stepped up seizures of American ships by the French navy. By mid-1797, the French had grabbed more than 300 U.S. merchant ships in a little over a year. This naturally outraged Americans, many of whom began to agitate for war with France.

In an effort to calm the waters, President Adams first thought of sending Vice President Jefferson, who was quite popular in France, to negotiate. But Jefferson, on the advice of James Madison, decided it was more politically prudent to keep an arms-length relationship with a president from the opposing political party. Adams's Federalist cabinet likewise vehemently objected to Adams's second choice, the Democratic-Republican Madison.

REMEMBER

So Adams eventually sent Virginia lawyer John Marshall and former Massachusetts Rep. Elbridge Gerry to join South Carolina's Charles Cotesworth Pinckney, who had been named U.S. minister to France by Washington before he left office. Unbeknownst to Adams, the French government had refused to recognize Pinckney's credentials and in essence had thrown him out of the country, although he was later recognized.

When news of Pinckney's humiliation did reach America, the clamor for war grew deafening. Then things got worse. In October 1797, the French foreign minister, Charles Maurice de Talleyrand, met for all of 15 minutes with the American negotiators and then left them cooling their heels for weeks.

In the meantime, a series of "informal" meetings took place with three Frenchmen who let it be known that formal talks would occur only if America agreed to lend France a lot of money and pay what amounted to a bribe of £50,000 (about $8 million in 2019 U.S. dollars) to Talleyrand himself.

Such arrangements were not unheard of in European diplomacy, but the American envoys were not buying it. "No, not a sixpence!" replied Pinckney, whose statement was later apocryphally amended to include "millions for defense, but not one cent for tribute!"

Eventually, Talleyrand agreed to meet. But by that time, the U.S. diplomats' dispatches of the bribery had reached Adams. When Republicans in Congress demanded they be made public, Adams agreed, but only after deleting the French bribe-seekers' names and replacing them with "X, Y and Z."

Congress reacted to the incident by ordering construction of a dozen new U.S. Navy warships (some of them merchant ships that were refitted), and authorizing the U.S. Navy to engage French warships. It also authorized creation of a sizeable army, to be led by George Washington (with, at Washington's insistence, Alexander Hamilton as second in command). But a much-feared invasion of America by France never occurred. Instead, America engaged in one of its quietest and least remembered conflicts.

Fighting a "quasi-war"

For a little more than two years, America and France duked it out in what became known as the *Quasi-War*, because neither side ever formally declared hostilities. That was just as well, because as wars go, it wasn't much. The U.S. Navy, which had all but disappeared after the Revolutionary War, worked itself up to 25 vessels, some of them small coastal "revenue cutters."

Almost all the fighting was at sea, mostly in the Caribbean and South Atlantic waters around the West Indies. The U.S. Navy lost one ship, while capturing or severely damaging several French frigates.

While the "war" continued, Adams appointed a new three-member delegation to seek a peaceful resolution. The trio — William Vans Murray, the U.S. ambassador to the Netherlands; Supreme Court Chief Justice Oliver Ellsworth; and former North Carolina Gov. William Richardson Davie — arrived in Paris in early 1800 to negotiate — again — with the French foreign minister Talleyrand. This time, however, Talleyrand had a new boss.

A 30-year-old Corsican general named Napoléon Bonaparte had seized control of France. The new French leader decided there were more important matters to deal with than fighting with America, such as conquering the rest of Europe. A deal — the *Convention of 1800* — was thus worked out that ended French raids on U.S. shipping and "indefinitely" suspended American claims for damages against the French.

Adams's decision not to undertake a full-scale war was widely unpopular among Americans. (For one thing, Congress had approved a land tax to finance the buildup of the military, the first direct tax it ever imposed.) The president had managed to infuriate pro-French Republicans by fighting, and anti-French Federalists by not fighting enough.

But it was a politically courageous act, since Adams knew he was quite probably dooming his chances for reelection. Indeed, Adams considered it his proudest accomplishment as president. He later wrote that a fitting epitaph for his final resting place might be "Here Lies John Adams, Who Took Upon Himself the Responsibility of Peace with France in the year 1800."

Aliens and Seditionists

The Quasi-War with France wasn't the only thing frightening and frustrating Federalist majorities in Congress. There was also a huge wave of French immigrants to America — as many as 25,000 by 1798 — who had fled either the terrors of the home country and wars in Europe, or a bloody slave rebellion on the French-controlled Caribbean island of Saint-Domingue (now Haiti).

They had been joined by thousands of what the Federalists labeled "wild Irish" immigrants who hated Britain for its long oppression of Ireland and naturally gravitated to supporting Jefferson's anti-British Democratic-Republican Party. Then there were the Republican "attack dogs" in the press.

In the Federalists' view, the French immigrants were potential saboteurs and spies. The Irish immigrants represented massive political reinforcements for the opposition party. And Republican-controlled newspapers were becoming intolerably irritating.

In fact, Federalists found Republicans in general were irritating — and vice versa. Mutual civility in Congress sank to levels that would embarrass fourth graders. The nadir was reached in February 1798, when Federalist Rep. Roger Griswold of Connecticut taunted Republican Rep. Matthew Lyon of Vermont about an old allegation Lyon had acted cowardly during the Revolutionary War. Lyon responded by spitting a mouthful of tobacco juice on Griswold. Two weeks later, Griswold retaliated on the House floor by attacking Lyon with a cane, whereupon Lyon grabbed a set of fire tongs and the two went at it — see Figure 17-1 — until colleagues pulled them apart.

FIGURE 17-1:
A comic portrayal of the fight between Reps. Matthew Lyon and Roger Griswold on the floor of the House of Representatives.

Passing a contentious quartet of laws

In the summer of 1798, the Federalist–dominated Congress passed a package of four bills to deal with the issues of unwanted immigrants, enemy aliens, and venomous editors. Known collectively as the *Alien and Sedition Acts*, they included

>> **The Naturalization Act,** which increased the residency period before someone could become a U.S. citizen from 5 years to 14 years. It was designed to prevent immigrants, particularly the Irish, from being eligible to vote in the short term.

>> **The Alien Enemies Act,** which gave the president authority to confine or deport aliens of an enemy country in time of war.

>> **The Alien Friends Act,** which authorized the president to deport any aliens he deemed "dangerous to the peace and safety of the country." Such deportations did not require a stated reason or any judicial proceeding.

>> **The Sedition Act,** which imposed fines of up to $2,000 ($41,000 in 2019) and jail terms of up to two years for those convicted of making "false, scandalous and malicious" statements about the president Congress or "the government of the United States." An important condition was added that allowed the truth of a statement to be offered as a defense.

Federalists contended the laws were needed to thwart Republicans' clandestine efforts to aid France. The Jeffersonians, claimed Federalist Rep. Robert Goodhue Harper of South Carolina, were "engaged in a most criminal correspondence with her (France's) agents, devoted to her service and aiding . . . the efforts of her diplomats." Federalists toasted President Adams on his signing of the acts: "May he, like Samson, slay thousands of Frenchmen with the jawbone of Jefferson."

Wielding "the jawbone of Jefferson"

Adams, who had not sought or supported the proposals, nonetheless defended his signature on them by claiming the acts were necessary wartime measures. "I knew there was need enough . . . and therefore I consented to them," he wrote. How much he really thought there was a need for the alien acts is questionable, since Adams rejected calls from some members of his cabinet to undertake mass deportations of "undesirable" aliens, and deported no one.

But Adams must have taken some quiet satisfaction regarding the Sedition Act, even though it was clearly a gross violation of the First Amendment. After all, even the most thick-skinned politician doesn't like to pick up a newspaper and read that he is a "repulsive pedant, a gross hypocrite and an unprincipled oppressor," as Virginia editor James Callender wrote about Adams, or that he is "blind, bald, crippled, toothless (and) querulous," as Philadelphia editor Benjamin Franklin Bache described the president.

Both Callender and Bache were among the 25 Americans convicted under the Sedition Act. Most were Republican newspaper editors. The non-editors included Republican Rep. Matthew Lyon of Vermont — the same fellow who had brawled with a fellow congressman on the House floor in early 1798. Lyon wrote that the Adams administration was guilty of "ridiculous pomp, foolish adulation, and selfish avarice." Lyon was fined $1,000 (about $20,000 in 2019) and sentenced to four months in jail, during which time he was reelected to Congress.

Another non-editor was Luther Baldwin, a New Jersey garbage scow pilot. As the president passed through Newark, a cannon salute was fired, to which a drunken Baldwin remarked, "I do not care if they fire thro' his arse!" A tavern keeper ratted on him, and Baldwin was fined $150 (about $3,100 in 2019).

Jefferson likened the acts to something from the 9th or 10th centuries. On the one hand, he counseled his fellow Republicans to keep their composure. "A little patience," he wrote to a friend, "and we shall see the reign of witches pass over, their spells dissolve, and the people, recovering their true sight, restore their government to its true principles."

REMEMBER

But Jefferson and James Madison secretly drafted what became known as the *Virginia and Kentucky Resolutions*. Approved by those states' legislatures, the resolutions contended the Alien and Sedition Acts were unconstitutional. As such, individual states had the right to ignore them.

Although no other state agreed to go along with the idea at the time, the resolutions planted the dark seeds of the *theory of nullification*: that states had the right to pick and choose which federal laws and policies they agreed with and would or wouldn't follow. In 1861, the theory would help propel 11 states out of the Union and plunge the nation into civil war.

As it turned out, public support for the laws waned rapidly once hostilities ceased with France, and it became obvious the sedition law was a partisan Federalist ploy to silence Republican press attacks. Three of the four laws either expired or were repealed by 1801. As president, Jefferson pardoned those still serving sentences under the Sedition Act, and Congress compensated them for any fines they had paid.

But an updated version of the Alien Enemies Act was still on the books in 2019. In fact, the law was the basis of the internment during World War II of more than 100,000 people living in America who were of Japanese descent, more than half of whom were U.S. citizens, not aliens.

The Revolution of 1800

The candidates in the 1800 presidential election were familiar faces. As in 1796, Thomas Jefferson and Aaron Burr formed the Democratic-Republican ticket. Incumbent John Adams was the Federalist choice for president, and his running mate, as in 1796, was a Pinckney. This time, however, it was Charles Cotesworth Pinckney, a Revolutionary War hero, diplomat — and the brother of Adams's running mate four years before.

But if the candidates were familiar, the rest of the election followed a scenario right out of *Alice in Wonderland*. To begin with, leaders of each party met secretly in *caucuses* (from an Algonquin Indian word meaning "adviser") to formally agree on whom to back and to plan strategy.

As in 1796, neither Adams nor Jefferson actively campaigned. But those who did so on their behalf managed to sink to depths seldom reached in U.S. political history. Nothing was off-limits. Adams, it was alleged, had imported English prostitutes for White House orgies. Election of the "Godless" Jefferson, prophesied Timothy

Dwight, president of Yale College, would mean "Murder, robbery, rape, adultery, and incest will be openly taught and practiced, the air will be rent with the cries of the distressed, the soil will be soaked with blood, and the nation black with crimes."

The "abuse and scandal" of the campaign, wrote First Lady Abagail Adams, was enough "to ruin and corrupt the minds and morals of the best people in the world."

"Fixing" New York

As he had in 1796, Alexander Hamilton tried to sabotage his fellow Federalist Adams by getting Federalist electors to each cast one of their two votes for Adams and Pinckney, except in South Carolina, where Adams would be left off enough ballots to give Pinckney the edge. As in 1796, it didn't work.

Instead, Hamilton was outmaneuvered in his home state of New York by his fellow New Yorker and arch-enemy, Aaron Burr. Burr was opportunistic, amoral and ambitious. In 1804, he would kill Hamilton in a duel and in 1807 he narrowly escaped a treason conviction in a scheme to establish an empire in Florida with British help.

But in 1800, the lawyer-turned-political boss set up brilliant grass-roots effort to elect a Republican majority to the New York legislature. That ensured the state's 12 electors — who under New York's system were selected by the legislature — would vote for Jefferson.

A frantic Hamilton tried to convince New York Gov. John Jay to call a special legislative session to change the state's method of selecting electors to a popular vote. "Scruples of delicacy and propriety ought to yield to the extraordinary nature of the crisis," he pleaded. But Jay refused to change the rules after the game was over. New York, which had voted for Adams in 1796, supported the Jefferson-Burr ticket, and it was enough to give the election to the Republicans.

"Jefferson is to be preferred"

As in 1796, the Constitution's goofy presidential election system resulted in chaos. Jefferson had indeed received 73 electoral votes to Adams's 65. But Burr had also received 73 votes, because each of the Republican electors had voted for *both* Jefferson and Burr.

Under the Constitution, the Federalist-controlled House of Representatives was to break the tie. Each state would have one vote, and the delegates from each state would vote among themselves to decide how the state would go. The winner would need 9 of the 16 states.

The Federalists did have a choice beyond either Jefferson or Burr. They could opt to let it remain deadlocked, in which case Secretary of State John Marshall (who was by this time also serving as U.S. Supreme Court chief justice) would become interim president until a new election was called. Few relished that approach because of the ominous precedent it might set, and because it could threaten the stability of the entire system of government.

Instead, the House pondered, argued, and horse-traded over the situation for six days — and 35 ballots — in mid-February 1801. On the first ballot, Jefferson won eight of the nine states he needed, but could not nudge any of the other delegations to his side. So in doubt was the outcome that Rep. Joseph Nicholson of Maryland was carried, through a snowstorm, from his sickbed to a cot in a room off the House chamber. His wife had to help steady his hand as he wrote down his votes.

Hamilton, meanwhile, decided that a man he considered politically delusional was better than a man he considered personally corrupt. In a blizzard of letters to Federalist representatives, Hamilton wrote that "Jefferson is to be preferred. He is by far not so dangerous a man. . . . As to Burr, there is nothing in his favor . . . he is (morally) bankrupt beyond redemption."

How effective Hamilton's lobbying was is unclear. There is some evidence to suggest Federalists were more persuaded by assurances from Jefferson he wouldn't fire all of the Federalists who held government offices.

In any event, on the 36th ballot, the deadlock was broken. Federalists in Vermont and Maryland changed their votes from Burr to abstentions, giving Jefferson majorities in those two states. In Delaware and South Carolina, Federalists also abstained, meaning those states did not vote. The final result was 10-4-2. Thomas Jefferson was the third President of the United States.

All Together Now

Shortly before noon on March 4, 1801, Jefferson left the Washington, D.C. tavern/boarding house where he had roomed as vice president, and walked the short distance to the Capitol to be sworn in as president.

An estimated 1,000 people crowded into the ornate Senate chamber, to witness what Jefferson himself had called "a peaceful revolution." The U.S. government was changing hands from one political party to another, without bloodshed. "The change of Administration," noted one observer, "which in every government and in every age have most generally been epochs of confusion, villainy and bloodshed, in this our happy country takes place without any species of distraction or disorder."

After Chief Justice John Marshall administered the oath, Jefferson spoke in a soft reedy voice. "Every difference of opinion is not a difference of principle," he said. "We have called by different names brethren of the same principles. We are all Republicans. We are all Federalists.

". . . . I know, indeed, that some honest men fear that a Republican government cannot be strong, that this government is not strong enough. But would the honest patriot . . . abandon a government which has so far kept us free and firm . . . I trust not. I believe this, on the contrary, the strongest government on earth."

His speech over, Jefferson walked back to his boarding house for lunch. He sat, as he had for his entire stay, at the foot of the table.

Chapter **18**

Aftermath

I t was a revolution like no other, "a revolution," in the words of the 18th century British statesman Edmund Burke, "made not by chopping and changing of power in any of the existing states (nations), but by the appearance of a new state, of a new species, in a new part of the globe."

In this chapter, I ask — and, with any luck, answer — a quartet of questions designed to help frame the import and enormity of the American Revolution.

So, How Big Was It?

Overstating the effects of the American Revolution on world history would be difficult. It's been estimated, for example, that more than half of the countries belonging to the United Nations in 2019 could trace their beginnings back to documents proclaiming their legitimacy as sovereign states and modeled on or inspired by America's Declaration of Independence.

In fact, it could be argued that just a single Revolutionary War battle in the fall of 1777 in eastern New York led to a French king having his head cut off; the end of the Spanish Empire in the New World; doubling the size of the United States;

firmly establishing Canada as a British colony; and hastening the settlement of Australia. That may seem a bit of stretch, but consider this:

>> In September and October 1777, American forces defeated a British army near Saratoga. The stunning victory, and surrender of the entire British force, helped convince French King Louis XVI to throw France's formidable military behind the American cause. That contributed greatly to America's military victory over the British in the Revolutionary War.

>> America's subsequent creation of a democratic republic provided a vivid example to the French of how effective an uprising against a tyrannical government might be. French revolutionaries used the U.S. Declaration of Independence as a template for drafting the *Declaration of the Rights of Man and the Citizen* in 1789. One of the casualties in the French Revolution that followed was Louis XVI — the same monarch who had helped America win its revolution.

>> Inspired by the U.S. and French revolutions and led by Simón Bolívar — the Venezuelan who became known as the George Washington of Latin America — much of Spain's colonial empire in Latin America revolted in the first three decades of the 19th century. By 1830, what are now the nations of Venezuela, Mexico, Argentina, Bolivia, Chile, Ecuador, Paraguay, Uruguay, and Peru had declared independence. In addition, the former Portuguese colony of Brazil and French colony of Saint-Domingue (now Haiti) had likewise successfully rebelled.

>> The loss of Saint-Domingue to a rebellion led by former slave Toussaint Louverture so irritated the French dictator Napoleon that he launched a major assault to retake the island. That ended in disastrous defeat for the French. The debacle helped persuade Napoleon to forget about a French Empire in the Americas. And that decision spurred France in 1803 to sell America 828,000 square miles of what became known as the Louisiana Purchase, for $15 million (about $335 million in 2019). That doubled the size of the United States.

>> After the U.S. victory in the Revolutionary War, as many as 80,000 Americans who had been loyal to the British fled to Canada. That had a radical demographic effect on the sparsely populated country, most of whose non-native inhabitants up to that time were of French descent. The influx of the loyalist Americans helped solidify Britain's cultural and political hold on Canada.

>> Prior to the Revolutionary War, America had served as a dumping ground for Britain's unwanted, which included a vast number of those convicted of various crimes. Faced with the post-war problem of where to send its excess convicts, Britain settled on its almost-empty colony of Australia. Between 1788 and 1868, an estimated 165,000 prisoners were transported to the Down Under continent.

Sure, lots of other elements are involved in each of these events that helped bring them about and influenced their outcomes. But there is no denying the American Revolution played a significant role in all of them.

What Kind of Revolution Was It?

Through most of the 20th century and into the 21st, a continual hot topic of debate among historians has been whether the American Revolution was a *conservative* or *radical* affair.

The conservative-event camp argues that the real aim of the Founding Fathers was a revolution in a literal sense: a 360-degree return to the rights, liberties and economic system that America had lived under during most of the 17th and first half of the 18th centuries. That was before the British government began looking for ways to raise revenues from its American colonies and started enforcing laws that benefited the mother country at the inconvenience of the colonists.

America's leaders, the conservative-revolution camp contends, had nothing new or particularly daring in mind in terms of a new form of government. They mostly just wanted the British to stop changing things. The proof of that, the argument goes, is that even after the Constitution was written and the new government framework it contained was established, the same people were still in charge. Slavery continued; women remained legally inferior; and voting was still largely limited to adult males who owned something of value.

But, the radical camp counters, the conservative revolution argument ignores the fact that an entirely new form of government resulted. The Founding Fathers came up with a fundamentally different view of the relationship between government and people. Under monarchies or autocracies, government serves the purposes of the one or the few, and operates through the labor and sacrifices of the many. In the model created by the Constitution, the government functions through the will of the people it serves, as expressed by the actions of the representatives they elect.

True, the radical camp concedes, the Founding Fathers ignored or sidestepped the inherent hypocrisy of a nation founded on lofty ideals of liberty, yet allowed slavery and treated half the populace as second-class citizens.

But they point out that the soundness of the governmental system the founders created has allowed it to gradually work to redress those wrongs: The 13th Amendment to the Constitution, for example, ended slavery in 1865; the 19th gave women the right to vote in 1920. These changes weren't reliant on the desires of individual rulers or even the whims of popular opinion. They came about as the result of Americans operating under a system, which when it was created, was a radical departure from governments of the time.

In the end, it may be futile to attempt to accurately categorize the American Revolution. A revolution is a massive upheaval, undertaken by a mass of human beings with different motives, aspirations — and levels of enthusiasm.

For example, John Hancock was a wealthy merchant; George R.T. Hewes, a poor shoemaker. Hancock presided over the group that drafted the Declaration of Independence; Hewes helped dump tea in Boston Harbor. Neither had anything to gain directly from rebellion. But both rebelled and risked their lives in doing so. Was Hancock a conservative hoping to go back to the good old days, and Hewes a radical pining for a new way of doing things? I don't know, and I don't think it matters. Assigning generalized labels to their reasons may be an interesting academic exercise, but not a whole lot more.

Why Did It Work?

As the citizens of scores of other countries around the world can attest, not every revolution works equally well. England underwent two revolutions in the 17th century. One resulted in the dictatorship of Oliver Cromwell; the other substituted one monarch for another. The French Revolution gave France — and the rest of the world — Napoleon. The Russian Revolution transformed the government from a corrupt and despotic regime to a corrupt and totalitarian regime.

But the American Revolution, however bumpy its path, succeeded. One reason was roots. Americans mostly derived their ideas about government from Britain, whose people had long wrestled with trying to balance the authority of the state with the liberty of the individual. By the time shots were fired at Lexington, many, if not most, Americans had also enjoyed decades of representative democracy, at least at the local level. Self-government was not a new experience. And unlike many other nations, America had escaped dominance by a single religious organization or secular interest group.

Then there was luck. America abounded in natural and economic resources. Life at the time of the revolution was generally pretty good in the colonies. The desperation faced by starving or war-torn nations on the verge of rebellion was absent and thus so was the desperate need to grab onto the first Cromwell or Napoleon to come along and offer a quick fix.

Finally, Americans settled on three key aspects to the system that helped ensure the revolution could mature. One was the system of checks and balances among the three branches of government — what the historian Richard Hofstadter termed "a harmonious system of mutual frustration."

While the system has certainly generated its fair share of friction, it has maintained a balance the Founding Fathers sometimes feared would be unobtainable. In 1974, for example, President Richard Nixon refused to release audiotapes recorded in his office to Congress, which was considering impeachment proceedings against Nixon. Nixon based his refusal on what he claimed was a "privilege" accorded to the executive branch. The U.S. Supreme Court ruled in favor of Congress. About two weeks after the court's decision, the president resigned.

The second key aspect of the America system that differentiated it from those of other revolutions was the recognition that the rights of the minority were every bit as important as the rights of the majority. As Thomas Jefferson put it in his first Inaugural Address, "Though the will of the majority is in all cases to prevail . . . the minority possess their equal rights, which equal law must protect, and to violate (this) would be oppression."

Finally, there is the elasticity of the Constitution. The document's framers recognized they weren't perfect and were thus unlikely to create a perfect blueprint for running the country. In the 230 years between 1789 and 2019, a total of 27 amendments were added to the Constitution. They guaranteed rights, made changes in the process of government — and in the case of Prohibition, made one societal activity illegal and then legal again.

What Can You Learn from It?

One of the most rewarding things about the study of history is its reassuring reinforcement of the fact that nobody is now, or ever has been, perfect. It naturally follows that nothing any human has ever done has been perfect.

That, as John Adams pointed out in answering letters from admirers in the first quarter of the 19th century, applied to both the Founding Fathers and their efforts. "I ought not to object to your reverence for (us)," he wrote one fan, "but to tell you a very great secret, as far as I am capable of comparing the merits of different periods, I have no reason to believe we were better than you are."

To another correspondent, Adams explained that "every measure of Congress from 1774 to 1787 inclusively, was disposed (of) with acrimony and decided by as small majorities as any question is decided these days . . . it was patched and pie-bald (irregular) then, as it is now, and ever will be, world without end."

So, one lesson to be learned from the American Revolution is that it's unreasonable to expect the political descendants of the Founding Fathers to be any more infallible than they — or the fruits of their labors — were.

Which raises a second lesson: The American Revolution wasn't finished with the end of the war, or the adoption of the Constitution, or the peaceful shift of power from one political party to another. It has been followed by a series of mini-revolutions, additions to the country's ever-changing menu of unresolved issues and unaddressed problems.

The menu's items have included the end of slavery; the preservation of the Union; the extension of suffrage and other rights to women; the establishment of a safety net of programs from Social Security to Medicare; the push for a color-blind justice system, and ongoing efforts to ensure that the scales of majority rule and minority rights remain in balance.

And that leads to a third lesson, and one I touch on in the Introduction to this book: The American Revolution isn't over. "On the contrary," wrote Dr. Benjamin Rush, physician, signer of the Declaration of Independence and Founding Father, "nothing but the first act of the drama is closed. It remains yet to establish and perfect our new forms of government and to prepare the principles, morals, and manners of our citizens for these forms of government after they are established and brought to perfection."

Dr. Rush's words were written in 1786. We're still working on perfection.

Chapter 19

Some Books Worth Perusing

Hundreds of books have been written about the American Revolution, from all kinds of perspectives and ideologies. The topic has been tackled broadly and specifically, as part of overall U.S. histories, or been explored down its scores of back alleys and side streets.

With that in mind, here's an admittedly eclectic and too-small list of titles you may find helpful in exploring the topic further.

Books to Explore

America: The Last Best Hope, Vol. I, **by William J. Bennett. Nelson Current Publishing, 2006.** Bennett served as secretary of education under President Ronald Reagan and was America's first drug czar as director of the Office of National Drug Control Policy. He writes in a breezy, conversational style, and acknowledges his goal is tell the positive side of U.S. history and balance a recent tendency toward emphasizing the country's warts.

A Patriot's History of the United States, **by Larry Schweikart and Michael Allen. Penguin Books, 2014.** Touted by conservative talk-show host Glenn Beck, this voluminous — 980 pages-plus — book is more argumentative than persuasive. The authors spend a fair amount of time disputing other interpretations of U.S. history, but still manage to cover issues and events in depth.

A People's History of the American Revolution: How common people shaped the fight for independence, **by Ray Raphael. The New Press, 2016.** Lauded by historian Howard Zinn, a self-described "democratic socialist," this book examines the actions of, and impacts felt by, "ordinary" groups of Americans during the Revolution, including women, Native Americans, and slaves. Well-researched, it downplays the influences of the Founding Fathers.

These Truths: A History of the United States, **by Jill Lepore. W.W. Norton & Co., 2018.** Harvard University history professor and New Yorker staff writer Lepore deftly combines analysis and narrative in this weighty (800-plus pages) summary of American history. The shadow of slavery lingers throughout the sections about the Revolution, which some readers will find thought-provoking, others irritating.

Conceived in Liberty, **by Murray N. Rothbard. Ludwig Von Miles Institute, 2011.** Rothbard was a revisionist historian, economist, and central figure in American Libertarianism, and all three callings come through in this four-volume set that starts with the Revolution's roots and ends with adoption of the Articles of Confederation. A treasure trove of details, and a novel interpretation of things — George Washington was a bumbling and not-too-bright despot?

The Penguin History of the United States, **by Hugh Brogan. Penguin Books, 2001.** Brogan is a well-known British historian and author and has a refreshing Brit's eye-view of the Revolutionary War.

The American revolution: A World War, **edited by David K. Allison and Larrie D. Ferreiro.** Smithsonian Books, 2018. An excellent and lavishly illustrated collection of essays by leading historians that show the global impact of the war.

Revolution Song: The story of America's founding in six remarkable lives, **by Russell Shorto. W.W. Norton & Company, 2018.** Shorto weaves the stories of individuals that range from George Washington to the Seneca war chief Cornplanter into what is essentially a nonfiction novel, with the American Revolution as a backdrop. In doing so, he manages to give equal weight to the truth of the times as well as the facts.

Desperate Sons: Samuel Adams, Patrick Henry, John Hancock and the secret bands of radicals who led the colonies to war, **by Les Standiford. Harper Collins, 2012.** Standiford focuses in on the Sons of Liberty and other groups that took a collection of colonial gripes to the next level — revolution.

1776, **by David McCullough. Simon & Schuster, 2005.** The master of narrative history is so good at telling a story that even people who don't care two figs for what happened a long time ago will find this book riveting.

American Dialogue: The Founders and Us, **by Joseph J. Ellis. Alfred A. Knopf, 2018.** It's a challenging read, but worth the effort. Ellis ferries readers back and forth between the lives and thoughts of four Founding Fathers — Jefferson, Madison, Washington, and John Adams — and the political and cultural climates of 21st-century America, to see how, and if, they relate to each other.

5

The Part of Tens

Chapter **20**

(At Least) Ten Things You Didn't Know about the Founding Fathers

Okay, you probably already know that George Washington's teeth were not his own, that Benjamin Franklin invented bifocals, and that Thomas Jefferson sometimes answered the door at the White House in his robe and slippers.

But did you know that Washington was quite a hoofer on the dance floor, Franklin invented a musical instrument that reportedly killed people, and Jefferson owned grizzly bears? I thought not. The Founding Fathers were a pretty interesting bunch. They had talents and shortcomings and eccentricities, just like the next guy. Here are ten quirks, traits, and other aspects of some of the men who made America great. Or at least interesting.

Twinkle-Toes George

The Father of Our Country wasn't exactly known for his charm. In fact, George Washington could be downright cold and aloof — except when it came to "cutting a rug." Yup, Washington was quite the dancer.

From minuets to cotillions, according to contemporary observers, George loosened up considerably on the dance floor, even in the midst of leading the American army during the war with Britain. "His Excellency danced upwards of three hours without once sitting down," one of his generals recorded. "The General danced every set, that all the ladies might have the pleasure of dancing with him," noted another observer.

Bonus fact: After retiring from public life, Washington operated one of the largest and most profitable whiskey distilleries in the country at his Mount Vernon Virginia plantation. Maybe that explains the dancing. . . .

Franklin's "Deadly" Instrument

Ben Franklin was at a dinner party in England when he heard musicians play a haunting melody on some water-filled wine glasses. Intrigued, the inveterate inventor went home and created the *glass 'armonica.* This instrument consisted of 37 glass bowls, threaded together on a metal spindle and color-coded to identify the different notes the bowls produced. Positioned horizontally, it was played by spinning the bowls and touching them lightly with one's moistened fingers. The resultant sound was both soothing and spooky.

But it also reportedly triggered maladies that ranged from deep depression to poisoning from the lead in the glass bowls. Scientific analyses have debunked all that, and the instrument is still here today. But Franklin also liked to start the day by sitting naked in front of an open window for 30 minutes, no matter how cold it was or who was walking by. He called the practice "air bathing." Makes you wonder if Ben didn't play one too many tunes on his 'armonica.

TJ and the Bears

Thomas Jefferson had a thing about the American West and its exotic animals. After all, he was the president who sent Lewis and Clark across the continent and told them to watch for wooly mammoths and giant ground sloths. So Jefferson must have been intrigued when the explorer Zebulon Pike sent him two grizzly bear cubs Pike had found in Colorado. Jefferson, however, was a smart fellow. He realized the cubs weren't always going to stay cubs. "These are too dangerous & troublesome for me to keep," he wrote to a granddaughter. Instead, the president gave the bears to a friend who ran a natural history/art museum in Philadelphia.

But it took two months to arrange the transfer, and in the meantime, the bears had to make do in cages (sorry, couldn't resist) on the White House lawn. Their museum stay did not end well. As they grew, they became wilder. One escaped and was killed while rampaging through a kitchen. The other was also eventually "put down." Both were stuffed and mounted for display. Perhaps it's just as well Lewis and Clark didn't find any mammoths or sloths.

Tom Paine's Bones

William Shakespeare wrote that "the evil that men do lives after them; the good is oft interred with their bones." He couldn't have been more wrong when it came to Thomas Paine. Born in England, Paine didn't arrive in America until 1774 just as things were heating up. He nonetheless became the Voice of the Revolution, whose essays in favor of independence electrified Americans. But Paine's contributions to the cause went unrewarded, to put it very mildly. After the war, Paine sailed home to England — and set about making powerful enemies. His incendiary writings in favor of the French Revolution got him accused of treason by the English. In France, he was at first lionized as a hero and then jailed by the radical leaders of the Reign of Terror that followed the French revolt. Finally freed, he returned to America, where in 1809 he died in New York at the age of 72.

Things continued to go badly. His funeral attracted only six mourners. (In contrast, Benjamin Franklin's Philadelphia sendoff drew 20,000.) Ten years after Paine's death, a fellow named William Cobbett disinterred Paine's body and took it to England for a proper and dignified reburial.

It never happened. Paine's remains were still unburied when Cobbett died in 1835. Exactly what happened to Tom Paine's bones is unknown. There were reports Cobbett's relatives turned some into buttons and sold the rest. On a happier note, Paine got plaques honoring him, both on the house where he was born in England and the house where he died in New York. To paraphrase the Bard, maybe the good is sometimes put on a building's wall. . . .

Sam Adams Really Made Beer (sort of)

Any Top 5 list of the American colonists the British government hated the most would have had to include Sam Adams. A second cousin to fellow Founding Father John Adams, Sam was a first-class rabble rouser. He helped organize the Sons of Liberty, the Boston Tea Party, and the militia group called the *minutemen*. He was a delegate to the Constitutional Convention and a Declaration of Independence signer. But he was a lousy businessman.

One of the businesses he helped run into the ground was started by his father. It involved producing malted barley, which was then sold to beer makers. Within a few years of taking the enterprise over, Sam went bankrupt.

Fast-forward to April 1985, when a Boston entrepreneur named James Koch began delivering his new beer to 32 bars, restaurants, and hotels in the Boston area. The beer, the label of which featured a colonial holding a foaming lager and bearing the words Patriot-Brewer, was called Samuel Adams Boston Lager. It helped spur a micro-brewery revolution in America and went on to become one of the largest and most-awarded craft brewers in the world. Koch said he picked Sam Adams as the company's icon because "I had always admired Samuel Adams's role in the American Revolution." Plus, it didn't hurt that like many of the Founding Fathers, Adams was not immune to the charms of fermented beverages.

The Price on Hancock's Head

His name has become a synonym for signature, as in "put your John Hancock on the dotted line." The reason, of course, is that Hancock's signature is the first to adorn the Declaration of Independence. Plus, it's almost twice as large as the next-biggest on the document and a whopping ten times bigger than the smallest. Why so big? "So the British Ministry can read that name without spectacles," Hancock is said to have explained. Those were bold words for a man with a hefty price on his head, but then Hancock was a bold guy.

A Harvard graduate, Hancock inherited the largest mercantile business in Boston from an uncle. Vexed by British duties and other rules regarding trade, he skirted the issue by becoming a smuggler. This move in turn vexed British authorities, who branded him a traitor and posted a hefty £500 bounty for his arrest — roughly $102,000 in 2018 dollars. In fact, one of the reasons British troops marched on Lexington and Concord on that fateful evening in 1775 was to nab Hancock and Sam Adams, who were hiding in Lexington. Paul Revere warned them in the nick of time. Hancock wanted to stay and fight, but was finally convinced that fleeing was smarter than being hanged.

During the Revolution, Hancock served as president of the Second Continental Congress. He had hoped to be put in charge of the continental army and was reportedly pretty bitter about losing out to George Washington. (He probably wasn't too happy about coming in sixth in America's first presidential election in 1789 either.) But Hancock got over it, becoming a key fundraiser for the revolutionary cause and eventually governor of Massachusetts. A major U.S. insurance company named itself after him. His name still prominently sticks out on the Declaration. And was he worried about that big price on his head? "Let them double their reward," he sneered.

I'll Trade You Six Hancocks for a Button

Quick! Name the second guy to sign the Declaration of Independence. Right! Button Gwinnett. Seriously. The delegate from Georgia. The one who died of gangrene in 1777 from a bullet wound he received in a duel with a bitter political rival. Yeah, that Button Gwinnett.

Gwinnett was a not-very-successful English-born plantation owner who moved to America in 1762. He apparently became a patriot largely because the county he lived in threatened to secede from the rest of Georgia if the colony didn't join the fight for independence. Whatever his motives, Gwinnett served in the army and the Georgia legislature and helped draft the colony's first constitution. A county near Atlanta is named for him. That's pretty much it. He's more of a Founding Uncle than a Founding Father.

Except for one thing. People who collect signatures of all 56 signatories of the Declaration of Independence — and there are such people — will pay a pretty penny for a Button Gwinnett. Why? Because only 51 are known to exist (most, apparently, on IOUs), and only 10 of those are in private hands. One of them sold in 2010 for $722,500. That's about 14 times what a really good John Hancock will cost you. By the way, the 2010 U.S. census counted 74 people with the first name Button. Not sure what their autographs are worth.

Whining — or Wining — about the Flag

Francis Hopkinson was a lawyer by profession but a designer at heart — and he had designs on some federal wine. Born in 1737 in Philadelphia, Hopkinson became one of America's first composers. During the Revolutionary War, he wrote popular satirical songs, poems, and pamphlets making fun of King George III and other British leaders. He was a Continental Congress member and signed the Declaration of Independence.

That alone would qualify him as a Founding Father. But Hopkinson also served as what was then the equivalent of Secretary of the Navy and in the Treasury Department. He also had a hand in designing U.S. currency and the Great Seal — and quite probably designed the American flag officially adopted by Congress in 1777.

In 1780, Hopkinson pointed out he had never been paid for his designs and humbly asked for "a quarter cask of the public wine." Congress demurred, so he eventually upped his price to £2,700 (about $4,000 in U.S. currency then; about $586,000 now). He got neither the wine nor the money. After months of stalling, Congress decided Hopkinson was already on the federal payroll and therefore deserved nothing extra and that others had probably helped with the designs. He did eventually get a consolation prize from President George Washington, who appointed him to the federal judicial bench in 1789.

That Betsy Ross flag story? It was based mostly on hand-me-down stories from her family, particularly a grandson, and there is no hard evidence she had anything to do with designing or making the first American flag.

A Justice in Jail

He may be one of history's lesser stars in the Founding Fathers firmament, but James Wilson does hold at least two distinctions in the group: He was the first U.S. Supreme Court Justice to die while on the high court's bench — and the first to be jailed. Not in that order.

Born in Scotland in 1742, Wilson came to America in 1766 and rose to prominence as one of the country's top legal minds. He not only signed the Declaration of Independence, but helped craft one of the key compromises in the effort to draft the Constitution, which was to count slaves as three-fifths of a person when proportionally divvying up federal aid and deciding how many representatives each state would have in Congress.

But he also had his troubles. During the war, he was suspected of hoarding supplies to drive up prices. In 1779, an angry mob attacked Wilson's house in Philadelphia where he and others, including fellow Declaration signer Robert Morris, had holed up. Before the riot was over, 5 people were dead and 17 wounded.

Later, after Wilson had been named by Washington as one of the first six U.S. Supreme Court justices, Wilson went broke in a land speculation scheme and was twice briefly jailed in a debtors' prison. At one point, he even went on the lam, fleeing to North Carolina to escape creditors — all the while remaining a Supreme Court justice. He died not only broke, but broken, in 1798.

The Little Guy on the Big Bill

If you can name the man whose likeness adorns the $5,000 bill, you're either a really dedicated currency collector — or spend waaay too much time online. For the rest of you, it's James Madison, fourth U.S. president and the smallest (5'4", about 100 lbs.) chief executive the county has ever had.

Madison was known by his contemporaries as Little Jemmy and by history as the Father of the Constitution. He was involved in virtually every aspect of drafting the document, from helping to write it to helping to sell it to the American public. Despite his diminutive size, he was one of only two presidents to be involved in an active military engagement while in office. That happened when he rode to the front lines to watch U.S. troops try to keep British forces from sacking Washington, D.C. during the War of 1812. (They failed, and Madison prudently fled.) Since you asked, the other president was Abraham Lincoln during the Civil War. Lincoln was also the tallest president. Don't you love historical symmetry?

Anyway, other things you may not know about Madison is that he was the last signer of the Constitution to die, on June 28, 1836. His doctor offered to try to keep him alive with stimulants so he could die on July 4, the same date as fellow presidents Thomas Jefferson, John Adams, and James Monroe, but Madison refused. He was 85 and figured another week wasn't a big deal.

Oh, and the $5,000 bill? It was only printed from 1928 to 1945 and used mainly to transfer payments between banks and other financial institutions. They are still legal tender, useable at mini-marts and gas stations, but if you have one, that would be one foolish expenditure: Collectors will pay as much as $300,000 for a five-grand bill in pristine condition. And I think I spend waaay too much time online. . . .

Chapter **21**

Ten Unsung Heroes of the American Revolution

t can be somewhat cynically said that politicians cause wars, generals plan them, privates fight them, and everyone else lives with the consequences.

Cynicism aside, here are quick looks at ten ordinary Americans who did extraordinary things during the American Revolution.

Joseph Plumb Martin

Joseph Plumb Martin began the Revolutionary War as a 15-year-old private from Massachusetts and ended it as a 22-year-old private. In between, Martin shivered at Valley Forge, roasted at the Battle of Monmouth, shot at people he hoped he didn't hit, and wept over the body of a friend bayoneted to death on the orders of Benjamin Franklin's Loyalist son.

Americans know all this because at the age of 70, Martin wrote a marvelous memoir he called *Private Yankee Doodle* (republished more recently as *Narrative of a Revolutionary Soldier,* published by Signet Classics). It's a remarkable story of an ordinary soldier, but one blessed with a splendid sense of humor and the quiet courage and determination that exemplified what kept the Continental Army going.

Martin did nothing particularly heroic, except persevere through incredibly trying conditions and live to tell people what it was really like to fight in the Revolutionary War: going day after day after day without adequate food, clothing, and shelter — and getting up to do it again. Come to think of it, that's pretty heroic.

"Molly Pitcher"

The name "Molly Pitcher" became the iconic composite of numerous women who followed their husbands to war, performing tasks such as fetching water, washing clothes, and nursing the sick and wounded. Several of them were also known to have fought alongside, or in place of, their husbands.

Joseph Plumb Martin (see preceding section) recorded one such incident at the Battle of Monmouth, when a woman whose husband was wounded took his place, helping to load a cannon. At one point, Martin wrote, "A cannon shot from the enemy passed directly between her legs without doing any other damage than carrying away all the lower part of her petticoat. Looking at it with apparent unconcern, she observed that it was lucky it did not pass a little higher, for in that case it might have carried away something else, and (then) continued her occupation."

Martin didn't name the woman, but she is most often identified as Mary Ludwig Hays. Impressed by her heroism, George Washington designated her a noncommissioned officer. Hays did not see action again, but was given a veteran's pension by the state of Pennsylvania before she died in 1832.

James Forten

At the age of 14, Forten joined the crew of an American privateer that was soon captured by the British navy. Most U.S. prisoners were doomed to horrific confinement in stinking prison ships anchored in New York Harbor. But Forten faced a worse fate: He was black, and even though he had been born free in Philadelphia, the British made no distinctions. Most captured African Americans were sold as slaves to the West Indies.

Forten, however, was lucky. He was befriended by the son of the British captain who had captured Forten's ship and was offered the chance to go to England. But Forten refused to repudiate his American citizenship. So instead of slavery, he was sent to a prison ship. There, he spent seven months huddled with a thousand other prisoners in a belowdecks enclosure that was less than three feet high. He was lucky again, when he was released in a prisoner exchange, whereupon he walked 100 miles home to Philadelphia.

After the war, Forten became a sailmaker. His business prospered, and he became a leading figure in the pre-Civil War abolitionist movement. In 2001, Forten was included by scholar Molefi Kete Asante as one of the 100 greatest African Americans.

Daniel Morgan

Okay, Daniel Morgan wasn't a private; he was a general. But there are at least 499 good reasons for remembering Daniel Morgan. He wore them on his back: While a member of the British Army (with his cousin, Daniel Boone) during the French and Indian War, Morgan was flogged for striking an officer. The 499-lash penalty was usually fatal, but Morgan escaped with scars and a lasting and understandable dislike of the British.

Born in New Jersey in 1736, Morgan got his nickname "Old Wagoner" from driving supply trains. When the Revolutionary War began, he formed a unit of sharpshooting frontiersman from Virginia and then marched them 600 miles in 21 days to Massachusetts without losing a man. "Morgan's Rifles" proved to be an invaluable fighting group. Often outnumbered, they used guerilla tactics, like shooting the British army's Indian guides first and then the officers. The British deemed it dishonorable; Morgan considered it effective.

Morgan rose to the rank of brigadier general and is recognized as one of the American army's best tacticians. After the war, he led federal troops to put down a rebellion against the young U.S. government and served a term in Congress. He died in 1802. And okay, he isn't completely unsung: There are statues of him in two different states and a county and national security school named after him.

Roger Sherman

You may not recognize this Founding Father's name, but it's the only one that appears on all four of what are considered America's Great State Papers: The Continental Association (which enacted a pre-Revolution boycott of British goods); the Articles of Confederation; the Declaration of Independence (which Sherman helped draft); and the U.S. Constitution.

Born in 1721, Sherman was a self-educated Connecticut lawyer and judge. He played key roles in working out the compromises that won approval for the Constitution and served in both houses of Congress before his death in 1793.

P.S.: A great-great-great grandson, Archibald Cox, would serve as a special federal prosecutor who helped bring down the presidency of Richard M. Nixon in 1973–74 — which probably would have been okay with Cox's ancestor: Sherman once said that the presidency was "nothing more than an institution for carrying the will of the Legislature into effect."

Nancy Hart

Nancy Hart was the wrong woman from whom to steal a turkey — or at least that's how the story goes. Born Nancy Ann Morgan around 1735 and a cousin of Gen. Daniel Morgan, this Georgia frontier dweller was described as a 6-foot-tall, red-haired, smallpox-scarred woman so feisty her Cherokee neighbors called her "Wahatche," or "War Woman." While her husband, Benjamin Hart, was off fighting for the American cause, Nancy Hart acted as a spy, hanging around British posts disguised as a feeble-minded man and keeping tabs on British troop movements and the activities of local Loyalists, or Tories.

The best-known story about Hart concerns a half-dozen British soldiers who confiscated a turkey from her farm and demanded she cook it for them. She complied — while quietly removing their weapons with the help of her daughter. Then she held them at gunpoint, killing one soldier and wounding another when they tried to rush her. The rest were hanged by her neighbors.

The story gained a shot of veracity in 1912, when railroad construction workers unearthed skeletal remains near what had been the Hart farm. Several of the skeletons had had their necks broken. That was good enough proof to help cement Hart's place in American Revolution history — and convince the folks in Georgia they were justified in naming a county after her — the only one of the state's 159 counties named after a woman.

Jeremiah O'Brien

Ever wonder why the United States Navy has had five different ships named after Jeremiah O'Brien? No? Well here's why anyway. Born in Maine in 1744 to a family in the lumber business, O'Brien and five of his brothers decided in early May 1775 to seize an American ship that was being forced to carry lumber for the British.

Having seized the ship, the O'Briens then led a group of their neighbors in an attack on a British navy schooner, forcing it to surrender in what is considered the first American naval victory of the Revolutionary War, even though there wasn't even an American navy yet. O'Brien later became the first captain in the Massachusetts Naval Militia. After the war, he was appointed a federal customs collector in his home port of Machias Maine.

Those U.S. Navy ships named after him? They include a torpedo boat and four destroyers. The liberty ship SS *Jeremiah O'Brien*, built in 1943 to ferry goods and troops during World War II, still floats in San Francisco Bay. And to top it off, film footage of the ship's engines was used to depict those of the doomed ocean liner *Titanic* in the 1997 film of the same name. "Titanic," not "O'Brien."

Daniel Bissell

Here's what Benedict Arnold, a woman's torn dress, and America's first military medal have in common: Daniel Bissell. Born in 1754, Bissell entered the Revolutionary War as a 22-year-old corporal from Connecticut. He served ably until August 1781, when he deserted to British-held New York City, eventually joining the British army and serving under the traitor Benedict Arnold. Only Bissell wasn't really a deserter; he was a spy.

Recruited by George Washington himself, Bissell spent 13 months in New York, suffering most of the time from a "fever" that kept him from fighting against his former comrades. He spent the time memorizing enemy positions and making maps and then found his way back to the American side with the info. For his heroics, Bissell was awarded the Badge of Military Merit, one of only three such awards given during the war.

The cloth badge was in the form of a purple heart. Although Washington was given credit for creating and awarding the badge, he apparently got the idea after Bissell accidentally tore a piece of his future wife's dress off while dancing with her at a party at which Washington was present. Bissell also served in the "Quasi War" with France, this time as an officer, and died in 1824. In 1932, the Purple Heart became the award given to those wounded or killed while in U.S. military service. Nobody gave any awards to Arnold.

Salem Poor

About six months after the Battle of Bunker Hill, 14 American officers took the time to petition the Massachusetts legislature to recognize the bravery during the battle of a soldier named Salem Poor. The petition, which was the only one of its kind after the battle, said Poor had "behaved like an Experienced Officer as Well as an Excellent Soldier." It didn't spell out exactly what he had done. But the fact he was there at all was remarkable in itself.

Salem Poor was born a slave on a Massachusetts farm in 1747. Somehow, he managed to save enough (£27, or about $6,500 in current currency) to buy his freedom at the age of 22. He joined the American cause in 1775 and reenlisted in 1776. Poor served through the Battles of Monmouth and Saratoga, and spent the miserable winter of 1777–78 with Washington's army at Valley Forge.

After the war, he had a tough go of it. Married four times, he lived for awhile in a Boston homeless shelter and was apparently run out of Providence Rhode Island for vagrancy. He died in 1802. But he did get a small measure of recognition in 1976, when the U.S. Post Office put his likeness on a 10-cent stamp to help commemorate America's Bicentennial.

Deborah Sampson

Deborah Sampson was the only woman to earn a full military pension for participation in the American Army during the Revolutionary War — and she earned it as a man. Sampson was born in 1760 near Plymouth, Massachusetts. After serving a stretch as an indentured servant, Sampson became a teacher for two years. Then in early 1782, she bound her small breasts in a linen wrap, straightened herself to her full height of 5 foot, 9 inches (some three inches taller than the average adult male), and enlisted in the army as Robert Shurtleff.

She was assigned to a light infantry unit, taking part in dangerous missions such as scouting, raiding parties, and foraging excursions. In a skirmish against a group of American Loyalists, Sherman was shot twice in the thigh. Fearful of her identity being discovered, she removed one of the musket balls herself, but the other was too deep. It remained in her leg the rest of her life.

Sherman served 17 months before she fell ill and was discovered. She was honorably discharged, eventually married a farmer, and in 1802 embarked on a year-long tour of lectures about her experiences. She began receiving a military pension from the state of Massachusetts in 1792, after waiting almost a decade. But it wasn't until 1816 that Congress finally granted her a federal pension, and that was in large part because of the intercession of a friend of hers with some pull — Paul Revere.

Sampson died in 1827. Like Jeremiah O'Brien, profiled earlier in this chapter, Sampson had a liberty ship named after her during World War II. And she got a shout-out as a history-making woman from actress Meryl Streep during Streep's speech at the 2016 Democratic National Convention.

Chapter **22**

Ten Quotes from or about the American Revolution

You could make a semi-plausible case that the German inventor Johannes Gutenberg should at least be considered a Founding Cousin. Yes, I know he died 44 years before Columbus first sailed to the Americas. But without Gutenberg's printing press, the Founding Fathers might have labored through the Revolution without one of their mightiest weapons: the printed word. Plus, it would have been tough to keep track of what they said.

So, here's a tip of the *tricorne* (that three-cornered hat they used to wear in the 18th century) to Gutenberg, along with ten profound, controversial, and/or humorous quotes from or about the American Revolution.

Or Else Just Give Us the Vote Now. . .

". . . In the new code of laws which I suppose it will be necessary for you to make, I desire you would remember the ladies and be more generous and favorable to them than your ancestors. Do not put such unlimited power into the hands of the husbands. Remember, all men would be tyrants if they could."

— ABIGAIL ADAMS TO HER HUSBAND JOHN, MARCH 31, 1776

At the time, John Adams was a delegate to the Second Continental Congress in Philadelphia. As much as he loved and cherished his wife, giving her and her gender a significant role in the new nation's government was not a high priority, or a priority at all. In fact, he wrote her back that it was a somewhat laughable notion. It would be another 144 years before the 19th amendment to the Constitution would give women in every state the right to vote.

And the Choices Are. . .

"Gentlemen may cry, 'Peace, Peace' but there is no peace. The war is actually begun! . . . The next gale that sweeps from the north will bring to our ears the clash of resounding arms! . . . Is life so dear, or peace so sweet, as to be purchased at the price of chains and slavery? Forbid it, Almighty God! I know not what course others may take; but as for me, give me liberty or give me death!"

— PATRICK HENRY, MARCH 23, 1775

Nearly every American kid who took eighth-grade U.S. history is at least somewhat familiar with Henry's dramatic speech before a meeting of Virginians trying to decide whether to take up arms and be ready to fight the British. But whether he ever said this is uncertain. There is no written text. In fact, the preceding quote was recorded years after Henry's death, by a biographer who cobbled it together from the recollections of those who heard Henry speak.

But whatever Henry's exact words were, the speech is generally credited with helping to convince Virginians in the audience that the coming fight was worth the risks. Which was probably a good thing, since Henry's audience that day included George Washington and Thomas Jefferson.

Sorry to Disappoint You, But. . .

"I had rather vote away the Enjoyment of (popularity) than the Blood and Happiness of my Countrymen . . . I had rather they should hate Me than that I should hurt them . . . (We) are Destroying a House before We have got another."
— THOMAS DICKINSON, NOTES FOR A SPEECH OPPOSING INDEPENDENCE, JULY 1, 1776

At the Second Continental Congress, Dickinson, an affluent and eloquent Philadelphia lawyer, argued against declaring independence saying it was premature to cut ties with Britain. He later abstained from voting on the independence resolution and declined to sign the Declaration of Independence. But he nonetheless fought in the Pennsylvania militia during the war, served as the first president of the state of Pennsylvania, and was a delegate to the Constitutional Convention.

Uh, Are You Sure, Your Majesty?

"Nothing important happened today."
— ENTRY IN THE JOURNAL OF KING GEORGE III, JULY 4, 1776

News traveled pretty slowly in those days. Or maybe the king meant nothing important happened in England on July 4, 1776. Or maybe he just didn't want to get anything for the 13 American colonies being born as a new nation. . . .

Take My Advice and Scram

"Go home sir, and endeavor to save the ruins of your ruined country . . . you are fighting for what you will never obtain, and we (are) defending what we mean never to part with . . . Let England mind her business and we will mind ours."
— THOMAS PAINE TO BRITISH GEN. SIR WILLIAM HOWE, IN "THE AMERICAN CRISIS, NO. 5," MARCH 21, 1778

In a series of 16 pamphlets, Paine wrote what were basically pep talks to keep up the spirits of Americans during the darkest days of the Revolutionary War. In this one, which he addressed to Britain's top commander, Paine mockingly saluted Howe on Howe's recent knighthood and suggested America couldn't wait to give him a fitting funeral.

"Except Us. . ."

". . . The horrors and devastations of war (were) happily terminated, and peace was restored between America and Great Britain, which diffused universal joy among all parties, except us. . .".
— BOSTON KING, A FORMER SLAVE, WRITING IN A LONDON MAGAZINE IN 1798.

King escaped from a South Carolina plantation and fled to the British Army, where he became an officer's servant and eventually was taken to New York City. When the war ended and American slave owners began hunting their former property, he fled to Nova Scotia and then to England, where he became a Methodist minister.

A Stimulated Simile

"A standing army is like an erect penis — an excellent assurance of domestic tranquility, but a dangerous temptation to foreign adventure."
— ELBRIDGE GERRY, 1787

Gerry, a Massachusetts delegate to the Constitutional Convention, was arguing against a proposal to allow for a full-time federal military. The delegates agreed to limit military funding to two years at a time and have Congress maintain control over its budget.

Keeping One's Feet Dry

"Monarchy is like a merchantman, which sails well, but will sometimes strike a rock, and go to the bottom, whilst a republic is a raft, which would never sink, but your feet are always wet."
— FISHER AMES, 1783

Ames was a Massachusetts lawyer and member of the first U.S. House of Representatives. He disliked the idea of a monarchy, but was leery of a government too reliant on popular opinion.

Looks Good So Far, But. . .

"Our Constitution is in actual operation, and everything appears to promise that it will last, but in this world, nothing can be said to be certain but death and taxes."

— BENJAMIN FRANKLIN, IN A LETTER TO FRENCH PHYSICIST
JEAN-BAPTISTE LE ROY, NOV. 13, 1789

The Constitution has lasted. Then again, so have death and taxes.

A Term of Endurance

"Standing in this presence, mindful of the solemnity of this occasion, feeling the emotions which no one may know until he senses the great weight of responsibility for himself, I must utter my belief in the divine inspiration of the founding fathers. Surely there must have been God's intent in the making of this new-world Republic."

— FROM THE MARCH 4, 1921, INAUGURAL ADDRESS OF PRESIDENT
WARREN G. HARDING

An affable fellow and a really terrible president, Harding is credited with coining the term Founding Fathers, or at least popularizing it to the point that it stuck in the American lexicon.

He actually used it first in his July 12 1920, speech accepting the Republican presidential nomination. In that speech, however, he used it to claim the Founding Fathers designed the U.S. governmental system so that political parties would be *"The effective agencies through which hopes and aspirations and convictions and conscience may be translated into public performance."*

If that's the case, someone should go back and check those blueprints again.

Appendixes

Appendix A

The Declaration of Independence

N CONGRESS, July 4, 1776.

The unanimous Declaration of the thirteen united States of America,

When in the Course of human events, it becomes necessary for one people to dissolve the political bands which have connected them with another, and to assume among the powers of the earth, the separate and equal station to which the Laws of Nature and of Nature's God entitle them, a decent respect to the opinions of mankind requires that they should declare the causes which impel them to the separation.

We hold these truths to be self-evident, that all men are created equal, that they are endowed by their Creator with certain unalienable Rights, that among these are Life, Liberty and the pursuit of Happiness. — That to secure these rights, Governments are instituted among Men, deriving their just powers from the consent of the governed, — That whenever any Form of Government becomes destructive of these ends, it is the Right of the People to alter or to abolish it, and to institute new Government, laying its foundation on such principles and organizing its powers in such form, as to them shall seem most likely to effect their Safety and Happiness. Prudence, indeed, will dictate that Governments long established should not be changed for light and transient causes; and accordingly all experience hath shewn, that mankind are more disposed to suffer, while evils are sufferable, than to right themselves by abolishing the forms to which they are accustomed. But when a long train of abuses and usurpations, pursuing invariably the same Object evinces a design to reduce them under absolute Despotism, it is their right, it is their duty, to throw off such Government, and to provide new Guards for their future security. — Such has been the patient sufferance of these Colonies; and such is now the necessity which constrains them to alter their former Systems of Government. The history of the present King of Great Britain is a history of repeated injuries and usurpations, all having in direct object the establishment of an absolute Tyranny over these States. To prove this, let Facts be submitted to a candid world.

He has refused his Assent to Laws, the most wholesome and necessary for the public good. He has forbidden his Governors to pass Laws of immediate and press-ing importance, unless suspended in their operation till his Assent should be obtained; and when so suspended, he has utterly neglected to attend to them. He has refused to pass other Laws for the accommodation of large districts of people, unless those people would relinquish the right of Representation in the Legisla-ture, a right inestimable to them and formidable to tyrants only. He has called together legislative bodies at places unusual, uncomfortable, and distant from the depository of their public Records, for the sole purpose of fatiguing them into compliance with his measures. He has dissolved Representative Houses repeat-edly, for opposing with manly firmness his invasions on the rights of the people. He has refused for a long time, after such dissolutions, to cause others to be elected; whereby the Legislative powers, incapable of Annihilation, have returned to the People at large for their exercise; the State remaining in the mean time exposed to all the dangers of invasion from without, and convulsions within.

He has endeavoured to prevent the population of these States; for that purpose obstructing the Laws for Naturalization of Foreigners; refusing to pass others to encourage their migrations hither, and raising the conditions of new Appropria-tions of Lands. He has obstructed the Administration of Justice, by refusing his Assent to Laws for establishing Judiciary powers. He has made Judges dependent on his Will alone, for the tenure of their offices, and the amount and payment of their salaries.

He has erected a multitude of New Offices, and sent hither swarms of Officers to harrass our people, and eat out their substance. He has kept among us, in times of peace, Standing Armies without the Consent of our legislatures. He has affected to render the Military independent of and superior to the Civil power. He has com-bined with others to subject us to a jurisdiction foreign to our constitution, and unacknowledged by our laws; giving his Assent to their Acts of pretended Legislation:

For Quartering large bodies of armed troops among us: For protecting them, by a mock Trial, from punishment for any Murders which they should commit on the Inhabitants of these States: For cutting off our Trade with all parts of the world: For imposing Taxes on us without our Consent: For depriving us in many cases, of the benefits of Trial by Jury: For transporting us beyond Seas to be tried for pretended offences: For abolishing the free System of English Laws in a neighbouring Province, establishing therein an Arbitrary government, and enlarging its Boundaries so as to render it at once an example and fit instrument for introducing the same absolute rule into these Colonies: For taking away our Charters, abolishing our most valuable Laws, and altering fundamentally the Forms of our Governments: For suspending our own Legislatures, and declaring themselves invested with power to legislate for us in all cases whatsoever.

He has abdicated Government here, by declaring us out of his Protection and waging War against us. He has plundered our seas, ravaged our Coasts, burnt our towns, and destroyed the lives of our people. He is at this time transporting large Armies of foreign Mercenaries to compleat the works of death, desolation and tyranny, already begun with circumstances of Cruelty & perfidy scarcely paralleled in the most barbarous ages, and totally unworthy the Head of a civilized nation.

He has constrained our fellow Citizens taken Captive on the high Seas to bear Arms against their Country, to become the executioners of their friends and Brethren, or to fall themselves by their Hands. He has excited domestic insurrections amongst us, and has endeavoured to bring on the inhabitants of our frontiers, the merciless Indian Savages, whose known rule of warfare, is an undistinguished destruction of all ages, sexes and conditions.

In every stage of these Oppressions We have Petitioned for Redress in the most humble terms: Our repeated Petitions have been answered only by repeated injury. A Prince whose character is thus marked by every act which may define a Tyrant, is unfit to be the ruler of a free people.

Nor have We been wanting in attentions to our Brittish brethren. We have warned them from time to time of attempts by their legislature to extend an unwarrantable jurisdiction over us. We have reminded them of the circumstances of our emigration and settlement here. We have appealed to their native justice and magnanimity, and we have conjured them by the ties of our common kindred to disavow these usurpations, which, would inevitably interrupt our connections and correspondence. They too have been deaf to the voice of justice and of consanguinity. We must, therefore, acquiesce in the necessity, which denounces our Separation, and hold them, as we hold the rest of mankind, Enemies in War, in Peace Friends.

We, therefore, the Representatives of the united States of America, in General Congress, Assembled, appealing to the Supreme Judge of the world for the rectitude of our intentions, do, in the Name, and by Authority of the good People of these Colonies, solemnly publish and declare, That these United Colonies are, and of Right ought to be Free and Independent States; that they are Absolved from all Allegiance to the British Crown, and that all political connection between them and the State of Great Britain, is and ought to be totally dissolved; and that as Free and Independent States, they have full Power to levy War, conclude Peace, contract Alliances, establish Commerce, and to do all other Acts and Things which Independent States may of right do. And for the support of this Declaration, with a firm reliance on the protection of divine Providence, we mutually pledge to each other our Lives, our Fortunes and our sacred Honor.

(Signed) John Hancock, Button Gwinnett, Lyman Hall, George Walton, William Hooper, Joseph Hewes, John Penn, Edward Rutledge, Thomas Heyward, Jr., Thomas Lynch, Jr., Arthur Middleton, Samuel Chase, William Paca, Thomas Stone, Charles Carroll of Carrollton, George Wythe, Richard Henry Lee, Thomas Jefferson, Benjamin Harrison, Thomas Nelson, Jr., Francis Lightfoot Lee, Carter Braxton, Robert Morris, Benjamin Rush, Benjamin Franklin, John Morton, George Clymer, James Smith, George Taylor, James Wilson, George Ross, Caesar Rodney, George Read, Thomas McKean, William Floyd, Philip Livingston, Francis Lewis, Lewis Morris, Richard Stockton, John Witherspoon, Francis Hopkinson, John Hart, Abraham Clark, Josiah Bartlett, William Whipple, Samuel Adams, John Adams, Robert Treat Paine, Elbridge Gerry, Stephen Hopkins, William Ellery, Roger Sherman, Samuel Huntington, William Williams, Oliver Wolcott, Matthew Thornton

Appendix **B**

The Bill of Rights: Amendments 1–10 of the Constitution

The Conventions of a number of the States having, at the time of adopting the Constitution, expressed a desire, in order to prevent misconstruction or abuse of its powers, that further declaratory and restrictive clauses should be added, and as extending the ground of public confidence in the Government will best insure the beneficent ends of its institution;

Resolved, by the Senate and House of Representatives of the United States of America, in Congress assembled, two-thirds of both Houses concurring, that the following articles be proposed to the Legislatures of the several States, as amendments to the Constitution of the United States; all or any of which articles, when ratified by three-fourths of the said Legislatures, to be valid to all intents and purposes as part of the said Constitution, namely:

Amendment I

Congress shall make no law respecting an establishment of religion, or prohibiting the free exercise thereof; or abridging the freedom of speech, or of the press;

or the right of the people peaceably to assemble, and to petition the government for a redress of grievances.

Amendment II

A well-regulated militia, being necessary to the security of a free state, the right of the people to keep and bear arms, shall not be infringed.

Amendment III

No soldier shall, in time of peace be quartered in any house, without the consent of the owner, nor in time of war, but in a manner to be prescribed by law.

Amendment IV

The right of the people to be secure in their persons, houses, papers, and effects, against unreasonable searches and seizures, shall not be violated, and no warrants shall issue, but upon probable cause, supported by oath or affirmation, and particularly describing the place to be searched, and the persons or things to be seized.

Amendment V

No person shall be held to answer for a capital, or otherwise infamous crime, unless on a presentment or indictment of a grand jury, except in cases arising in the land or naval forces, or in the militia, when in actual service in time of war or public danger; nor shall any person be subject for the same offense to be twice put in jeopardy of life or limb; nor shall be compelled in any criminal case to be a witness against himself, nor be deprived of life, liberty, or property, without due process of law; nor shall private property be taken for public use, without just compensation.

Amendment VI

In all criminal prosecutions, the accused shall enjoy the right to a speedy and public trial, by an impartial jury of the state and district wherein the crime shall have been committed, which district shall have been previously ascertained by law, and to be informed of the nature and cause of the accusation; to be confronted with the witnesses against him; to have compulsory process for obtaining witnesses in his favor, and to have the assistance of counsel for his defense.

Amendment VII

In suits at common law, where the value in controversy shall exceed twenty dollars, the right of trial by jury shall be preserved, and no fact tried by a jury, shall be otherwise reexamined in any court of the United States, than according to the rules of the common law.

Amendment VIII

Excessive bail shall not be required, nor excessive fines imposed, nor cruel and unusual punishments inflicted.

Amendment IX

The enumeration in the Constitution, of certain rights, shall not be construed to deny or disparage others retained by the people.

Amendment X

The powers not delegated to the United States by the Constitution, nor prohibited by it to the states, are reserved to the states respectively, or to the people.

Appendix C

Key Events of the American Revolution

July 10, 1754: Delegates from several colonies meeting at Albany New York agree to the formation of a permanent union for purposes of mutual defense, expansion to the west, and dealing with Native Americans. Colonial assemblies, however, reject the plan.

Feb. 10, 1763: The Treaty of Paris goes into effect, ending the French and Indian War. Britain gets all of Canada, all of America east of the Mississippi River, Florida, and some Caribbean islands. It cements Britain's place as the most powerful nation in the world.

March 22, 1765: Parliament passes the Stamp Act, requiring government-issued paper stamps or prestamped paper for almost all legal documents as well as everything printed on paper. The act is bitterly resented and all but ignored in the American colonies.

Nov. 1, 1768: British troops arrive in Boston in an effort to quell civil disturbances.

March 5, 1770: The Boston Massacre occurs when British troops fire on a crowd in a Boston street. Five citizens are killed and six wounded. The incident inflames resentment among Americans about the presence of British troops.

Dec. 16, 1773: The Boston Tea Party takes place when men wearing Native American disguises board three British ships in Boston Harbor and dump hundreds of pounds of tea into the water, as a protest to British duties imposed on the tea. The action outrages British officials, who retaliate by closing Boston Harbor to all shipping.

Sept. 5, 1774: The First Continental Congress begins meeting in Philadelphia. Delegates endorse a boycott of British goods and agree to meet again in May 1775 if things aren't better.

April 19, 1775: American militia clash with British troops at the Massachusetts towns of Lexington and Concord, marking the beginning of the American Revolutionary War.

May 10, 1775: The Second Continental Congress convenes at Philadelphia.

Jan. 10, 1776: Thomas Paine publishes *Common Sense,* a pamphlet urging the colonies to break free from British dominance. The pamphlet becomes a huge best-seller.

July 4, 1776: The Second Continental Congress approves the *Declaration of Independence.*

Aug. 27, 1776: American forces under Gen. George Washington are routed at the Battle of Long Island. Washington narrowly escapes capture and is eventually forced to retreat into Pennsylvania.

Dec, 25–26, 1776: In a daring move, Washington crosses the ice-choked Delaware River on Christmas night and surprises a force of German mercenary soldiers at Trenton, New Jersey. The victory, along with another win a few days later at Princeton, are huge boosts to flagging American morale.

Oct. 17, 1777: More than 5,000 British troops surrender at Saratoga, New York. The U.S. victory sparks Congress to pass the Articles of Confederation, creating a new U.S. government.

Feb. 6, 1778: Impressed by the victory at Saratoga, France formally recognizes the United States of America as an independent nation and agrees to join forces against Britain.

Jan. 17, 1781: American troops smash a British force at the Battle of Cowpens in South Carolina, thanks to a clever ruse by Gen. Daniel Morgan.

Oct. 19, 1781: A large British force under the command of Gen. Charles Cornwallis, hemmed in by U.S. and French forces at Yorktown, Virginia, surrenders. The victory effectively ends the American Revolutionary War, in America anyway.

Sept. 3, 1783: Spain, France, and America sign separate peace treaties with Britain in Paris. Final ratification of the treaties is completed by May 1784.

Dec. 23, 1783: George Washington resigns his commission as commander in chief of the American army, giving up the opportunity to assume any role as a de facto U.S. monarch.

Sept. 17, 1787: A convention of delegates approves a new constitution for the United States. In July 1788, New Hampshire becomes the ninth state to ratify the document, which goes into effect March 4, 1789.

Feb. 4, 1789: George Washington becomes the first U.S. president.

Dec. 15, 1791: Virginia ratifies the Bill of Rights, thus putting the first ten amendments to the U.S. Constitution into effect.

July 7, 1798: America begins an undeclared, or *quasi,* war with France, over unpaid Revolutionary War debts and what amounted to the solicitation of a bribe by French officials to open negotiations. The "war" ends in September 1800.

July 14, 1798: Congress passes the Sedition Act, which makes it a crime to print or voice remarks about the federal government or federal officials that are deemed "malicious." Fourteen individuals, all of them members of the Democratic-Republican Party and most of them journalists, are jailed under the act. The act becomes a major issue in the presidential election of 1800 and helps lead to the election of Thomas Jefferson. The new president pardons those convicted under the act.

March 4, 1801: Thomas Jefferson, the Democratic-Republican Party candidate, becomes the third U.S. president, succeeding Federalist Party presidents Washington and John Adams. Jefferson's assumption of office is significant, among other reasons, for marking a peaceful transition of power from one political party to another.

Index

C

cabinet, 267–269

Cabot, John, 22

Cabrillo, Juan, 20

Callender, James, 293

Calvert, George, 46

Calvin, John, 15

Calvinism, 15

Camden, South Carolina, 152

camp fever, 139

Canada, 300, 341

caravels, 18

Caribbean Islands, 206, 341

Carleton, Guy, 172, 196

Carlos I (king of Spain), 23

Carpenter's Hall, 114

Cartier, Jacques, 21

casinos, 54

Catherine the Great (empress of Russia), 128, 169

Catholic Church, 14–15, 22, 24

Cavaliers, 60

Cayuga, 78

Champlain, Samuel de, 22

Charles I (king of England), 36, 46, 60

Charles II (king of England), 48, 61, 65, 104

Charles III (king of Spain), 167

Charleston, South Carolina, 152, 163, 196

Cherokee Indians, 205

Chesapeake Bay, 154

chief justice, 271–272

Chile, 300

Church of England (Anglican Church), 22, 37, 42, 93–94

circuit courts, 270

circumnavigation, 20

city-states, 14

clergymen, salaries of, 92–93

Clinton, Bill, 17

Clinton, George, 250, 280

Clinton, Henry, 120, 149, 163, 169, 206, 213

Cobbett, William, 313

Coercive Acts, 112, 115

Collins, James, 175, 179, 192

colonies

colonizing for religion and profit, 29–31

currencies, 72

dates of establishment, 59

economic goals, 70–71

England's salutary neglect of, 59–61

government, 73–74

Jamestown, 31–36

Massachusetts Bay Colony, 41–43

opinion of average Britons on, 159

overview, 8, 9–11

Pennsylvania, 47

Plymouth, 38–40

population, 68–69

religion, 43–46, 75–77

slave trade, 69–70

standard of living, 72–73

taxes, 158

trade laws, 71–72

Columbus, Christopher, 18–19, 23

Committee of 11, Constitutional Convention, 235

Committee of Detail, Constitutional Convention, 235

Committee of Postponed Parts, Constitutional Convention, 235

Committee of Style, Constitutional Convention, 235

committees of correspondence, 99

common law, 270

Common Sense (Paine), 127–128, 144, 160, 227, 342

communications lines, British problems, 163

Conceived in Liberty (Rothbard), 306

Conciliatory Resolution, 115

Concord, Battle of, 117–118, 119, 159, 314, 342

Concord Hymn, 118

conditional ratification, 254

Confederation Congress, 209, 236, 249–250, 256

Confederation of the United Colonies of New England, 56

Congregational Church, 42

Congress of the Confederation, 203, 237–251

Connecticut

Confederation of the United Colonies of New England, 56

duties on goods, 206

gradual manumission laws, 241

Loyalists in, 177

neighbor-against-neighbor conflicts, 175, 177

presidential election in 1796, 285

quarrels with other colonies, 57

ratification of Constitution, 253

slavery law, 184

Connecticut Plan, 239–240

conquistadores, 20

Industrial Revolution, 174

inferior courts, 269

inferior tribunals, 236

inflation, 189–190, 199

Innocent III (pope), 16

Intolerable Acts, 112

Irish immigrants, 291

Iroquois Confederacy, 78, 82, 150, 187–188

Isabella I (queen of Spain), 18, 19

Isle of Wright, 170

J

Jackson, Andrew, 133, 185

Jackson, Elizabeth, 185

Jackson, William, 246

James I (king of England), 23, 26, 29–30, 36, 37, 46, 60

James II (king of England), 63, 79

Jameson, John Franklin, 246

Jamestown, 31–36, 214

James-Towne weed, 66

Jay, John. *See also* Founding Fathers

background, 212, 222–224

First Continental Congress, 114

as Founding Father, 222–224

Jay Treaty, 288–289

quotes from, 279–280

resignation as chief justice, 271

resumé, 222

role in 1800 presidential election, 295

on slavery, 215

Treaty of Paris, 173

votes in first presidential election, 260

Jay Treaty, 288–289

Jefferson, Thomas. *See also* Founding Fathers

on Alexander Hamilton, 285–286

background, 212, 224–225, 278–279

bears, 312–313

on Coercive Acts, 113

Constitutional Convention, 233–234

on creation of bank, 277

Declaration of Independence, 130–131

drinking, 217

election as president, 295–296, 343

as Founding Father, 224–225

on George Washington's resignation, 199

inaugural address, 303

inauguration as president, 296–297

on insurrection, 66

"jawbone" of, 293–294

on King George III, 160

on Marbury v. Madison, 273–274

Northwest Territory proposal, 204

on public debt, 275

quotes from, 1, 66, 199

resumé, 224

Second Continental Congress, 124

on slavery, 181, 215

Virginia and Kentucky Resolutions, 294

on Washington's presidency, 267

Jenifer, Daniel, 171

Jenkins, Robert, 80

Jeremiah O'Brien (ship), 323

Jimson weed, 66

John (king of England), 16

Johnson, Samuel, 95, 97

Johnson, William, 187

joint-stock companies, 26

Jones, John Paul, 151–152, 172

judicial review, 273

Judiciary Act of 1789, 269

K

Kalb, Johan de, 166

Kentucky, 173, 284

Kerber, Linda, 185

key events, 341–343

King, Boston, 328

King George's War, 80–81

King James Bible, 30

King Philip (Native American chief). *See* Metacom

King Philip's War, 55–56

Kings Mountain, Battle of, 179

King William's War, 79

Knopf, Alfred, 213

Knox, Henry, 124, 140, 198, 261, 268

Koch, James, 313

L

Lafayette, Marie-Joseph-Paul-Yves-Roch-Gilbert du Motier du, 166, 172, 188, 197, 201

Land Ordinance of 1785, 204

Laud, William, 41, 60

Laurens, Henry, 169

Lavoisier, Antoine-Laurent de, 165

Lawes, Divine, Moral and Martiall, 33

leadership, British problems, 163

League of Armed Neutrality, 169

learning, 293

Lee, Arthur, 165

Lee, Charles, 139, 149

Lee, Richard Henry, 130, 250, 251

Le Havre, 170

L'Enfant, Pierre Charles, 257

Lennox, Charles, 160

Leo X (pope), 24

McCullough, David
    1776, 307
McGillivray, Alexander, 188
Mechant's Exchange, 270
Melville, Herman, 54
Mennonites, 177
Menorca, 170
mercantilism, 70
merchant class, 14
Metacom, 55
Mexico, 168, 300
Michigan, 204
Middle Ages, 14
midnight judges, 273
military drafts, 176
Minden, Battle of, 162
Minorca, 168
Minute Men, 116, 137, 313
Mississippi, 173
Mississippi River, 288
Mittelberger, Gottlieb, 76
Mobile, 170
Moby Dick (Melville), 54
Mohawk, 78
molasses, 98–99
"Molly Pitcher", 320
money supply, 189–190
Monmouth, Battle of, 320
Monmouth Courthouse, 149
Monroe, James, 250, 254, 258
Montgomery, Richard, 122–123, 138
Moors, 18
Moravians, 177
Morgan, Daniel, 147, 321, 342
Morgan, Joseph Plumb, 149
Morgan, Nancy Ann, 322
Morgan's Rifles, 321
Morris, Gouverneur, 240, 242, 246–247
Morris, Robert, 189, 200–202, 268, 317

Morris Note, 202
Morrison, Samuel Eliot, 40
Morristown mutiny, 190–191
Mount Vernon plantation, 182, 207, 312
Mullins, William, 38, 40
Murray, John (Lord Dunmore), 123
Murray, William (Earl of Mansfield), 97
Murray, William Vans, 290
Mysore, 168, 171

N

Narragansett Bay, 171
Narragansett tribe, 53, 55
Narrative of a Revolutionary Soldier (Martin), 319
Natchez, 170
National Archives, 17, 133, 246
national debt, 95, 274, 278
National Gazette, 279
nationalists, 208, 232
National Legislature, 236
nation-states, 16
Native Americans
    aftermath of American Revolution, 188
    casino, 54
    colonial relations with, 49–50
    Creek Indians, 113, 205
    Iroquois Confederacy, 78, 82, 150, 187–188
    King Philip's War, 55–56
    land ownership, 50
    Narragansett tribe, 53, 55
    neutrality of, 187
    Onandaga tribe, 150
    Opechancanough, 51
    overview, 8
    Pequots, 53–54
    Pocahontas, 32

Pontiac's War, 90
Powhatan, 32, 50–51
Seneca Indians, 78, 81
Virginia wars, 50–52
Wampanoag, 40, 54–55
Naturalization Act, 292
natural rights, 204
Navigation Acts, 61
navigation rights, Mississippi River, 173
Ndongo, 34
negars, 34
Nehru, Jawaharlal, 174
neighbor-against-neighbor conflicts, 175–178
Netherlands, 48, 57
New Amsterdam, 48, 62
Newburgh conspiracy, 191
New Deal, 269–270, 280
New England, 56–57
Newfoundland, 21, 173
New France, 22, 25
New Hampshire
    Constitutional Convention delegates, 234
    Dominion of New England, 63
    gradual manumission laws, 241
    presidential election in 1796, 285
    protests and riots, 209
    ratification of Constitution, 254, 343
    seats in House of Representatives, 242
New Hampshire Gazette, 234
New Haven, 56, 57
New Jersey, 206, 208, 253
New Jersey Plan, 238
newspapers, 58
New World, 18–23

gradual manumission
laws, 241

opposition to Constitution,
252

presidential election in
1796, 285

ratification of Constitution,
256

religious freedom, 46

Richard I (king of England), 17

right of habeus corpus, 204

rights, 204, 337–339

rights in civil cases (Seventh
Amendment), 339

rights of accused persons
in criminal cases (Sixth
Amendment), 338

Rights of Man, The (Paine),
227

right to bear arms (Second
Amendment), 338

Robertson, James, 179

Rochambeau, Jean-Baptiste
Donatien de Vimeur,
171, 205

Rodney, Caesar, 132

Rogues Island. *See* Rhode
Island

Rolfe, John, 33–34

Roman Empire, 157

Roosevelt, Franklin, 269–270

Ross, Betsy, 316

Rothbard. Murray
Conceived in Liberty, 306

Rotunda for Charters of
Freedom, 133, 246

Roundheads, 60

Royalists, 60

Rubenstein, David M., 17

rum, 23

Rush, Benjamin, 1–2, 180,
217, 304

Russia, 169

Russian Revolution, 302

Rutledge, Edward, 114, 143

Rutledge, John, 241, 243, 271

S

Saint-Dominique, 291, 300

Saints, 37

Salem, 112

salutary neglect, 59

Sampson, Deborah, 323

Samuel Adams Boston
Lager, 313

Sandys, George, 35, 36, 38

Saratoga, Battle of, 147–148,
167, 300, 342

Savannah, Georgia, 152,
163, 196

scalps, 150

Schuyler, Philip, 122, 139

Schweikart, Larry
*A Patriot's History of the United
States*, 306

Scott, William, 192

Second Amendment, 338

Second Continental Congress,
122, 124, 315, 326, 342

secularism, 15–16

Sedition Act, 292, 294, 343

seditionists, 291–294

Senate, 237, 256–257

Seneca Indians, 78, 81

Separatists, 37

Serapis (ship), 151

1776 (McCullough), 307

Seventh Amendment, 339

Seven Years War, 81

Sewall, Samuel, 75

Shakers, 177

Shakespeare, William, 313

Shallus, Jacob, 246

Sharp, Granville, 97

Shays, Daniel, 208–209

Sherman, Roger. *See also*
Founding Fathers
background, 228–229
Bill of Rights, 259
Connecticut Plan, 239
Constitutional Convention, 234

Declaration of Independence,
130–131

as Founding Father, 228–229,
321–322

quotes from, 322

resumé, 228

as signer of all four
documents, 216

ships, 151–152

Shorto, Russell
*Revolution Song: The story of
America's founding in six
remarkable lives*, 306

Sierra Leone, 183

sinking fund, 274

Six Nations, 78

Sixth Amendment, 338

slavery/slaves
anti-slavery, 215
Catholic Church and, 24–25
Constitutional Convention,
241–243
cost, 69
Ethiopian Brigade, 123, 182
fighting for the American side,
181–182
Founding Fathers on,
214–216
gradual manumission
laws, 241
in Jamestown, 34–35
laws, 97
overview, 9
population, 69
prohibition of, 204
rebellion, 70
recognition as problem,
214–215
serving on the British side,
182–183
slave states, 216
slave trade, 242–243
in Spanish colonies, 24–25
state laws, 184
three-fifths of a human,
241–242

Smith, John, 31–32

Smith, William, 206

Sons of Liberty, 101, 109

South Carolina
  abolition in, 214
  Declaration of
    Independence, 132
  presidential election in
    1796, 285
  protests and riots, 209
  ratification of Constitution, 254
  slave trade in, 243
  war debts, 275

Spain
  disputed territories, ceding of,
    288–289
  Great Invasion of 1779, 170
  New World exploration, 20
  peace treaty with Britain, 174
  relations with U.S., 205
  Spanish Empire, 20
  supplies for American army,
    167–168

Spanish Armada, 170

Squanto, 40

St, Malo, 170

Stamp Act, 100–102, 341

Standiford, Les
  *Desperate Sons: Samuel Adams,
    Patrick Henry, John Hancock
    and the secret bands of
    radicals who led the colonies
    to war*, 307

Starving Time, 32–33

State House Speech, 253

Stewart, Charles, 97

Stimson, Henry L., 229

Stoddard, Samuel, 50

Strangers, 39

Streep, Meryl, 324

St. Vincent, 170

Suffolk Resolves, 115

sugar, 23

Sugar Act, 98–99, 100

sugar cane, 23

Sullivan, John, 150

sunshine patriots, 145

Superintendent of Finance, 200

supply lines, British
  problems, 163

Supreme Court, 269–270, 271

supreme tribunals, 236

Sweden, 169, 288

T

Talleyrand, Charles Maurice de,
  289–290

taxation
  on American colonists, 158
  excise taxes, 274
  on imported goods (imposts),
    201–202
  on molasses, 98–99
  repeal of, 172
  slave trade and, 242–243
  stamps, 100–101
  on tea, 101
  on whiskey, 276–277
  without representation, 96

tea, 104

Tea Act of 1773, 110, 111

tenant forming, 215

Tennessee, 173, 205, 284

Tenth Amendment, 339

Thanksgiving, 65

Thayendanegea (Mohawk
  leader), 187

theory of nullification, 294

*These Truths: A History of the
  United States* (Lepore), 306

Third Amendment, 338

Thirteenth Amendment,
  301–302

Thirty Years War, 16

tobacco, 23, 33–34

Tocqueville, Alexis de, 94

Toleration Act (1649), 46

Tories. *See* Loyalists

Townshend, Charles, 96–97,
  102

Townshend Acts, 102, 105, 109

Treaty of Paris, 341

Treaty of Tordesillas, 20

Trenton, New Jersey, 145, 342

Triangular Trade, 70

tricorne, 325

Trumbull, John, 199

Trump, Donald, 213

Tuscarora, 78

Twain, Mark, 228

Twelfth Amendment, 286

Twentyseventh
  Amendment, 260

U

undelegated powers kept by
  the states and the people
  (Tenth Amendment), 339

unsung heroes of American
  Revolution
  Bissell, Daniel, 323
  Forten, James, 320–321
  Hart, Nancy, 322
  Martin, Joseph Plumb,
    319–320
  "Molly Pitcher", 320
  Morgan, Daniel, 321
  O'Brien, Jeremiah, 322–323
  Poor, Salem, 323–324
  Sampson, Deborah, 323
  Sherman, Roger, 321–322

women in American Revolution, 184–186, 320, 322, 324

world wars, 79–81

writ of habeus corpus, 97

writs of assistance, 92

Wycliffe, John, 15

Wyoming Valley, 150

Y

Yeardley, George, 36

Yorktown, surrender of, 154–155, 343

Z

Zenger, John Peter, 75

Zinn, Howard, 306

About the Author

Steve Wiegand is an award-winning journalist and history writer. His 35-year journalism career was spent at the *San Diego Evening Tribune,* where he was chief political writer; *San Francisco Chronicle,* where he was state capitol bureau chief; and *Sacramento Bee,* where he was a special projects writer and politics columnist.

Wiegand is the author, coauthor, or contributing author of eight books, including *U.S. History For Dummies* (Wiley), which is currently in its fourth edition and has been published in both Chinese and German; *Lessons from the Great Depression For Dummies* (Wiley); the *Mental Floss History of the World* (Collins); and *Papers of Permanence* (McClatchy). His latest book, *The Dancer, the Dreamers and the Queen of Romania* (Bancroft), will be released in February 2020.

He is a graduate of Santa Clara University, with a bachelor's degree in American history and literature, and has a master's degree in mass communications from San Jose State University.

He lives in Arizona.

Dedication

To Ceil and Erin, who have made my life a revelation and a revolution.

Author's Acknowledgments

A big thank-you to Project Editor Kelly Ewing, Technical Editor Troy Guthrie, and Executive Editor Lindsay Lefevere. Everything right about this book is the doing of these folks, the goofs are the doing of yours truly.

Finally, thanks to my mom for having given me the inspiration to read books, so I could someday write them, and to my dad for giving me the sense of humor not to take it — or myself — too seriously along the way.

Publisher's Acknowledgments

Executive Editor: Lindsay Lefevere
Project Editor: Kelly Ewing
Technical Editor: Troy Guthrie
Editorial Assistant: Matthew Lowe
Sr. Editorial Assistant: Cherie Case
Proofreader: Debbye Butler

Production Editor: Siddique Shaik
Cover Image: © kreicher/iStock.com

Leverage the power

Dummies is the global leader in the reference category and one of the most trusted and highly regarded brands in the world. No longer just focused on books, customers now have access to the dummies content they need in the format they want. Together we'll craft a solution that engages your customers, stands out from the competition, and helps you meet your goals.

Advertising & Sponsorships

Connect with an engaged audience on a powerful multimedia site, and position your message alongside expert how-to content. Dummies.com is a one-stop shop for free, online information and know-how curated by a team of experts.

- Targeted ads
- Video
- Email Marketing
- Microsites
- Sweepstakes sponsorship

20 MILLION PAGE VIEWS EVERY SINGLE MONTH

15 MILLION UNIQUE VISITORS PER MONTH

43% OF ALL VISITORS ACCESS THE SITE VIA THEIR MOBILE DEVICES

700,000 NEWSLETTER SUBSCRIPTIONS TO THE INBOXES OF *300,000* UNIQUE INDIVIDUALS EVERY WEEK

# of dummies

Custom Publishing

Reach a global audience in any language by creating a solution that will differentiate you from competitors, amplify your message, and encourage customers to make a buying decision.

- Apps
- Books
- eBooks
- Video
- Audio
- Webinars

Brand Licensing & Content

Leverage the strength of the world's most popular reference brand to reach new audiences and channels of distribution.

For more information, visit dummies.com/biz

PERSONAL ENRICHMENT

Staying Sharp
9781119187790
USA $26.00
CAN $31.99
UK £19.99

Facebook
9781119179030
USA $21.99
CAN $25.99
UK £16.99

Guitar
9781119293354
USA $24.99
CAN $29.99
UK £17.99

Investing
9781119293347
USA $22.99
CAN $27.99
UK £16.99

Beekeeping
9781119310068
USA $22.99
CAN $27.99
UK £16.99

Digital Photography
9781119235606
USA $24.99
CAN $29.99
UK £17.99

Meditation
9781119251163
USA $24.99
CAN $29.99
UK £17.99

Pregnancy
9781119235491
USA $26.99
CAN $31.99
UK £19.99

Samsung Galaxy S7
9781119279952
USA $24.99
CAN $29.99
UK £17.99

iPhone
9781119283133
USA $24.99
CAN $29.99
UK £17.99

Crocheting
9781119287117
USA $24.99
CAN $29.99
UK £16.99

Nutrition
9781119130246
USA $22.99
CAN $27.99
UK £16.99

PROFESSIONAL DEVELOPMENT

Windows 10
9781119311041
USA $24.99
CAN $29.99
UK £17.99

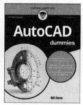
AutoCAD
9781119255796
USA $39.99
CAN $47.99
UK £27.99

Excel 2016
9781119293439
USA $26.99
CAN $31.99
UK £19.99

QuickBooks 2017
9781119281467
USA $26.99
CAN $31.99
UK £19.99

macOS Sierra
9781119280651
USA $29.99
CAN $35.99
UK £21.99

LinkedIn
9781119251132
USA $24.99
CAN $29.99
UK £17.99

Windows 10
9781119310563
USA $34.00
CAN $41.99
UK £24.99

SharePoint 2016
9781119181705
USA $29.99
CAN $35.99
UK £21.99

Fundamental Analysis
9781119263593
USA $26.99
CAN $31.99
UK £19.99

Networking
9781119257769
USA $29.99
CAN $35.99
UK £21.99

Office 2016
9781119293477
USA $26.99
CAN $31.99
UK £19.99

Office 365
9781119265313
USA $24.99
CAN $29.99
UK £17.99

Salesforce.com
9781119239314
USA $29.99
CAN $35.99
UK £21.99

Coding
9781119293323
USA $29.99
CAN $35.99
UK £21.99

dummies.com

dummies
A Wiley Brand

Learning Made Easy

ACADEMIC

9781119293576
USA $19.99
CAN $23.99
UK £15.99

9781119293637
USA $19.99
CAN $23.99
UK £15.99

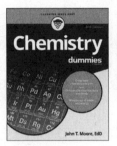

9781119293491
USA $19.99
CAN $23.99
UK £15.99

9781119293460
USA $19.99
CAN $23.99
UK £15.99

9781119293590
USA $19.99
CAN $23.99
UK £15.99

9781119215844
USA $26.99
CAN $31.99
UK £19.99

9781119293378
USA $22.99
CAN $27.99
UK £16.99

9781119293521
USA $19.99
CAN $23.99
UK £15.99

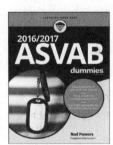

9781119239178
USA $18.99
CAN $22.99
UK £14.99

9781119263883
USA $26.99
CAN $31.99
UK £19.99

Available Everywhere Books Are Sold

dummies.com

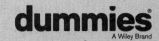

Small books for big imaginations

9781119177173
USA $9.99
CAN $9.99
UK £8.99

9781119177272
USA $9.99
CAN $9.99
UK £8.99

9781119177241
USA $9.99
CAN $9.99
UK £8.99

9781119177210
USA $9.99
CAN $9.99
UK £8.99

9781119262657
USA $9.99
CAN $9.99
UK £6.99

9781119291336
USA $9.99
CAN $9.99
UK £6.99

9781119233527
USA $9.99
CAN $9.99
UK £6.99

9781119291220
USA $9.99
CAN $9.99
UK £6.99

9781119177302
USA $9.99
CAN $9.99
UK £8.99

Unleash Their Creativity

dummies.com

dummies
A Wiley Brand